THE DESIGNER'S SOURCE OF ARTISTS AND ARTISANS

THE GUILD®

KRAUS SIKES INC.
MADISON, WISCONSIN

PUBLISHER: **Toni Fountain Sikes**
President
James F. Black, Jr.
Vice President
Susan Fee
Board Member
Vicki Finke
Production Manager
Karen A. Stocker
Marketing Director
Patricia K. Rahm
Bookkeeper
Yvonne Cooley
Secretary

SALES REPRESENTATIVES: **Susan Fee**
Liz Fisher
Lois Gilligan
Andrea Moriarty
Kelly Rude
Cynthia Snook
Lyn Waring

PRODUCTION AND DESIGN: **Planet Design Company**
Madison, Wisconsin
(608) 256-0000
U.S. Lithograph, typographers
New York, NY
(212) 673-3210
Susan Troller
Writer/Editorial Consultant
Toppan Printing Co.
Color Separations, Printing, Binding

PUBLISHED BY: **Kraus Sikes Inc.**
228 State Street
Madison, WI 53703
(608) 256-1990

DISTRIBUTION: This book is exclusively
distributed by
Rockport Publishers, Inc.
Rockport, Massachusetts

THE GUILD:

ISBN 0-9616012-8-0
ISSN 0885-3975

Printed in Japan

TABLE OF CONTENTS

DOING BUSINESS WITH ARTISTS   **5-8**

THE COMMISSIONING PROCESS   **9-18**

METAL FURNITURE   **19-32**

FURNITURE   **33-74**

THE NEW CRAFTS MOVEMENT IN AMERICAN CULTURE   **40**
Paula Rice Jackson, Editor-in-Chief, Interior Magazine

PAINTED FINISHES   **75-84**

FLOOR COVERINGS AND TEXTILES   **85-94**

TAPESTRIES   **95-110**

THE PERSONALIZATION OF CRAFTS   **106**
Jack Lenor Larson, President Emeritus
American Craft Council

ART QUILTS   **111-124**

FIBER INSTALLATIONS   **125-156**

ARTISTS AS A COLLECTIVE NOUN   **148**
Lawrence B. Perkins, Founding Partner
Perkins and Will

PAPER AND MIXED MEDIA   **157-190**

AN OBJECT LESSON   **160**
David Rockefeller, Jr. Trustee, Museum of Modern Art

ON THE CUTTING EDGE   **176**
Douglas Greenwood, Director of Public Relations, AIA

WALL INSTALLATIONS/OTHER MEDIA   **191-226**

TILES AND MOSAICS   **227-242**

LIGHTING AND ACCESSORIES   **243-256**

SCULPTURAL OBJECTS   **257-272**

VESSELS AND BASKETS   **273-298**

THE GALLERY AS A RESOURCE   **300-303**

RESOURCES/A LISTING OF GALLERIES   **305-333**

INDICES   **335-343**

This book is dedicated to the artists, consultants, gallery owners, designers, architects and their clients who believe that the world should be filled with beautiful things.

Dimitrios Klitsas (see page 79 in The Architect's Source) created the hand-carved wood chest that is used for the background of the book jacket. Ilias Kanavaros, photographer.

Cover artists (left to right): Top Row: Martha Chatelain, p. 163; Karen Singer, p. 241; Faith O'Heron, p. 180; Middle Row: Tim Bissétt, p. 277; Kerri L. Buxton, p. 245; Michael K. Hanson & Nina Paladino, p. 280; Bottom Row: Culin Colella, p. 48; Beverly Plummer, p. 184; Johanna Okovic Goodman, p. 80.

Photographers: Marvin Sloben, p. 163; Deborah Boardman, p. 241; Owen Melenka, p. 277; Borge B. Anderson, p. 245; Rick Waller, p. 280; Rick Albert (and designed by Deborah Reiser), p. 48; Robert Goodman, p. 80.

At THE GUILD we've learned that the relationship between designers and artists is not just theoretically a good idea. We know it works.

When we began THE GUILD six years ago as a publication that marketed American craft work to interior designers and architects, we found ourselves in the front ranks of a design revolution. A revolution that celebrates the soaring inventiveness of the human mind and the practiced skill of the human hand in creating beautiful, one-of-a-kind solutions to design problems. After well over half a century of Modernism's spare design vocabulary regulating what we may or may not use in spaces where we live and work and play, the language of design is becoming more diverse, more deeply textured and more eloquent.

At THE GUILD we believe the voices of craft artists have been some of the most forceful in encouraging the changes we're witnessing. What they say through their work is that beauty may have function and function may have beauty. Or, the function might simply be beauty. Because unique, hand-crafted ornamentation and objects give a lustre and human-scale resonance to our environment, increasing numbers of designers and architects want to work with artists to create the kind of space this newly-enriched language of design is capable of imagining. Meanwhile, a visually literate public has become enthusiastic about design. This growing arts audience is sophisticated and confident, ready to assess, reject or embrace what it likes or doesn't like. It demands that design be fresh, challenging and, above all, not rigidly wedded to narrow notions of correct color and line.

From the beginning, THE GUILD's role has been to serve as liaison between the design team professionals including architects, landscape architects, art consultants and interior designers. Much of my incentive in developing THE GUILD as a sourcebook came from working with craft artists who were discouraged because the exquisite work they were doing seemed to have no broader audience than a loyal regional clientele. Meanwhile, many designers were insisting that they craved experimentation with detail and, yes, some ornamentation, but they claimed that the kinds of artisans capable of doing the quality work they wanted were not to be found.

I figured these two groups needed each other and so from our first edition, THE GUILD became a quiet matchmaker. I knew we couldn't guarantee that every marriage between design professionals and artists would succeed but it seemed to me they at least deserved a first date.

Today, with a full-fledged Renaissance in crafts upon us, architectural elements as well as one-of-a-kind pieces of furniture and furnishings are finding a welcome place in American design and architecture. And at THE GUILD we've learned that a working relationship between designers and artists is not just theoretically a good idea. We know it works.

For example, take our friend the Boston architect who designed a spectacular private residence half way across the country in the Midwest. Complicated by weather delays and the logistical difficulties of trying to remote-control many of the construction details, the project was well on its way to becoming a nightmare of competing tensions between client, builder and designer.

The kitchen, particularly, was a battleground where furious issues of control and aesthetics were being contested. The architect required cabinetry that followed a curved wall. The builder, representing the kitchen showroom with whom he routinely worked, insisted it couldn't be done, at least not with standard pieces familiar to him. The client, who was having personal problems of his own, was close to giving the entire project up.

Designers and architects, like us, have learned that working with individual artists is not just creatively satisfying, but that it's good business as well.

After six years of working with thousands of the top craft artists ... we've discovered that the pleasure we take from our artists/friends' extraordinary work is nearly matched by the pleasure of doing business with them.

At this point the architect discovered a small cabinet shop run by artisans, a husband and wife design/fabrication team. Naturally they could build cabinets that followed the wall's curve, and certainly they could follow the architect's design and of course they found it easy and rewarding to pick up on the themes and motifs they saw throughout the house and apply them to their work. Not only could they do all these things, they did them pleasantly, promptly and professionally. Furthermore, they loved the kitchen, they loved the job, and they made sure the client knew how they felt about it. In the end, the architect got the design he specified, and a far happier client as well. The builder was able to keep his crew on schedule. And the kitchen itself was the most luminous room in the house, a source of enormous satisfaction to all who had anything to do with it.

We don't pretend that every relationship involving an artist has an ending where everyone falls in love and then lives happily ever after. But we know the business of artistic collaboration between designers and craftspeople is growing and steadily

gaining acceptance. And we know there's good reason for this increasing interest. Certainly much of it is the result of the design professionals' renewed fascination with ornamental form, and the sheer quality and beauty of contemporary North American crafts. But we also have to believe that designers and architects, like us, have learned that working with individual artists is not just creatively satisfying, but that it's good business as well.

The artists that we've dealt with over the years are intensely visionary, but they're also enthusiastic team players. They know how to read blueprints. They're conscientious about timing and scheduling and installation. They're comfortable dealing with sub-contractors who may be necessary to get the work in place. In many cases, they will know more about the safety codes that pertain to their specific material than the designer.

Knowledgeable and thoroughly professional, these artists bear little resemblance to the romantic stereotype of the sullen character incapable of operating in the real world. Instead, they do what they say they're going to do, they do it on time, and they do it within the allotted budget. They're a pleasure to work with, and they are uncompromisingly honest with their client's time and money.

After six years of working with thousands of the top craft artists

at THE GUILD, and commissioning a number of them for our own projects ranging from office renovation to furniture design and from architectural glass to fine cabinet work, we've discovered that the pleasure we take from our artists/friends' extraordinary work is nearly matched by the pleasure of doing business with them.

Several years ago I realized that part of the appeal of my work and my attraction to exquisitely crafted objects, was a growing appreciation for the details that make up the fabric of human life. In what often seems like a chaotic impersonal world, I find reassurance and comfort knowing that the human spirit is still capable of creating beautiful, unique things, drawing from reservoirs of skill and imagination. And in a time when there's almost an assumption that business relationships are hard-edged and adversarial, my dealings with the artists of THE GUILD have reminded me that virtues of competence, consideration, creativity and honesty put the fun back into the most demanding work.

Toni Fountain Sikes

Publisher

THE GUILD'S GUIDE TO GETTING GREAT WORK WITHOUT TEARING OUT YOUR HAIR

Because THE GUILD operates as a kind of matchmaker between artists and design professionals, we have considerable interest in how the matches that begin here turn out. We want to help these relationships work by doing everything we can to make the contact between artist and designer satisfying and profitable.

We also want to make it easier for designers to create new professional alliances with artists. And we'd especially like to reassure those who have been reluctant to try such collaboration because of their concerns about how the process works.

This article is a how-to guide to the commissioning process...how it comes about, who is involved, the steps to take and when to take them, what to prepare for, and how to avoid problems.

We hope it answers some questions and offers encouragement to design professionals seeking to work directly with artists and artisans.

If we begin at the beginning, we have an incomplete or unbuilt space and a client. Every project — whether the development of a major institution or a room to be redecorated — will have as its first and guiding influence the client and his pocketbook.

"As an artist I have two goals for the initial meeting with clients who are interested in doing collaborative work. The first is to educate them about what I do and how I do it. The second is to reassure them about the process."
Maya Radoczy, glass artist

By far the most important part of getting great work is choosing a great artist — or at least the right artist for your particular project and pocketbook. The selection is the decision from which all others will flow, so it's worth devoting time and study to the selection process and to season the process with both wild artistic hopes and hard-nosed realism. The right choices at this early stage will make things go easier later on.

Some clients will be very interested in helping select the artist, and once the choice is made, working closely with him or her. Others will want only minimal involvement, leaving most of the decision-making to the design team.

Whoever is making the decision, there are several ways to find the right artist. Obviously, we recommend browsing through the pages of THE GUILD. Not only does our book show a wide range of some of the top work available, it also has the advantage of weeding out people who may not really want to work with designers and architects on commissioned pieces. Every artist included THE GUILD is looking for collaborative work — that's why they're here. Many of these artists already have a strong track record of working with designers, architects and their clients. You gain from their professionalism and experience. If you don't see exactly what you like in THE GUILD or you want to know who else may be available, there are a number of other routes to go in the selection process.

Sometimes you may see work you like at a gallery or at a craft fair. Ask for artist names and business cards. Design magazines often feature artists, along with contact information. Your own colleagues may yield more names. If the project is a large one, you may go through a request-for-proposal process that can draw responses from all over the continent or around the globe.

"As time goes by, we're finding that the relationships we have with architects are getting better and better. As we trust each other more, they feel freer to let us do some of the head scratching and design."
Mark C. Nichols, metalworker

A qualified art consultant will also have a wide network of artists to choose from. If the complexity of your project warrants using an art consultant in the selection process, make sure the consultant is sophisticated and experienced enough to really provide guidance through the rest of the process of working with the artist. This should mean the ability to help negotiate the technical details of a very specific contract, including issues like installation, insurance, storage, transportation and gauging possible engineering costs.

Make your initial selection on the basis of what you like about an artist's past work. When you make the first contact, either via telephone or a letter, be prepared to provide information about the size and scope of your project, the budget, the deadlines and even the materials and colors you have in mind. If you do. This will help the artist tailor his or her response more specifically to you, which will yield a better sense of whether this is the right person for your project.

Most experienced craft artists will be pleased to provide you with a portfolio — usually on slides, but sometimes printed. Don't, however, expect to see the exact piece you're looking for in a portfolio. Remember, you're choosing an artist at this point, not a piece of art. Look for creativity, command of the materials or technology, and also how the work seems to fit the specific environment.

Once you've made a tentative selection based on a portfolio, along with the artist's past experience and reputation, it's time to get serious. Even though some designers and architects still believe artists are too "unbusinesslike" to worry much about such things as building codes, lighting specifications, deadlines and budgets, you will find the great majority of craft artists who seek commissioned work will be very conversant with contract details. Most designers find that the craft artist's professionalism and thorough knowledge of subject, materials and their requirements regarding code, safety and engineering is complete and reassuring.

After you've narrowed your choice to a small number of artists, or maybe only one, and you've learned that he, she, or they are interested and available, it's time to set up your first, no-obligation meeting.

The purpose of this meeting is to find out if the chemistry is right — whether you have the basis to build a working relationship. It's also the time to confirm that the craft artist has the necessary skills to undertake your project. Be thorough and specific when asking questions. Choosing an artist is much like choosing an advertising agency or, for that matter, an architect or designer. If it feels like you might have trouble working together, it's wise to heed these early warning signs. But if all goes well and you decide to move ahead with the artist, your second meeting will be to agree on a budget and timetable, establish a method of work, and sign a contract.

Your rules at this second meeting should be that silence is not golden and ignorance is not bliss. Now is the time for possible misunderstandings to be brought up and resolved, not later after the work has been half done and deadlines loom.

2. CREATE A COLLABORATIVE ATMOSPHERE

"For a collaboration between design professionals and an artist to work well, it's as important for everyone involved to come at the process as well as the project in a creative way."
Susan Fee, landscape architect and art consultant

Perhaps you have seen it happen. The designer has planned a perfectly balanced space and, at the last minute, the client installs a piece of art that, while beautifully made, has the unintended effect of destroying the harmony of the lines, colors or space. Or the client chooses a work that requires totally different lighting, or needs a different structure for support. Such last minute changes can ruin both budgets and relationships. You can avoid this by bringing the craft artist into the process at the earliest possible stage — at about the same time you are hiring the general contractor or are completing the final design.

While choosing the artist or artists who might contribute their creative energy and work to a project when it is still mostly unformed space may seem unnecessary and premature, this is a wise investment for several reasons. Early inclusion of the artist helps ensure that the collaborative effort will go smoothly throughout all phases of the project. If the artist is respected as part of the team, his work can benefit the project's overall design. Concentrating his talent on what may be a relatively small but vital focal point, the artist frees the designer to concentrate on the rest of the space.

From the beginning, the space is designed with the art in mind, and the art is created to enhance the space. As a result, there are no unpleasant surprises about size or suitability of the artwork to the space. Furthermore, when art is planned for early on and is a line item in the budget, it's far less likely to be cut at the end of the project when money and energy for defending design decisions are running low.

Naturally, the scope of the project will determine the number of players to be involved with the artist. A room redecoration will probably include just the client and the interior designer while the construction of a large public building can involve a cast of hundreds, including engineers, insurance underwriters, bankers, construction workers and attorneys to say nothing of the staff of architects, draftsmen, designers and art consultants. It's a good idea to designate one person to serve as liaison with the artist to avoid mixed signals.

13

3. SEEK TWO-WAY UNDERSTANDING

Be sure the artist understands the technical requirements of the job, including traffic flow in the space, the intended use of the space, the building structure, maintenance, lighting and environmental concerns. Keep the artist appraised of any changes you make that will affect the work in progress. Did you find a certain material you specified unavailable and replace it with something else? Did the colors change? Did the available space become bigger or smaller? These may seem like small changes to you, but they could have a profound impact on an artist's planning and work.

At the same time, the artist should let you know of any special requirements his or her work will place on the space. Is it especially heavy? Does it need to be mounted in a specific way? Must it be protected from theft or vandalism? What kind of lighting is best? Remember that you are partners. Don't assume that all changes will be resisted or resented by the artist. Artists who choose to work in a collaborative way have learned to understand design changes.

Most artists experienced with commissioned work factor the notion of a continuing design dialogue into their fee. There is an unfortunate belief — harbored by some architects, designers and, yes artists too, that a willingness to change and compromise somehow indicates a lack of commitment or creativity. On the contrary. The ability to compromise on execution, without compromising on artistic quality, is a mark of professionalism which is found in a growing number of craft artists. We recommend looking for this quality in the artist you choose, and then respecting it by treating the artist as a partner in the decisions made affecting his or her work.

Of course, part of working together is making clear who is responsible for what. Since few designers and architects — and even fewer contractors — are used to working with artists, the relationship is custom-made for misunderstanding. Without a firm understanding from the outset — nurtured by constant communication — things can easily fall through the cracks.

"It's important for people to be honest and realistic with each other from the beginning, and to make a real effort to speak each other's language."
Susan Fee, landscape architect and art consultant

It is a truism in any kind of business that it is much cheaper to get the lawyers involved at the beginning of a process than after something goes wrong. A contract or letter of agreement will assure you and the client that the artist will complete his or her work on time and to specifications, and it will assure the artist that he or she will get paid the right amount at the right time. That just about eliminates the biggest conflicts that can arise.

Contracts should be specific to the job. Customarily artists are responsible for design, production, shipping and installation. If someone else is to be responsible for installation, be sure you specify who will do it and who will pay for the installation. If it is not the artist, it usually is the client. With a large project, issues like insurance and liability may need to be considered. They should be discussed up front and if the artist is not familiar with the requirements it may be wise to use an art consultant or attorney to clarify things.

Payments usually are tied to specific points in the process. These serve as check points to make sure the work is progressing in a satisfactory manner, on time and on budget. Payment customarily is made in three stages, although this certainly depends on the circumstances, scope and complexity of the project.

The first payment usually is made when the contract is signed. It covers the artist's time and creativity in developing a design specific to your needs. You can expect to go through several rounds of trial and error in the design process, but at the end of this stage you will have detailed drawings and — for three-dimensional work — a macquette, or model, that everyone agrees upon. The artist usually charges a fee to cover the costs of the macquette and his design time.

The second payment is generally set for a mid-way point in the project and is for work done to date. If the materials are expensive, the client may be asked to advance money at this stage to cover materials costs. If the commission is cancelled during this period, the artist keeps the money already paid for work performed.

Final payment usually is due when the work is installed. If the piece is finished on time, but the building or project is delayed, the artist customarily is paid on delivery, but still has the obligation to oversee installation.

Other considerations that should be included in a contract are copyright (the artist usually retains copyright with certain restrictions), maintenance, and warranty. Many contracts are written with an arbitration clause. In case of dispute, an arbitration panel made up of art experts often can render a better judgment than a court and for much less cost.

"A lot of artists really have their act together. They know how to work with us; they're a pleasure to deal with. I encourage other designers to use them."
Teri Figliuzzi, interior designer
Kohn Pedersen Fox Conway

The partnership between artists and designers is an old and honorable one. Many venerable blueprints will indicate, for example, an architect's detail for a ceiling with the scrawled note, "Finish ceiling in this manner." The assumption, of course, is that the artisan working on the ceiling has both the technical mastery and the aesthetic skill to create a whole expanse of space from a detail that comes from the mind and pen of the architect.

We believe today's new breed of craft artist is capable of such relationships, and we're delighted to see increasing numbers of design professionals including artists on their teams. After too many years of the crafts being separated from design we're happy to be a part of a renewed interest in collaboration.

An architect we know is an avid art collector and has the highest respect for artist, but is hard-nosed about hiring artists for his projects. He asks: "Will working with an artist make my work easier? And will it make my work better?" After six years of watching more and more artist and design professionals forge satisfying partnerships, we can respond honestly with "Yes, probably," and "Yes, most certainly."

SOME SIMPLE RULES

Although it's true that managing the collaborative efforts of creative people may not be quite as simple as getting a convention of conflict resolution counselors to work together, it doesn't have to be scary, especially if you know ahead of time where there are likely to be problems and misunderstandings.

Art consultant Susan Fee, who has a background as a landscape architect, is an enthusiastic advocate for artists working on commission with design professionals. But even she admits there are some horror stories about conflicts that sour relationships and leave the organizers feeling bitter. "Most artists are a real pleasure to work with — highly professional and deeply creative. They can contribute immeasurably to a project. Following some simple rules throughout the process can keep the project on track and save a lot of headaches.

"The architect and design people are most concerned about timing and the schedule. They have anxieties that the art will look different from what is promised, and they are afraid the artist will flake out on them. For his part, the artist is afraid he will get burned on payment, and will be treated like a second-class citizen. I try to reassure people that none of this needs to happen."

Fee suggested several rules to help avoid the most likely problems that can create conflict and sabotage the collaborative effort.

■ Bring the artists into the project as early as possible.

■ Be organized and as specific as possible about the scope and range of the project, even in early meetings before the final decision about selecting an artist is made.

■ Be honest and realistic, and expect the same from the artist. When the artist has been selected and you're getting down to the details regarding deadlines, responsibilities and specific project requirements, don't avoid the areas where there seem to be questions.

■ Choose an artist based on a solid portfolio of previous work. And remember that it's less risky to use an artist you know has worked on projects that are similar in size and scope, and who you know can handle the demands of your kind of job.

■ Consider hiring an art consultant or additional trouble shooter if the commission is particularly large or complex. The consultant should help with complicated contract arrangements and details, and should make certain that communication between artists and support staff (including sub-contractors and engineers) is thoroughly understood.

■ Trust your instincts when you're choosing an artist. Like selecting an advertising agency or an architect, choosing an artist is based partly on chemistry. You need to like the work, and respect the artist, but you also have to work with him or her.

When the mix is right, says Fee, and the collaboration process works well, it not only benefits the project, but is a pleasure for all the people connected with it. This should be the goal for every collaborative effort.

METAL FURNITURE

21 Chris Axelsson

22 Peter Handler

23 Russell C. Jaqua

24 Rob Johnson

25 Ray Lewis

26 Albert Paley

27 David A. Ponsler

28 Brian F. Russell

29 Jeffrey Sass

30 Steve Smith

31 Brian Swanson

32 Sculpture Studios Wooldridge

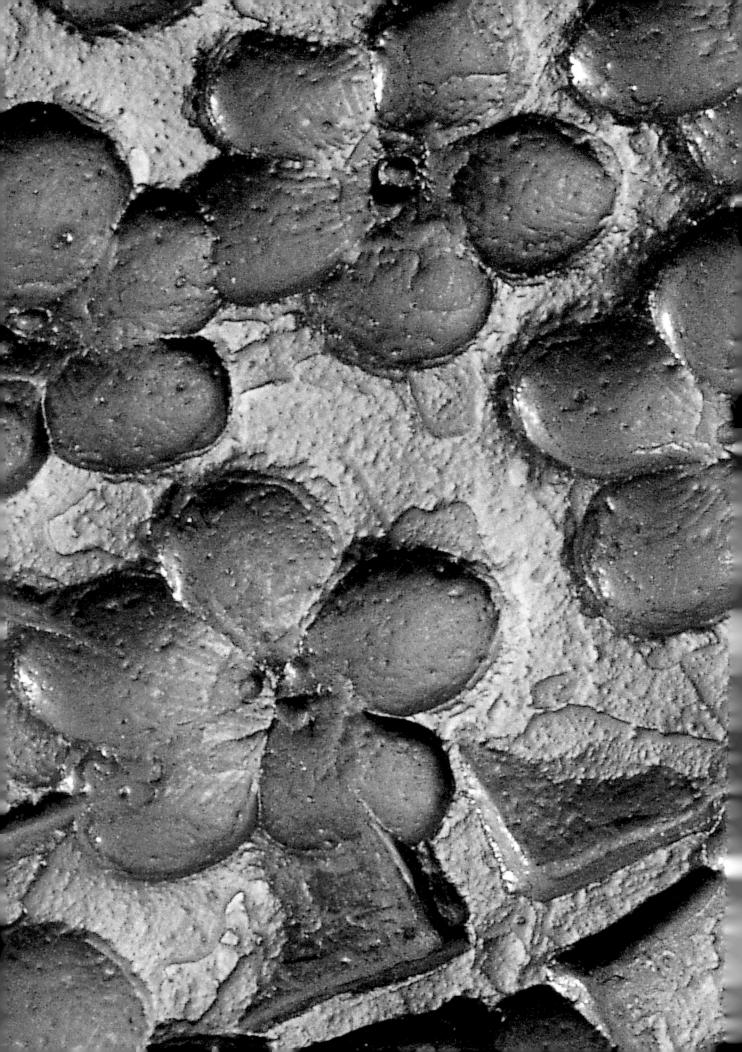

hris Axelsson

elsson Metalsmith
. Box 22-2598
rmel; CA 93922
one: (408) 624-3909
: (408) 624-3579

e metalworking skills have been achieved
offer the highest standards in reviving
iod ironwork and fashioning contemporary
igns. Chris Axelsson's work is hand-forged
d lends an organic quality to materials
h as iron, copper and bronze.

nored with numerous gold medals from the
ional Ornamental Metals Association, the
t's private and corporate commissions
ude sculpture, lighting, gates and furniture.
e of fine furnishings is offered in the form
ables, beds, lamps, candleabras and
place implements. Axelsson is accustomed
working closely with architects, owners and
gn firms. Installation is available
onwide. A design and production period
quired for major commissions.

iries are welcomed.

ured is a California King Iron Bed. Forged
fabricated mild steel, with quartz crystal.

Peter Handler

Peter Handler Studio
2400 W. Westmoreland Street
Philadelphia, PA 19129
(215) 225-5555 FAX (215) 225-3964

Peter Handler designs and produces custom and limited production anodized aluminum, glass and granite furniture for the home and office. Using high-strength clear adhesives to join metal and glass or stone, he creates furniture which is eminently functional, yet esthetically and structurally minimal.

Working with an excellent commercial anodizer, Handler produces a broad range of colors, frequently developing new hues to meet his clients' needs. Anodized aluminum, with its luminous color spectrum, has a hard, permanent surface that is highly resistant to scratches and stains, retaining its beauty with a minimum of care.

Retail prices range from $1300 for an occasional table to $6000 for a conference table.

Delivery time ranges from two to four month Catalog and aluminum samples are availab upon request.

"Dinner Trolley", 24" x 33" x 29".

"Elemental", Coffee Table, 40" x 48" x 15".

"Chess Master", Chess Table and Chess Set, 30" x 30" x 28".

"Gyro", Coffee Table, 44" x 48" x 14."

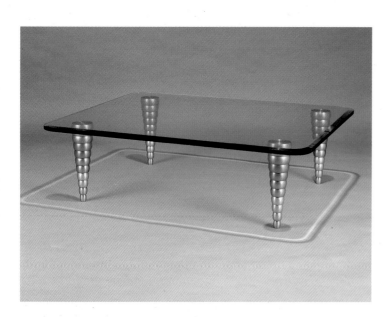

ussell C. Jaqua

nba Forge
19 Blaine St.
t Townsend, WA 98368
06) 385-5272

The "Plate Graffique" technique developed by Russell Jaqua is illustrated in the elegant transformation of a durable material, steel, into visually light-active tables.

Over the past seventeen years, Jaqua has exhibited nationally and internationally. He is represented in several museum collections.

The table tops are forged of 1/2" plate, hot worked into a decorative relief; all edges are softened by chamfering. The legs are 1 1/4" forged tapers tenoned through the top.

Harmony among these elements is assured by the process of being wrought.

The Forest and Floral collections portray natural patterns and are offered on a limited production basis. Size and height changes will be accepted on commission. End tables shown with a wax finish are priced at $450 F.O.B.

e Fir 16" x 48" x 16" ht.

Wild Rose 16" x 16" x 18" ht.

Blossom 16" x 16" x 18" ht.

Rob Johnson

Rob Johnson Furniture
949 Amsterdam Avenue
New York, NY 10025
(212) 865-6027

A self-taught artist with no formal design training, Rob Johnson both designs and executes his line of contemporary furniture. Mr. Johnson's seating, tables and lighting are available in galleries and stores in New York City. Matte Black and Grinded Steel, plate glass and industrial rubber materials ensure strength and durability. Rob Johnson collaborates with glass artist Jerry Morrell and leather artist Toshiki to expand his own skills and to showcase the work of others in his frameworks of steel. Commissions are done promptly and correctly. Retail prices available on request.

(Right) Warrior Lamps—Telescope to 11 ft. tall.

(Below) Adult seating at Soho Gallery location.

ay Lewis
una Collection
). Box 1095
ariposa, CA 95338
9) 966-5484

y Lewis creates chairs of fantasy and
ction. They are equally impressive in a
rporate collection or residential setting.

e chairs are made of sand-cast aluminum
y, hand-polished to a fine silver tone.
ats are black leather. Each limited edition
air is numbered and signed by the artist.

ey are at once collectible art and fine
ndcrafted furniture.

Eagle Chair was the recipient of the 1990
ne Award for Metal Sculpture. The trio was
tured at the Atlantic International Museum
rt and Design.

Fauna Chairs are shown in numerous
eries and in corporate and private
ections throughout the U.S.

h chair is $2,800. Please allow 4 to 6
eks for delivery. A brochure is available on
uest.

) Impala Chair.

tom) Dolphin, Impala and Eagle Designs.

tography by Marvin Silver.

Albert Paley

Paley Studios, Ltd.
25 North Washington Street
Rochester, NY 14614
(716) 232-5260 Fax (716) 232-5507

Known for producing large-scale sculpture and a wide range of architecturally related work, Albert Paley and his studio also create individual and unique functional objects in steel and bronze including tables, plant stands, lecterns, door pulls, sconces, and candle holders along with other works of decorative art. All work is designed and produced by Paley Studios.

(Below) © Paley Studios, Ltd. 1990. Series and edition items. Photo by Bruce Miller.

David A. Ponsler

Wonderland Products, Inc.
72 Lenox Avenue
P.O. Box 6074
Jacksonville, FL 32236
(904) 786-0144
FAX (904) 786-0145

David Ponsler's hand forged "bed of roses" features heavy twisted bars and delicate ribbons and roses. It is finished in natural oils and waxes which allow the inherent beauty of the iron to show through.

This model is queen size and retails for $5,000.00. Please inquire for information and pricing on other sizes, variations and custom designs.

David Ponsler also does a wide variety of architectural metal products for which you can request literature.

Southwest inquiries should be directed to Baggett Associates/Dallas, Houston.

Brian F. Russell

Brian Russell Designs
2537 Broad Avenue
Memphis, TN 38112
(901) 327-1210

Brian Russell excels in creating exciting and original forged steel furniture and architectural details for interior designers, architects, corporations and private clients. Based on historical precedents and constructed with a dedication to craft and materials, the limited edition tables are priced from $1500–4000. Gates, railings and screens may be finished for interior or exterior use and are priced on an individual basis. Installation is available throughout the U.S. Other products include door handles, knockers, fireplace accessories, sculpture, candelabrums, lighting and other architectural and furniture pieces. Brian Russell's work is shown on both coasts, with a listing and portfolio available.

(Shown here) Monologue Table, steel and marble, 20" x 24" x 27", Phyllis Morris, Beverly Hills

rian Swanson

16th Avenue West
3l nd, WA 98033
5) 827-0398

resented By
A Gallery
Occidental Ave. South
tle, WA 98104
167-8283

wanson's vision is inspired by the cast
chine parts, tools, and appliances that
cts. His designs highlight the function
uty of parts made during an earlier
ing durable for indoors or out.

novation, humor, and elegance
und in his pieces.

frey
tique sense of design is evident along with
heirl orward handling of materials.

queens n with design teams are
orporates elines negotiable.
vannah. Ec
ects som $800-$4,000.
racious
ironda g Chair.   (Bottom) Counsel Chair.

Wooldridge Sculpture Studios

Stephen E. Wooldridge
1264 West 206 Street
Sheridan, IN 46069
(317) 758-6076

Stephen E. Wooldridge has been working in metal for over 30 years. He has studied Design and Sculpture at Dayton Art Institute and advanced Sculpture technique at Herron Art Institute. He has extensive experience in the welding, fabrication and finishing of ferrous, non-ferrous metals, and exotic alloys through training with the US Navy. His work has been viewed through out Northern America and Europe.

He is currently building limited edition sculptural furniture, and site specific sculpture for indoors and out.

Stephen works closely with architects, designers, and private clients and is able to handle all aspects of design, construction, transportation and installation.

Brochures and additional details are available upon request.

FURNITURE

35 Lincoln Alden

36 Andrew Pate Design

37 Eric W. Bergman

38 Carter Gustav Blocksma

39 Mark T. Bolesky

41 Lynette Breton
   Ann Flannery

42 Micheal Cabaniss

43 Stephen M. Cabitt

44 James M. Camp

45 Warren Carther

46 Tony Clarke

47 Jeffrey Cooper

48 Culin Colella

48 Culin Colella

50 Jeremiah de Rham

51 Ron Diefenbacher

52 Thomas J. Duffy

53 Kevin Earley

54 Micheal Emmons

55 Brad Greenwood

56 Frank Garvelink

57 John Hein

58 William Hewitt

59 Boyd A. Hutchison

60 Ira A. Keer. A.I.A.

61 Loy Davis Martin

62 Peter Maynard

63 Peter Maynard

64 Modern Objects

65 Norman Petersen

66 Ronald C. Puckett

67 Ronald C. Puckett

68 Martha Sears

69 Brad Smith

70 Mamie Spiegel

71 David Stenstrom

72 The Century Guild

73 Gary Upton

74 Wm. B. Sayre, Inc.

coln Alden

Design
132
ifford, VT 05070
562-5110
765-4314

Designer and furnituremaker Lincoln Alden specializes in creating distinctive tables uniting stone and wood. Fine hardwoods are selected for color and grain to accent the natural beauty of polished marble and granite insets. With over 40 stone choices from around the world, clients can specify color and texture to suit any residential or corporate setting. Integrity in construction and simplicity in line reveal the quiet elegance of Alden Design furniture.

Prices start at $900.00 for cocktail tables. Delivery time ranges from 2–4 months. Design consultation, brochure and stone samples available upon request.

(Left) Cocktail table, 24"w x 40"l x 17"h, walnut, curly rose marble.

(Right) Writing desk, 35"w x 50"l x 30"h, cherry, walnut inlay, Vermont Verde Antique marble.

Andrew Pate Design

Box 199A, RD 3
Greenwich, NY 12834
(518) 692-7676

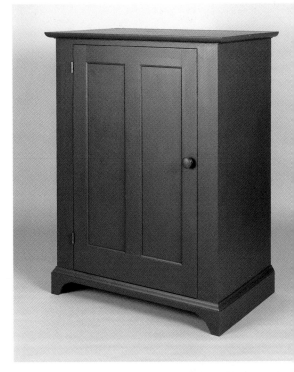

Andrew Pate and Ray Mullineaux design and build fine furniture, cabinetry, and architectural wood work.

They welcome inquiries from architects, designers and collectors; and encourage active participation of clients in the design process.

Attention to detail, material selection, and the tradition of high quality craftsmenship in wood are hall marks of their work.

Professional services include design consultation, production, contracting and installation.

(Right) Shaker cupboard, 45" tall, painted pine, $3900.

(Below) Oval Bar, 40" tall, curly red oak, birdseye maple, pink marble, $10,500.

ic W. Bergman

ophile Inc.
Greene Street
w York, NY 10012
2) 925-4956

Bergman started Neophile in 1984. The
dio produces a comprehensive line of
niture, lighting and decorative accessories.
of the pieces are hand-made and
d-painted. Glass designs are cut and
d-blasted in-house.

chure and price list are available upon
uest. Custom colors are available on most
es. Commissions for residential and
mmercial installations as well as display
d special events props are welcomed.

Carter Gustav Blocksma

Designforms
15675 Gorton Road
Grass Lake, MI 49240
(313) 475-8751
FAX; (313) 475-0350

Carter Blocksma has been designing and manufacturing furniture and cabinetry for over fifteen years. His company produces custom and limited production pieces for residential and commercial application nation-wide. Blocksma's work has been recognized by "Fine Woodworking" and exhibited at the "International Furniture Fair" in New York.

Prices range from $900.00 to several thousand depending on the complexity of the commission. Allow 8–12 weeks for delivery once a blueprint (or model) and price contract have been settled.

Architectural and interior design collaboration is encouraged.

Additional information available.

RECENT COMMISSIONS

Giorgio Armani, IL

TRW Building, MI

Hobbs & Black Architects, MI

Matthew C. Hoffmann Jewelers, NY

(Below, right) "Deco Drama" 49" x 24" x 80" Mahogany, Wenge, Sapele Veneer, Curly Maple.

(Bottom left) "Dancing Chairs" 21" x 21" x 36 White Oak, Curly Bubinga.

rk T. Bolesky
m Carpentry
. Diamond Street
field, OH 44902
526-9663

reation of our limited production
ure is accomplished through the mind of
esigner and the hands of our master
man.

ums include wood, glass, stone, and
made materials available in any finish
ied. Bolesky excels in reproductions,
ntial and commercial works on a limited
ction basis.

workmanship, quality materials, limited
ction by three master craftsmen in our
. We work closely with you in creating
pecial furniture that will fit your vision
pace.

ure and promotional video available for

White oak and wenge inlayed cedar
s with dovetail joints.

THE NEW CRAFTS MOVEMENT IN AMERICAN CULTURE

As we become more sophisticated about the way we live and work, more aware of the rich options that growth and maturity bring to everyday experience, the desire to express individual choices about our tastes and values intensifies. Warmth and character take precedence over more conventional offerings. We look to artists and collectors to stretch our understanding of what it is possible to discover, to acquire, to live with and ultimately, to share.

What is unique in the world holds a great mystery. We appreciate the role that study and discipline plays in the life of the dedicated artist and craftsperson. The issue of the culture providing a stage for such sustained performance becomes deeper.

It is reassuring to note that the American corporation continues to contribute its part to the nurturing of fresh talent. Contemporary custom furniture, site-specific work of art—sculpture, fiber art, glassmaking and metalwork—and all manner of handworked interior architectural details are continuing to find their way to the uppermost reaches of the corporate culture. These modern Medicis are in turn guided and supported in their decisions by some of the country's leading architectural and design firms who themselves serve as brokers between the board room and the studios and workshops where this work is being commissioned.

Now, as the century closes, a renewal of the ideal of craft as both a serious artistic pursuit and a contributing part to daily life is taking hold.

"There is an entire generation of craftspeople working in furniture, glass, metal, tile and fiber who are making beautiful objects designed to shape or inhabit our environment," says Patricia Conway, president of the prestigious New York architectural interiors firm of Kohn, Pedersen, Fox, Conway, whose new book, *Art for Everyday* (Clarkson Potter) presents the works of what she styles the New Crafts Movement. Mrs. Conway's interiors for such clients as Equitable Life Assurance Society, Capital Cities/ABC, Morgan Grenfell and the St. Moritz Hotel in New York City, attest to her commitment to bringing the work of artists and craftspersons into contact with new and old traditions. "Their work is highly individualistic, intensely personal and constantly evolving. It may even be that, given their youth, their best is yet to come," she says.

Through exposure to such fine public interiors, we all have access to those forces which help us define and refine our tastes. These objectives have an appeal that is immediate, an application that is universal and whose experimentation keeps American craftspersons in the very forefront of fresh, new thinking by which we all continue to profit.

Paula Rice Jackson
Editor-In-Chief,
Interiors Magazine
New York, New York

ynette Breton
nn Flannery

eton Flannery Woodworks
South Street
eeport, ME 04032
7) 865-4142

nette Breton and Ann Flannery formed their
siness in 1985, after 20 years of combined
perience. Each trained in the West
parately coming East to nurture their love
the traditional forms of furniture and
oden boat building. After romancing that
t of their careers, they formed Breton
nnery Woodworks. Their focus is the union
ween traditional construction methods
n designs of today, to create antiques of
norrow.

ecializing in custom woodwork and design,
r work includes high quality built-ins, solid
d furniture, doors and staircasing.

chair pictured here was recently honored
being selected from 10,000 photographs
he cover of Fine Woodworking Design
k Five.

se write or call for more information.

Southwestern style twin headboard and table.

estern style end chest, 32"w.x 26"h.x20"d.

Southwestern style reading chair, 19"w.x 41"h.x19½"d.

Michael Cabaniss

P. O. Box 142
Davenport, CA 95017
(408) 426-4819 or (408) 426-9418

The artist, through the skillful knowledge of his tools and craft, has forged a body of work that speaks quietly about comfort and function and the natural beauty of wood.

To achieve structural integrity, dovetail and mortise-and-tenon joinery is utilized. All parts are interlocked together, then pinned or lightly glued. Great attention is also given to design that accommodates the seasonal expansion and contraction of wood.

Every piece is dated and identified by the artist's hand-carved signature.

All inquiries are invited.

(Right) *BUREAU #2*, 54 X 36 X 24 inches, Black Walnut, Peroba Rosa, Gabon Ebony, Aromatic Red Cedar.

Photography is by Tony Grant of Santa Cruz, California.

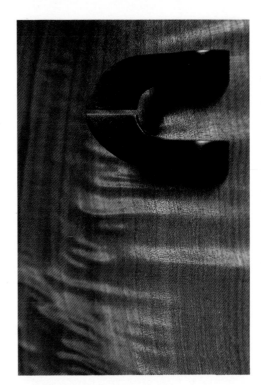

Stephen M. Cabitt

Stephen M. Cabitt Company
Cabinetmakers/Designers
? Strathmore Road
Brookline, MA 02146
(617) 734-4286

Stephen Cabitt has designed and built furniture for architects and designers in the Boston/New York area for the past fifteen years. He is comfortable working in a classic or contemporary format and enjoys collaborating with other designers. His commercial installation experience is invaluable on large scale pieces.

Projects range from breakfronts and armoires to limited production of contract furniture for corporate clients. Libraries are a specialty.

Historical commissions include the Old Corner Bookstore for the Boston Globe, the Paul Revere House, Isabella Stuart Gardner Museum, and Museum of Transportation.

He is pleased to review drawings and provide prompt quotations. A brochure is available on request.

(Upper right), Old Corner Bookstore, Boston, MA.

Mahogany Corner Cupboard.

James M. Camp

J. Camp Designs
11 Longford Street
Philadelphia, PA 19136
(215) 333-2899

J. Camp creates expertly crafted wood pieces to accommodate your specific needs. A broad range of sculptured designs may be had including tables of all kinds—game, cocktail, and conference; music stands, clocks, and also creative wall sculpture. Camp works primarily in walnut with hand-rubbed linseed oil finish. Other woods are available upon request.

Camp has been in business in the Philadelphia area for 25 years. The artist is available for consultation. Prices range from $500–$10,000.

Warren Carther

Warren Carther Glass Studio
3 Roslyn Road
Winnipeg, Manitoba
Canada R3LOH5
(204) 453-2496

Warren Carther received his glass education studying with Bill Carlson in New York and later under Marvin Lipofsky at C.C.A.C. in California (B.F.A. 1978). He has been creating architectural and sculptural glass for 16 yrs., often collaborating with architects and designers.

His attention is now turning to carved glass tables, both as limited editions and unique pieces. Price range: $10,000.–$20,000.

Carther's technique is to fire on color and to carve deeply with abrasive blast into very thick, sometimes laminated glass.

The artist's work is found across Canada, parts of the U.S., Europe and Japan. At this printing he is producing a mullionless carved glass wall 25'hx20' for the new Canadian embassy in Tokyo.

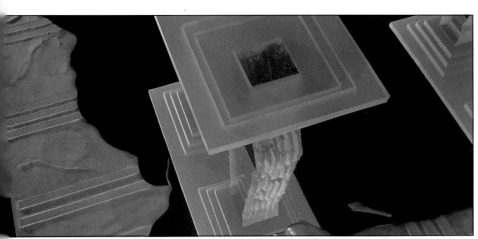

Detail: Laminated and carved table.

Detail: Mullionless carved glass wall 90" x 78" x ¾"

Laminated and carved glass table, 120" x 54" x 29"h, weight 1500 lb.

rear photo showing Mullionless support 90" x 78" x ¾".

Tony Clarke

Clarke Fine Furniture
One Cottage Street 5th Floor
Easthampton, MA 01027
(413) 527-2127

Tony Clarke offers a wide range of design and fabrication possibilites; marquetry, parquetry, custom veneering, inlay, relief and sculptural carving, decorative joinery, turning, and stained glass. Clarke's work is often characterized by strong geometric shapes, bold inlays, and graceful curves.

Clarke's architectural work has included kitchen's, wet bar's, offices, staircases, a wide range of built-in cabinetry, custom moldings, and furniture.

A high standard of quality and respect for budgetary and scheduling requirements is brought to every project. Prices for furniture range from $1000.00 to $20,000.00.

(Above) Wet bar-cherry with stained glass and underlit glass tile counters. Architect: Jeff White. Photo: Scott Miles-Landmark Photography.

(Below) Armoire-curly koa, wengé, and mahogany. 90"H x 50"W x 22"D. Photo: David Levy.

effrey Cooper

esigner of Sculptural Furnishings in Wood
5 McDonough Street
tsmouth, NH 03801
03) 436-79

for Kids?

ese chairs are lifetime treasures, ruggedly
lt, each handcarved with its own
ividuality. They are to be enjoyed by kids
m 1 to 100!

ces start at $1000. Commissions for any
mal and portraits of special pets are
lcome. Chairs measure 14 x 16 x 28H
d a matching table is available to make
et

mal chairs won the 1989 Stewart Nelson
rd by ballot of the visitors at the Living
n Craft Show, 56th annual League of NH
ftsmen's Fair.

lama, Saddlehorse, Springbok (a type of gazelle), Giraffe

Culin Colella

Ray Culin
Janis Colella
632 Center Avenue
Mamaroneck, NY 10543
(914) 698-7727

(Bottom) Photographic Print Chest, By Janis
Colella. 69" x 28" x 33". Bubinga and ebony.

(Top Left) Art Nouveau Fireplace Carving, By
Janis Colella. 65" x 10" x 50". Curly Maple.

(Top Right) Writing Desk, By Ray Culin
(Designed by Deborah Reiser). 60" x 24" x 29"
Satin wood and ebony.

Photos: Rick Albert

ulin Colella

Culin
is Colella
Center Avenue
maroneck, NY 10543
4) 698-7727

Culin and Janis Colella bring together
pecial marriage of backgrounds in
hitecture, furniture design, sculpture,
d woodworking.

distinctive blend of artistic flair and
ention to detail has raised the combination
he fanciful and the practical to an
orm. This is profoundly evident in their
gn and production of unique furniture,
inetry, sculpture, architectural
odworking, and specialty finishing.
e-ranging services, from design to
rication, include one-of-a-kind and limited
ion pieces, as well as contract furniture.

s by Culin/Colella, which incorporate
thirty years of experience, are on display
urlington House, Phillip Brothers, and
corp, and may be found in many fine
nes and galleries in the tri-state area.

ails are available upon request.

(Top) Jan's Jewelry Box, By Ray Culin.

12" x 7 1/2" x 4". Curly maple, ebony, dyed
maple, and polished lacquer.

(Bottom Right) Armoire, By Ray Culin. 30" x 24"
x 90". Bird's eye maple, ebony and
transparent polished lacquer.

(Bottom Left) Writing Desk, By Ray Culin
(Designed by Deborah Reiser). 28" x 60" x 29".
Curly maple, bird's eye maple and dyed
veneer.

Photos: Rick Albert

Jeremiah de Rham

de Rham Custom Furniture
43 Bradford Street
Concord, MA 01742
(508) 371-0353

Jeremiah de Rham specializes in the design and building of custom commission furniture for private clients and architects. From simple and elegant law office furniture to the fine art of carefully joined classic Chinese furniture, de Rham produces uncompromising quality of design and construction. All work is built with an eye to detail, from careful wood selection at the start through to the final, beautiful hand rubbed finish.

See work in Guild 5. Preliminary design fee of $100. Prices start near $1,000.

Commission prices dependent upon design and wood. Collaboration invited. Call for scheduling information.

(Top Right) Lawyer's office desk. Cherry. 30 1/2"h.x 40"w.x78"l.

(Top Left) Office side table. Cherry. 28"h.x 20 1/2"w.x56"l.

(Bottom) Coffee table. East Indian rosewood. Single board panel top. 17"h.x21"w.x52"l.

on Diefenbacher

n Diefenbacher Designs
32 Big Bend
ouis, MO 63122
4) 966-4829

m design to delivery, Ron Diefenbacher
s a professional approach in assessing
nts' needs and developing creative
tions. Combining artistic skill and an ability
work well with architects, interior designers,
d private parties, Diefenbacher creates
ature pieces which stress the individuality
ach new project. These unique designs
placed in many private collections,
cutive offices, and fine galleries across the
ntry.

enbacher has a Master of Arts in Furniture
gn and teaches Woodworking and
iture Design at Washington University in St.
s.

tom left) Pescadero Lamp: teak, ebony,
per.

tom right) Detail, Pescadero Lamp.

right) Writing Desk: padauk.

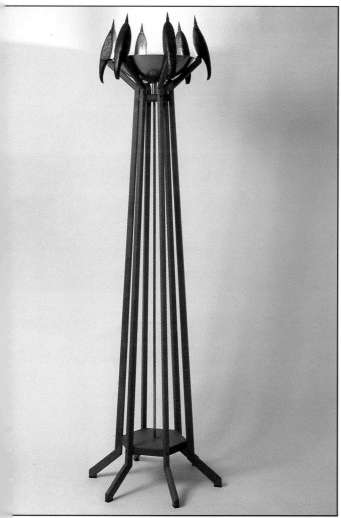

Thomas J. Duffy
Duffy's General & Specific Millwork
52 E. River Street
Ogdensburg, NY 13669
(315) 393-8553
Fax (315) 393-4827

Studio crafts are alive, well and available from Tom Duffy. From one-of-a-kind designs and fabrications to collaborations with other crafts artist, promise is made good.

Duffy's range of work is from design/build furniture to unusual architectural woodworking and boat building (see Architectural Wood page).

More information upon request.

(Clockwise) Bench: Holly veneer, English Harewood, purplehearts—dyed wood, inlay and gold leaf, 14½" x 16½" x 34".
Collection: Boston Museum of Fine Arts, 198.

Pentimento™: Folding Screen, 76" x 76", dro matched Holly with dyed wood inlays, curly maple frame, 1987.

Detail: Inlay—dyed woods in Holly Veneer, 1990.

Chair Within A Chair: Pentimento™, 23" x 29 39". Drop matched Holly dyed wood inlay, 1990.

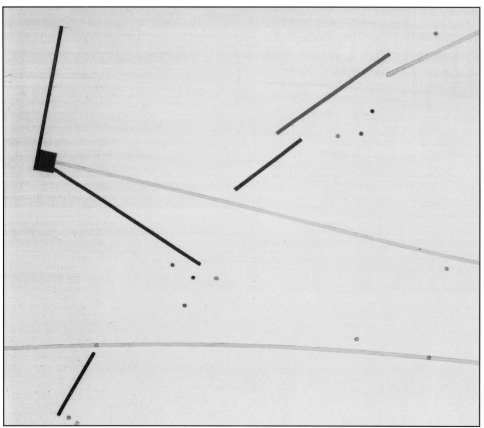

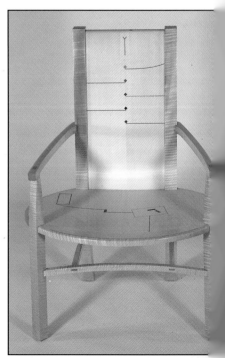

Kevin Earley
1 E. Wilson Street
dison, WI 53703
3) 256-5171

For twenty years Kevin Earley has designed and built furniture which blends the practical with the beautiful. He combines wood and veneers, metal, glass, stone and fabric to meet the individual demands of residential and business clients.

Innovative use of inlay is a hallmark of his work.

Prices begin at $2,000 with delivery time from two to six months.

(Clockwise) Sofa d'Amore—cherry, inlay, wool upholstery 77w. x 31h. x 28d.
Detail of d'Amore.
Hat Cabinet—Cypress & ebony, oil and paste wax finish 22w. x 65h. x 16d.
Sideboard—Walnut, dyed inlay, gold leaf, catalyzed varnish finish—42w. x 50h. x 21d.
Photos: Lois Stauber.

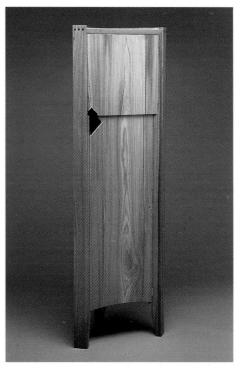

Michael Emmons

Laughing Willows
Partington Ridge
Big Sur, CA 93920
(408) 667-2133

Michael Emmons designs and builds furniture with the focus on bringing the essence of nature into the living space. Using the hardwoods of the California coast, he works primarily with eucalyptus, for its expressive character and silky surface texture.

He works with interior and restaurant designers, as well as individual clients, and will build pieces for specific situations. Upholstery available: leather, handpainted canvas, and cuttings from Turkish kilims. Emmons' work has been featured in Metropolitan Home, House Beautiful, N.Y. Times Home Magazine, Elle Décor, and Town and Country.

Prices start at around $600.

Catalog available: $3.00.

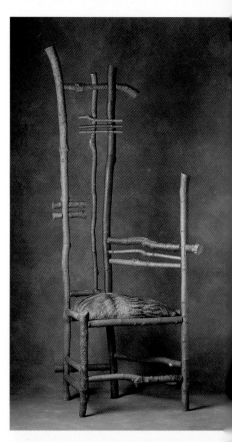

ad Greenwood

eenwood Designs
24 Idaho-Maryland Road
vada City, CA 95959
5) 273-8183

Brad Greenwood combines natural form and function in furniture that has rustic character and simplistic style. The materials are primarily oak branches, complemented by other fine woods.

He designs and crafts a complete line of furniture, beginning with selection and cutting of trees and stripping of bark. Instead of nails and screws, mortise-and-tenon joints and carved pegs solidly unite the wood. The smooth, hand-sanded finish distinguishes

Greenwood furniture from other works of similar style.

Strength, comfort and quality are incorporated into each unique design, and every piece is signed and numbered.

Greenwood has participated in a number of custom projects and considers specific requirements in each commission. Delivery time is eight weeks or more. For additional information, please contact the studio.

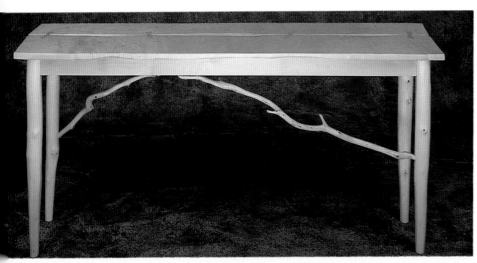

Frank Garvelink

52558 Burlington Road
Marcellus, MI 49067
(616) 646-9055

Frank Garvelink specializes in heirloom quality rocking chairs, handcrafted from solid walnut and cherry for individual and corporate collections.

Garvelink's designs harmonize the natural structure and grain of the wood with the natural structure of the human form. Curved spindles to fit the back, chair seats deeply contoured for comfort, laminated runners with brakes, all insure beauty and comfort.

(Top) High Back Rocker Cherry, Soft Maple 48"h.x28 1/2"w.x41"l. Price range $1600–$2000.

(Lower) Bow Back Rocker Black Walnut, Soft Maple 37"h.x24"w.x36"l. Price range $1300–$1500.

Delivery Time is 3–6 months.

ohn Hein

Woodland Avenue
enton, NJ 08638
09) 883-4573

hn Hein's wood furniture contains a blend
traditional and contemporary aesthetics.
raditional respect for nature and purity
craftsmanship combined with a
ntemporary structure are the aesthetic
nciples influencing their design and
nstruction. Furniture is joined with
ortise-and-tenon and dovetail joints, and
ead of screws to reinforce crucial joints,
ved pegs are used. Hein chooses woods
ntaining suggestive patterns, woods he
mbines to create warm and subtle
niture, furniture with gentle surfaces and
gant lines. Most pieces cost between
000 and $9,000 depending on size, number
drawers, and complexity of design.

o) "Side Table" of cocobolo, American
ck walnut, and Ceylon satinwood (32" x
x 14").

ttom) "Spalted Maple Door Cabinet" of
ple, East Indian rosewood, and walnut (66"
" x 10").

William Hewitt
Witticks Design
46 River Road, RFD
South Deerfield, MA 01373
(413) 527-5973

William Hewitt has run a custom furniture and cabinet shop for the last eight years. His work has generally involved pieces designed to fit into existing spaces while expressing his own solution. His work emphasizes the use of solid wood construction and woods of contrasting colors.

William is accustomed to collaborating with clients concerning ideas and due dates. He will provide drawings for projects of major scale for a design fee, while bids are supplied free of charge.

oyd A. Hutchison

tchison Woodworking
). Box 928 (Route 7)
effield, MA 01257
3) 229-3280

d Hutchison builds custom furniture one
ce at a time utilizing timeless Shaker
igns which are faithfully reproduced or
ughtfully adapted for contemporary living.
finest domestic cabinet woods are used
is furniture along with traditional,
e-tested joinery of uncompromised quality
d flawless, hand-rubbed finishes which
duce durable surfaces that enhance the
auty of the fine woods used.

allation services are available for built-in
ces. Send for brochure.

right) Canterbury side table reproduction.

tom) The Shaker Wall at Round Hill Farm.

Ira A. Keer, AIA

P.O. Box 50115
Minneapolis, MN 55405
(612) 871-8802

Ira Keer's whimsical furniture is designed to be used. With each piece he aims to elicit an emotion, enticing the beholder into its matrix of concept, craftsmanship and utility.

Keer's furniture designs inject fantasy and playfulness into ageless architectonic elements and period styles. His conceptual furniture ideas now emerging in three dimensions, have been exhibited in select galleries and museums. His work is recognized in a wide range of publications and has won numerous design awards.

A practicing architect, Keer's designs are executed by a spirited collaboration with select Minnesota craftsmen. This collaboration ensures excellence of design as well as the finest construction, materials and finishes.

He produces both one-of-a-kind pieces and limited edition works. Special orders, collaborations and commissions are encouraged. More information, brochure upon request.

T. SQUARES: An Armoire ©1988. Curly maple, brazil and ebonized walnut; 73 1/2"h x 34"W x 22 1/2"D; Fabrication, Bruce Kieffer; Photography, Bill Zuehlke.

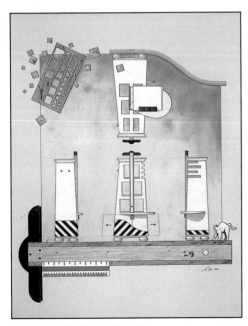

oy Davis Martin

y D. Martin Furniture
00-A Park Boulevard
lo Alto, CA 94306
5) 856-2834

Every design from Loy D. Martin answers to the individual environment and needs of the client. The result is an unusual range of stylistic expression and technique. Trained in aesthetics and the history of furniture styles, Loy Martin has shown in major west coast galleries and in national publications like American Craft and Design Book Four. Some pieces are frankly contemporary while others make allusions to design vocabularies of different eras. Richness and rarity of materials and the highest standards of workmanship characterize each piece.

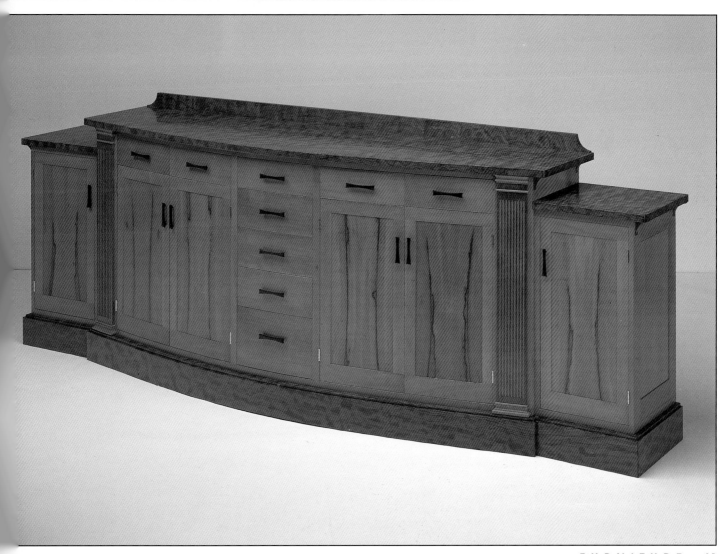

Peter Maynard

Peter Maynard and Associates
P.O. Box 77, Main Street
South Acworth, NH 03607
(603) 835-2969

As a master furnituremaker, Peter Maynard offers excellence in design in a broad range of styles. He has evolved his own aesthetic statement with Classical Chinese, Native American, European and other influences.

For eighteen years he has worked with both designers and private individuals to create fine furniture and architectural installations.

Prices and photos of additional designs are available upon request.

Card table, closed.

Card table, solid curly maple with ebony and rosewood inlays. 30"h.x36"l.x18"d. (36"d. when opened)

ng table, tilt mechanism.

g table, painted bases with red oak top and base detail. Dimensions vary according to clients' requirements. $1950.

Modern Objects

Michael Aguero
Michael Sarti
18 Marshall Street
South Norwalk, CT 06854
866-0334   Fax 866-9469

Their cumulative knowledge and experience in all phases of design have had innovative results for Michael Aguero and Michael Sarti with the introduction of Modern Objects an affordable addition to the ɘ2rt2 furniture and home accessories market.

Their criteria are pure use of materials, simple design and engineering, beauty and strength. The choice of materials such as wood, glass, steel and marble is derived from an architectural aesthetic. They are crafted so that the natural beauty and textures are enhanced and then combined with such elements as unusual patinaes, exotic papers, leather hinges and natural fibers.

Their initial concept of designing a line of products inspired by architectural form has established this team as a major contributing force to a trend that has become the strongest influence in the design of home furnishings today. A brochure is available upon request.

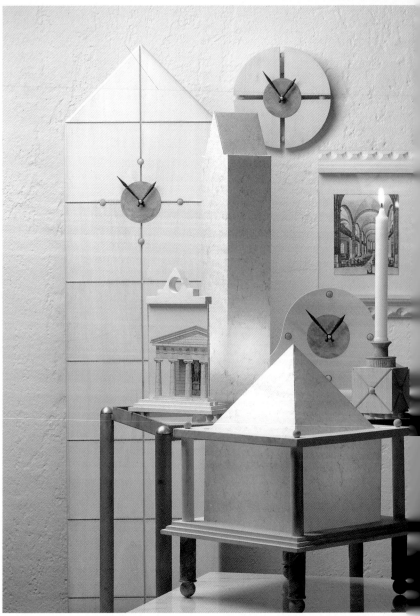

orman Petersen

Treat Avenue
Francisco, CA 94110
5) 431-1100

Norman Petersen accepts commissions to design and build pieces for private, commercial, and public spaces. His work includes both interior and outdoor pieces. At present he is working on a series of chairs and tables based on an African tribal motif. His work is shown in galleries throughout the U.S. and is in the permanent collection of the San Francisco Museum of Modern Art. Contact Norman Petersen's Studio for information on pricing and current exhibitions.

born–1941

Stanford University, Academy of Art in Munich, San Francisco Art Institute.

1966–79 Designer, Teacher, Builder in California and France.

1979–present Designs and builds furniture in his San Francisco studio.

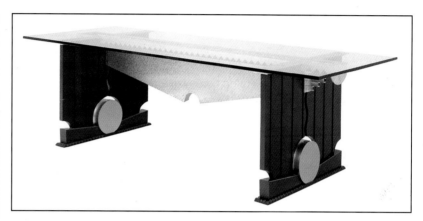

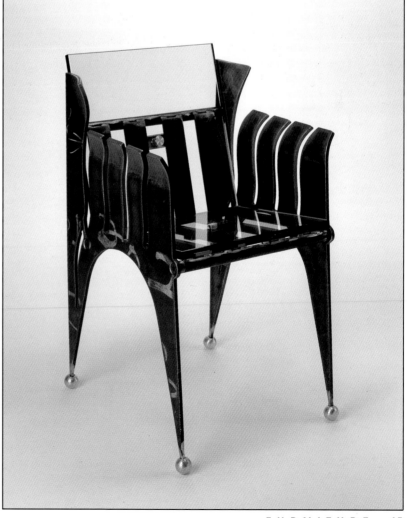

Ronald C. Puckett

Ronald C. Puckett & Company
P.O. Box 9549
Richmond, VA 23228
(804) 752-2126

"Ron uses the colors of wood to define the forms and shapes of his furniture, like a painter uses color, creating elegant, fluid, and regal furniture."

Veena Singh
Gallery owner
Sansar Gallery
Washington, D.C.

Ron Puckett is available for both corporate and residential commissions. His furniture can be seen in interior architect Patricia Conway's *Art for Everyday*, the *Guild 4 & 5* as well as galleries in Washington, D.C., Philadelphia, Pa. and East Hampton, N.Y. Recent corporate commissions include Southern Progress Corporation, Birmingham, Alabama, and the MONY headquarters in New York. Ron was a Merit Winner in the Kraus-Sikes 3rd American Crafts Awards. Photos of current works are available from the artist.

(Top)"Night Moves Desk," detail, leather, padouk, wenge, maple, 29"h X 72"w x 36"d.

(Bottom right) "Night Moves Desk," padouk, wenge, maple, leather, 29"h x 72"W x36"d.

(Bottom left) "Metropolis Chair," bubinga, wenge, leather, 35"h x 34"w x 32"d.

onald C. Puckett
nald C. Puckett & Company
). Box 9549
hmond, VA 23228
4) 752-2126

(Clockwise) "Lap of Luxury," mahogany, fiddleback mahogany, wenge, fabric, 34"h x 66"w x 32"d.

"Atlas Table," bubinga, wenge, 28"h x 28"d.

"Pawling Cabinet," figured maple, cherry, wenge, padouk, slate, 56"h x 42"w x 24"d.

"Bow Front," bubinga, wenge, 34"h x 56"w x 20"d.

Martha Sears

P.O. Box 1153
Washington Green, CT 06793
(413) 567-7433

Martha Sears designs and builds provocative table sculptures using mixed media—ceramics, glass, wood and plastics. Visually intriguing and challenging one's sense of balance yet structurally sound. Pieces range from game tables to coffee tables to runners to conference tables.

A portfolio is available upon request. Commissions are accepted.

(Right) Commission, chess table, mixed media, 29"x32"x32", Springfield, MA.

(Below left) Coffee table, mixed media, 50"x30"x27".

(Below right) Installation, side table (foreground) and coffee table (background).

rad Smith

dford Woodworking
0 Fisher Road Box 157
rcester, PA. 19490
5) 584-1150

Bradford Woodworking was established in 1980 by Brad Smith upon graduating from the School for American Craftsmen at Rochester Institute of Technology.

Brad has concentrated on a line of stools and chairs which are characterized by legs resembling ax handles. These legs are made on an 1850's vintage ax handle lathe which he has modified to suit his needs and to create unusual spiraling surface textures.

Average delivery time is 4 weeks. More information available upon request.

(Top Left) Ax Handle Stools. Five heights 18"–30" with or without backs. Retail price range $110.–210.

(Top Right) Fork Chairs. 18" high at seat front. 31" over-all height. $240.

(Bottom) Farm Series Tables. One of a kind pieces.

Price range $500.–1000.

Mamie Spiegel

147 West 15 Street
New York, NY 10011
(212) 675-4972

Shown here are a few of the wide variety of tables Mamie Spiegel makes. Made of clay tiles affixed to a sturdy plywood base, each piece comes with a set of plates handmade to complement the table.

The standard tables measure approximately 3 ft. by 6 ft., and seat six people; but they can be built to any dimensions required.

Her work has appeared in numerous magazines, books and galleries. She received an NEA grant, and her work has been featured in two shows at the American Craft Museum in New York.

Spiegel also collaborates with designers and architects on fireplaces, doorways, bathrooms and other tile installations.

The price of a table seating six and matching plates is $3,600. For further information, please contact the artist.

avid Stenstrom

Park Street
tland, ME 04101
7) 772-7643
7) 774-9298

David Stenstrom makes custom furniture inspired by the strong, sophisticated designs and character of 17th and 18th Century American country furniture. He uses traditional construction, mostly native woods, and sometimes paint to make pieces that are friendly and easy to live with. He would like to work with your design ideas and requirements. His shop is capable of small production runs. Price quotes are available on request. The usual delivery time is 2 to 6 ·months but he will try to accommodate your schedule.

Pencil post bed—maple and red lacquer,

Desk—antique Southern yellow pine,

Owls eye chair—ebonized mahogany and paint,

Pilgrim chest—oak and paint.

The Century Guild

Nick Strange
PO Box 13128
Research Triangle Park NC 27709
(919) 598-1612

By commission: design, fabrication, installation of exceptional one-of-a-kind contemporary or traditional pieces for corporate, residential or ecclesiastical spaces. Brochure upon request.

(Top right) Curved Section:
architect-designed boardtable for Glaxo Inc.
(27' by 12'; mahogany, cherry, marble).

(Bottom right) Upper Portion:
architect-designed columbarium cabinet for Saint Thomas Church Fifth Avenue (New York, NY), showing triple-door detail (quarter-sawn white oak, mahogany, ebony).

(Below) Corner Detail: executive desk (ash, olive ash burl, ebony).

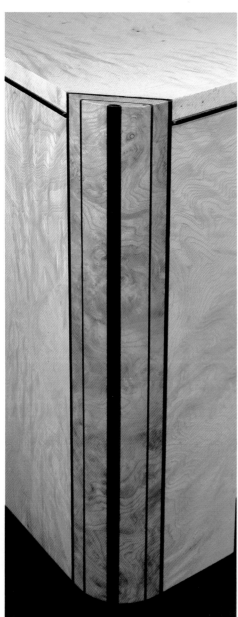

ary Upton
ry Upton Woodworking inc.
56 Loma Rica Drive
ass Valley, CA 95945
5) 273-1449

Combining Hardwoods, Granite, and Metals, Gary Upton creates furniture that is on the cutting edge of design and function.

Since 1976 Gary's work has been featured in Fine woodworking, Northern California Home and Garden, and Sacramento KCRA-TV Evening Magazine.

Custom Commission/Limited Production, brochure and price list are available.

Audio System (Bottom) 89" x 24" x 79h" in figured maple, granite, anodized aluminum, ebony & ebonized mahogany. The upper cabinet hinges from back to access connections.

Hall Table (top) 30" x 18" x 36h" granite, maple, ebonized mahogany.

Wm. B. Sayre, Inc.

One Cottage Street
Easthampton, MA 01027
(413) 527-0202
(413) 527-0502 Fax

Fine commissioned furniture executed to the designs of specifying architect, interior designer, or residential customer.

Working in the finest hardwoods available, collaborating in a wide range of other media to produce heirlooms of distinction and innovation.

Full design services available. Complete production facilities.

Brochure available upon request.

Australian lacewood, zinc etching plate, bevelled glass.

© 1990 Wm. B. Sayre. Inc. Hall table designed by William Sayre.

PAINTED FINISHES

77 Laura Bender
John Early

78 Laura Dabrowski

79 Rosemary Fox

80 Johanna Okovic Goodman

81 Yoshi Hayashi

82 Malakoff & Jones

83 Gregory D. Sheres

84 Wendy MacNaughton

ura Bender
nn Early

ainters
Palm Avenue
esa, CA 91941
462-0159

Early and Laura Bender create fine
ages in a folding screen format for
ntial and commercial settings in
poration with designers, architects, and
e clients. Bender and Early work in
ge of styles from painterly to collage-
ed, using representational, abstract, and
t motifs.

wood screens are of fine furniture quality
ealed for durability. Screen proportions,
er of panels, etc. are part of the artist/
design process. Prices start at $1500.
nclude a 3-D scale model.

ainters also produces murals, panels,
ls, and paint finishes. Complete
nation is available.

eens shown, 6 1/2'h x 5'w, wood and
paint.

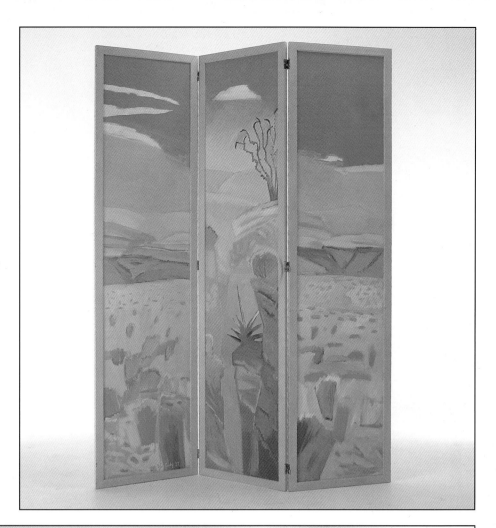

Laura Dabrowski

LAURA D'S
Folk Art Furniture, Inc.
106 Gleneida Avenue
Carmel, NY 10512
(914) 228-1440

"Playfulness and creativity join with superior craftmanship in the world of Laura Dabrowski." Indianapolis Museum of Art

Laura Dabrowski, a.k.a. "Laura D", goes for more pizzazz." Maggie Malone, *Newsweek*

Laura D. brings humor and an unmistakable presence to the world of handpainted childrens furniture. Her durable line of birchwood cows and cats, rabbits and bull terriers as well as bowlegged roosters and more was inaugurated with the birth of her son Cody. Each piece features bold brush work and fabric like patterns.

Laura D's work can be seen at FAO Schw Neiman Marcus, and many fine stores ar galleries. Prices from $100.00 to $10,000 fc an outdoor play house. A color brochure available for $2.00. Adult size pieces are also available.

2nd Place Furniture Award, Bruce Museu Greenich, CT.

osemary Fox

. Box 186
arsville, NY 12409
4) 679-6132

First a painter/illustrator, Fox began decorating furniture when she "rescued" an old dresser.

Her work's been shown by Museum American Folk Art, national magazines, including *House Beautiful* and *Victoria* and drawn accolades at shows. Working mainly in polyurethane-sealed acrylic, she's superbly proficient in all styles, including trompe l'oeil, faux and decorative finishes, and is particularly strong in developing innovative pictorials.

She'll paint customers' things or have them made to order. Also keeps inventory of interesting pieces from auctions and antiques shops. Will do floorcloths, canvases, etc., too, and travels for projects like murals and pianos.

Enjoys collaborating with clients, using her comprehensive library of historical and contemporary references to create unique museum-quality objects.

Prices: $200 to $10,000.

Johanna Okovic Goodman

Okovic / Goodman Studio
718 S. 22nd Street
Philadelphia, PA 19146
(215) 546-1448

Johanna Okovic-Goodman uses "found chairs" to create functional sculpture. These wood chairs are built up directly with acrylic medium or stuffed and painted to create a unique objet.

The colors are protected with multiple coats of polyurethane. Goodman's color and execution are of the highest quality. Only natural wood chairs are used. The Santa Fe and Folk Art styles featured employ mixed media: ribbon, fabric, beads, hemp, oil cloth, and hand-made paper. All add to the three-dimensional qualities without sacrificing functionality.

Clients can use their own chairs or the artist will supply them. Prices range from $250 to $800. Two week delivery.

Goodman's work is featured in galleries and stores across the country.

Photos by Robert Goodman.

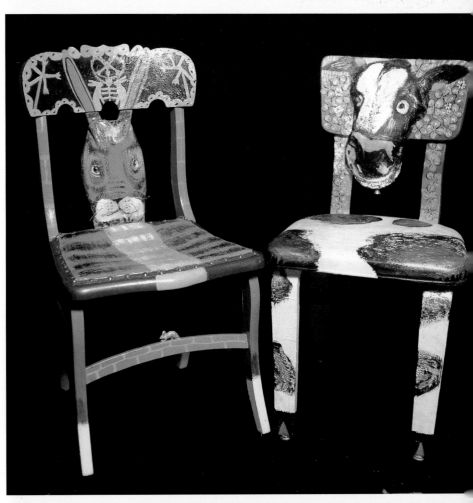

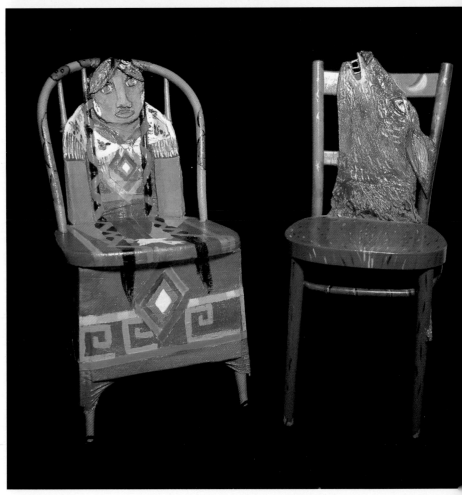

oshi Hayashi
Ninth Street, 3rd Floor
n Francisco, CA 94103
5) 552-0755, (415) 924-9224

hi Hayashi creates twentieth century
erpretations of traditional Japanese
quer art, with a keen awareness of the
st details. He produces a wide variety of
inal designs, which range from traditional
modern. His designs on screens, boxes,
iture and decorative objects are
ntemporary reflections of Hayashi's
anese heritage.

work has been exhibited in the V. Brier
ery, Gump's and Neiman-Marcus in San
ncisco, Nikko Hotel and Galleria Design
ter's shears & window.

nmissions are accepted.

Malakoff & Jones

Peter Malakoff and Norman Jones
Schoonmaker Building
10 Liberty Ship Way #4139
Sausalito, CA 94965
(415) 332-7471
(415) 332-2481 Fax

Peter Malakoff and Norman Jones have designed and built art cabinetry and furniture in the San Francisco area for the past eight years. With their knowledge and appreciation of both ancient and foreign cultures, they demonstrate in their work a distinctive interplay between craft and fine art, with a sensitive attention to detail.

They welcome innovative commissions from the architectural, corporate and private worlds.

Pictures of "Egypto-Deco Pharaoh Cabinet," inspired by objects found in Tutankhamun's tomb. Privately commissioned. Completed 1/8/89. 120"w. (180"w. open) x 90"h. x 28"d. Materials: Sycamore, satinwood, ebony, ivory, gold, lacquer.

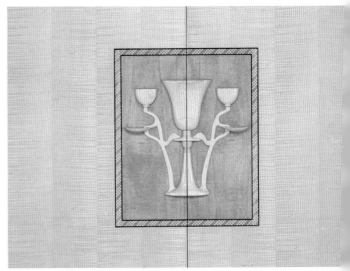

Gregory Sheres

Gregory Sheres Studio
2 NW 52nd Terrace
ami, FL 33178
5) 477-4200

Greg Sheres brings fine art to furniture, For a canvas, the artist uses such materials as emerald pearl granite imported from Sweden and travertine marble imported from Italy. Every table is cut by the artist's own hand; an original painting is then applied to the stone, and then finished with lasting layers of acrylic resin. Heavy stainless steel is then shaped, molded and welded to form a one of a kind base as inspired by the table top.

The artist works closely with clients to incorporate their custom specifications.

Allow 2–3 months for completion of project.

Brochure available upon request.

Prices range from $1,900–$11,000.

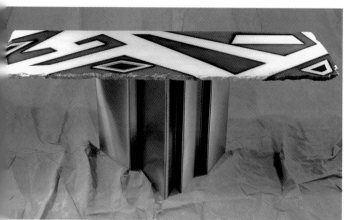

tine console table, 60" x 18" x 29".

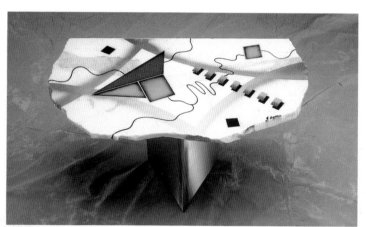

White marble end table, 32" x 22" x 19".

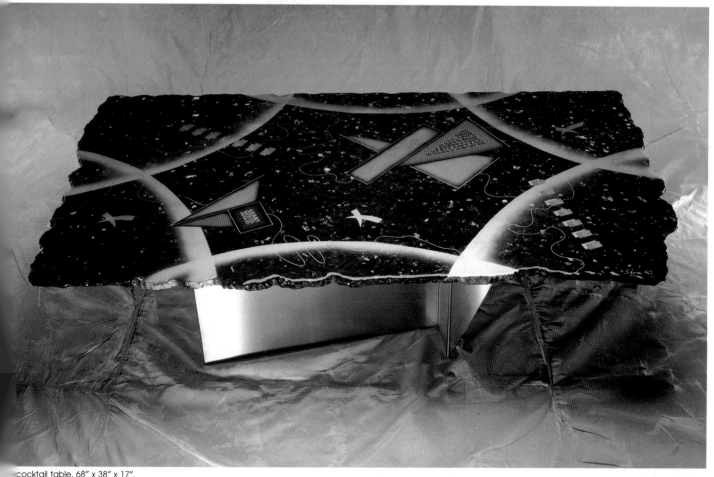

cocktail table, 68" x 38" x 17".

Wendy MacNaughton

"Interior Graphics"
88 Poverty Hollow Road
Newtown, CT 06470
(203) 426-9747

Wendy MacNaughton's work is both elegant and functional. She specializes in decoratively painted finishes on furniture, folding screens, painted floors, trompe L'oeil, stenciling and floor cloths.

MacNaughton offers the designer both execution of work on site and producing one of a kind studio pieces. While using a wide range of styles, she can also replicate existing fabric patterns and motifs for specific client needs.

Working in oil or acrylics depending on the piece, a final 2–4 coats of polyurethane is applied for durability. Due to the wide range of pieces available, pricing and time schedules will vary, with the exception of floorcloths and murals which are priced per foot.

MacNaughton's work was recently featured in "Hi Chic," a Japanese interior design magazine.

FLOOR COVERINGS & TEXTILES

87 Pamela Bracci
    Kathy James

88 Kathy Cooper

89 Anne Landford Dalton

90 Marilyn Forth

91 Nancy Lubin

92 Jennifer Mackey

93 Jill Wilcox

94 Barbara Zinkel

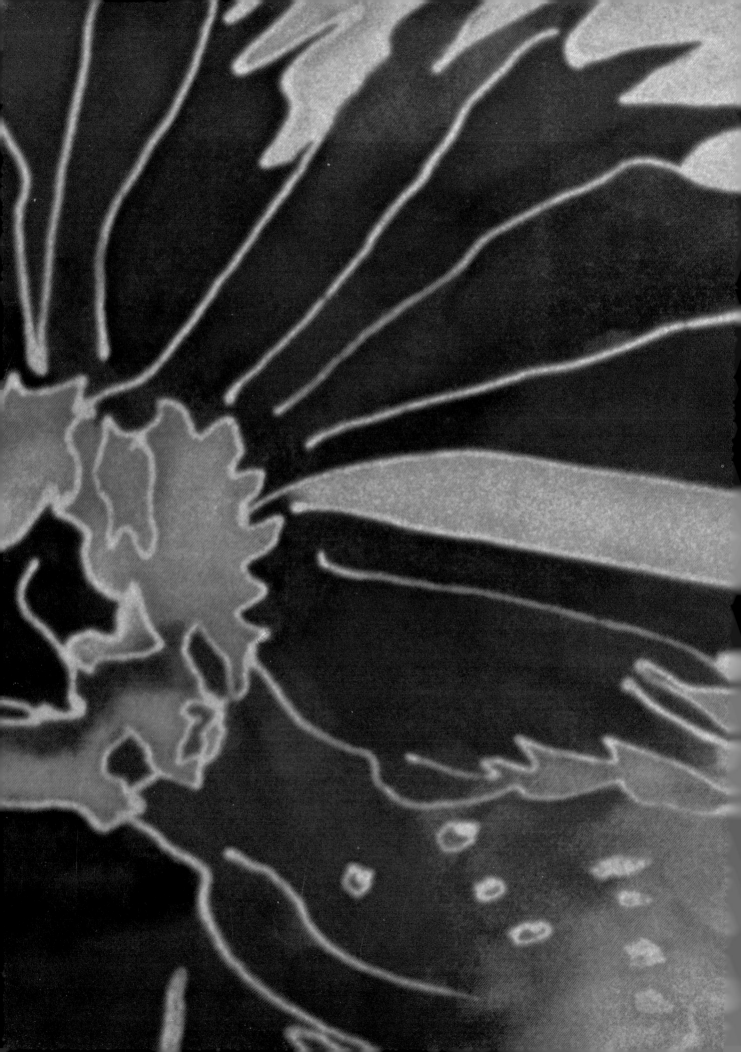

amela Bracci

cci and James
Hamilton Avenue
verhill, MA 01830
8) 465-5938
8) 388-6771

athy James

Sherwood Forest
ter, NH 03833
3) 778-3885

w much time is spent looking for fabrics
t work well together? Handmade cloth
rs flexibility in design, color, and materials.
cci and James, with a ready-made
aboration of handpainted and
dwoven fabrics, will match, integrate and
cent to meet specific client needs.
nolstery, tableware, pillows and other
cessories for the home and office are
ilable and show that strong graphic
gn and distinctive use of color that are
hallmarks of their work.

ht) Featured here is a table runner set.
se sets are available to accompany or
ent any selected tableware designs.

es will vary because of the custom nature
he work, but delivery times are
onable. Requests for additonal
rmation are welcome.

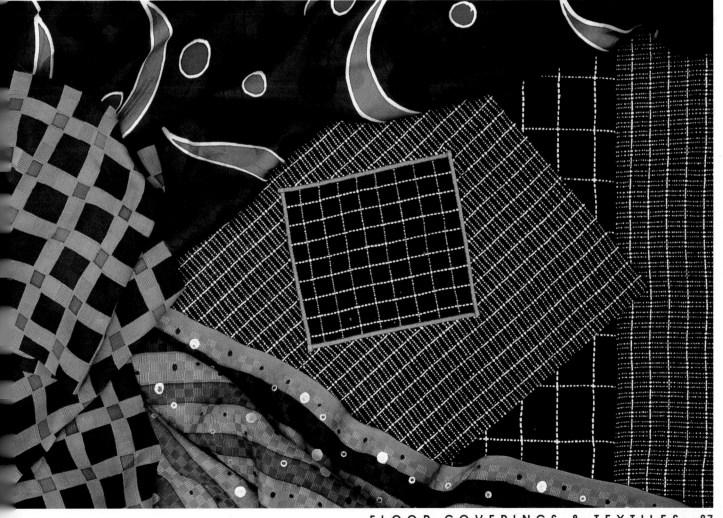

Kathy Cooper

Orchard House Floorcloths
Route 5 Box 214
King, NC 27021
(919) 994-2612

Kathy Cooper specializes in custom designed floorcloths. Large sizes are available and priced per square foot. Cooper uses a wide range of imagery in her work including abstract, floral and whimsical depictions of animals and vegetables.

Floorcloths are intended for practical use on hard-surface floors, or may be hung on walls. Made of heavy canvas, each floorcloth is hand-painted and receives several coats of varnish for a durable, yet flexible, surface.

Colors will not fade. Floorcloths can be cleaned with mild soap and a damp mop. Periodic waxing is recommended to protect the varnish.

Cooper's canvases have been featured in New York magazine, Country Living, House Beautiful, Metropolitan Home, Better Homes and Gardens Decorating and Country Home.

A catalogue is available.

"Zigzag Border with Confetti Center" © 1990
8' x 12' Private residence, Baltimore, MD.

ne Lanford Dalton
ner/Artist in Fiber
Shenna Boulevard
Jorth, TX 76114
625-9558

Dyed and handwoven silks in washes of color are the specialty of Anne Lanford Dalton. Applications of Dalton's silks range from large sculptural fiber art installations, to upholstery and interiors textiles, to production lines.

Dalton earned a Master of Fine Arts Degree in Fibers/Printed Textiles from Texas Woman's University and has 16 years experience weaving and dyeing. Her minor field of study during postgraduate work was interior design.

Working from design problem, to concept, to presentation, sampling, and approval, to completed project, Dalton develops custom designs to address client needs, including custom palettes. Every project is completed with care and expertise.

Pricing, delivery, and terms are determined by the size and scope of a project. Please inquire regarding custom projects, works available, and production lines.

Marilyn Forth

416 David Drive
N. Syracuse, NY 13212
(315) 458-3786

Marilyn Forth produces paintings on silk which possess a great deal of visual depth and color clarity. She uses a very high grade of silk and Procion Fiber Reactive Dyes. The flowers in her artwork seem to move and grow and be alive. Her wall panels and framed work bring the garden inside. Any combination of flowers may be ordered. Commissions range from $250 to $4,000. Commissions begin with sketch and color study on silk. Panels are washable and fade resistant. Installation services available. Delivery in 4 to 6 weeks. Marilyn Forth has taught Textile Arts courses c Syracuse University.

(Left) "Pansies" John Michael Kohler Arts Center, Sheboygan WI, 4 ft. x 6 ft.

(Top right) "Crocuses and Windflowers" 45" b 45".

(Bottom right) "Garden Bouquet" 45" by 45"

ncy Lubin

rn Maine Weavers
arl Street
en ME 04843
236-4069

Lubin hand weaves custom designed
from luxury fibers including silk, alpaca,
and mohair.

years Nancy has been a national
ce for uniquely designed throws for
designers. The throws, which can be
ved all year, frequently appear in major
design magazines.

exhibits regularly at prestigious
al craft fairs and trade shows.

rn Maine Weavers has a well stocked
ory of throws for immediate delivery.

ct Western Maine Weavers for more
ation.

x 72" plus fringe. Mohair Throws.

Jennifer Mackey

Chia Jen Studio
P.O. Box 469
Scotia, CA 95565
(707) 725-2626

Mackey's handpainted natural fibers are contemporary and refreshing. Chosen for practicality and richness, silks, cottons and linens are also durable and easily cleaned. Her design element often evokes a Japanese mood via color/space/textural depth ratios. Mackey designed and studied throughout the U.S. and Europe. Her work has been represented in several national publications, galleries, and specialty stores.

Jennifer Mackey welcomes collaborations and private or corporate commissions. Her fabrics have been used for many nontraditional textile applications. Custom fabrics start at $60 yard and installations start at $50 per sq. ft. Call or write for brochure.

(Top) Custom table linens for Neiman-Marcus.

(Bottom right) Reverse appliqued silk curtains, 96" x 72".

(Bottom left) Floor canvas.

ll Wilcox

W 20th Street, 4th Floor
w York, NY 10011
3) 858-0868

ether for the residential or commercial
rior, Jill Wilcox creates hand-painted and
pliquéd textiles in one of a kind and limited
tions. These works are suitable for banners,
hangings, and bedcovers.

wall hangings are of cotton canvas and
-fading, heat treated textile paint,
ereas fabrics for bedcovers can vary
cording to the client's wishes. Retail prices
ge from 90.00 to 200.00 per sq. ft. and
very time varies by project.

Wilcox's work is included in corporate and
ate collections in the U.S. and Europe and
been published in:

Guild, 1987.

gn Journal, April 1989.

temporary Crafts for the Home, Bill Kraus,
).

left) "Lattier/Sunlight," wallhanging, 4' x 5'.

right) "Terra cotta Collage," bedcover

om) "Kingston Trees #2," wallhanging,
5'.

Barbara Zinkel

333 Pilgrim
Birmingham, MI 48009
(313) 642-9789

Barbara Zinkel is internationally known for her limited edition serigraphs. Their saturated hues and large, graphic elements are expressionistic and coloristic in spirit. The prints are produced on 100% rag paper, signed and numbered by the artist. Her work is included in many corporate and private collections.

Zinkel's serigraphs are in collections of:
Chase Manhattan Bank, N.A., Atria West, NY
Proctor & Gamble, Corporate Headquarters, Cincinnati, OH
Steelcase, Inc., Grand Rapids, MI
Texas Instruments, Dallas, TX
Rabo Bank, Eibergen, the Netherlands
Landmark Systems, Vienna, VA

Barbara Zinkel is currently featuring a custom rug design with 35 colors in reds, greens, purples, navy in combination with neutral tones. It is professionally hand-tufted and hand-carved. It is 100% wool fiber and is 9 1/2' x 12' in size. It retails for $14,000. Custom sizes are available and require four months for delivery. Samples are available.

(Top right) "Interlude," serigraph, 39" x 44". Edition size: 250, $450

(Bottom) Detail from custom wool rug design by Barbara Zinkel

TAPESTRIES

97 Carol Atleson

98 Lynda Brothers

99 Joan Griffin

100 Martha Heine

101 Silvia Heyden

102 Victor Jacoby

103 Michelle Lester

104 Antonia Lowden

105 Dianne McKenzie

107 New York Tapestry Artists

108 Julia Schloss

109 Elinor Steele

110 Nancy Wines-DeWan

arol Atleson

Ruskin Road
herst, NY 14226
6) 834-9384

nderfully rich in color and texture, Carol
eson's imaginary landscapes have been
ibited nationally and chosen for
dential, corporate and public spaces.
se unique inlay weavings, exceptionally
able and easily installed and maintained,
be commissioned in single or multiple
els to accommodate any size and color
cifications. A two month minimum is
uired from the initial color study to
pleted weaving.

right) "Aquarial View," 43"w. x 56"h.

tom) "Rockbound", Real Associates,
nor, PA, 85"w. x 44"h.

Lynda Brothers

McKeon Art Consulting
Laurie L. McKeon
1404 Foothill Road
Ojai, CA 93023
(805) 646-7917

Lynda Brothers designs and weaves tapestries for corporate and residential spaces. Her versatile techniques encompass sophisticated abstract and representational themes.

She has experience in large scale collaborations, up to 3,375 square feet, with architects and designers. Collectors of her work in the United States, Africa and Europe include: Medical Advertising and Design, Fuji Bank, Coldwell Banker, Pacific Telephone, Marriott Hotel. The artist completes approximately 20 square feet per month. Prices range from $200–$450 per square foot. Installation available.

Woven tapestry, hand-dyed wool, mohair and metallic fibers, 14' x 7', Beverly Hills, California.

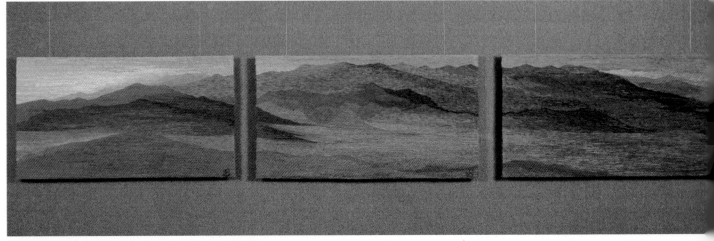

"TANTROPTYCHON", woven tapestry, wool and mohair, 3' x 17'.

an Griffin
Design Studio
ke Street
mondsport, NY 14840
569-2256

om designed tapestries by Joan Griffin
been commissioned for corporate
es, conference rooms, libraries, hospitals
orivate residences. They are woven of
ium wool and silk to ensure durability,
of installation and maintenance.

ommissioned tapestries, scaled drawings
yarn samples are presented for approval
irm delivery date and cost. Retail price
e is $175–250 sq. ft. Complete information
ble upon request.

Right) Detail "Fantasy Flight", 5' x 7'.

.eft) "Spring Garden", 6' x 9'.

om): "Wings", 5' x 3'.

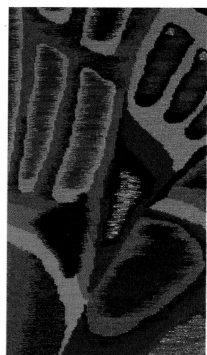

Martha Heine

7 Haggis Court
Durham, NC 27705
(919) 479-3270

Martha Heine designs and weaves tapestries for corporate clients and residential areas.

With variegated and European novelty yarns she explores movement with subtle transitions of color. Large spaces are broken up into detailed imagery. She suggests diptych or multiple pieces for a project wider than 5 ft.

A maquette and yarn samples are submitted to meet the needs of the client. The artist welcomes private and corporate commissions for site-specific projects. Prices range from $140.–to $175.-per sq. ft.

Collections and commissions include: Duke University Eye Center, Wachovia Bank and Trust, Glaxo, Inc., NCNB, Inc., Southern Bell Telephone, R.J. Reynolds. IBM, Fuqua Industries, Peoples Security Insurance, and numerous private collectors.

(Right) Uplifting Chords, 48" x 60".

(Below) Cascading Light, 48" x 60".

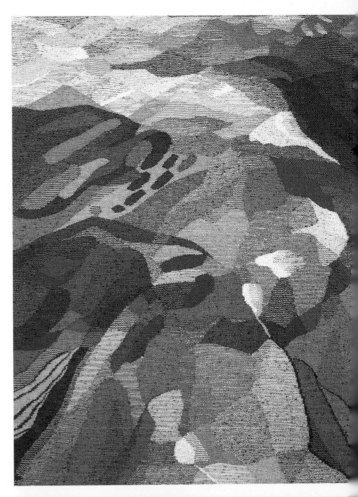

ilvia Heyden
29 Montgomery Street
rham, NC 27705
9) 489-0582

Contemporary tapestry-weaving is a unique, still unexplored art form. While classical tapestries are predesigned pictures in wool, Silvia Heyden's work follows its own means of expression in the process of weaving. Silvia Heyden discovers unexpected relations between woven texture, color and form, which give new life and energy to our surroundings.

1989 commissions for public buildings include: Main Lobby, Renaissance Plaza, Greensboro, North Carolina and 'Art in Architecture Project' of Maryland Community Recreation Center, Chevy Chase, Maryland

'Sonatina', 60" x 52"

Victor Jacoby

1086 17th Street
Eureka, CA 95501
(707) 442 3809

The tapestries of Victor Jacoby are woven of fine wools and cotton. They have been exhibited throughout the U.S. and in Canada and France.

Commissioned tapestries are designed for both corporate and residential spaces. Themes vary from landscape and floral to figurative. Price is $150 per square foot.

Clients include AT&T, Kaiser-Permanente, Marriott Corporation, SEIU and Shearson, Lehman, Hutton.

(Top left) "Afternoon Shadows" 32 x 30 ©1989.

(Top right) "Autumn Shadows" 48 x 36 ©1990.

(Bottom) "Roses" 61 x 97 ©1989.

Michelle Lester

West 17 Street
w York, NY 10011
2) 989-1411

chelle Lester's watercolors and drawings
ve been the basis for her studio's
duction since 1971. The original
rks-on-paper are available and can be
ordinated with her tapestries.

mes are varied—from landscapes and
als through abstractions on other themes.

nts include Honeywell, Neiman Marcus,
aco, IBM, General Electric, TRW, and R.J
nolds, Sheraton Grande Tokyo, Japan,
AS Medical Ctr. Yanbu, Saudi Arabia, and
in's Communication, NYC and Chicago.

o) "Two Trees," 8' x 6 ' ©1988.

tom) "April Showers," 6 1/2' x 9 1/2 ' ©1989.

Antonia Lowden

Contemporary Design-Woven for the Wall
401 Court Street
Reno, NV 89501
(702) 826-3655

Award Winning Designer/Artist Antonia Lowden has been working with Architects and Interior Designers for ten years. An MFA/Graduate of Fiberworks/JFK University she is known for her Woven Tapestries and Oil Pastel Paintings. Her works are in many private and corporate collections, and hang in Banks and Hospitals.

(Pictured below left) Oil Pastel Painting "Interior Landscape" 2' x 3'.

(Right) Commission for St. Mary's Hospital, Reno, NV. 3' x 15'.

(Bottom) The American Tapestry Alliance 'Award of Excellence' winning "Vision Mountain" tapestry 12' x 6',

Artist is available for installation. Most commissions require 6–8 weeks. Cost $200 sq/ft.

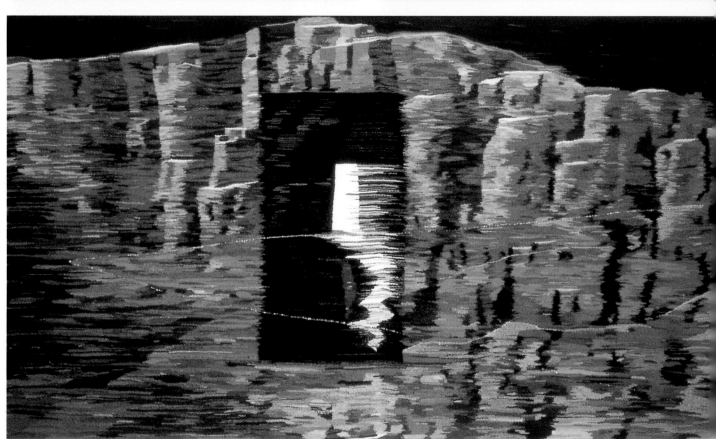

anne McKenzie

ne McKenzie Design
Box 337
Sea Ranch, CA 95497
) 785-2567

ne McKenzie's studio designs and
aves large-scale tapestries for corporate
ections, public art installations and
dential interiors. Over the past 15 years,
nts have included: Bank of America; San
cisco Design Center: Gibson, Dunn and
cher, attorneys; Washington National
ance; and numerous private collectors.

Kenzie also collaborates with fine artists,
preting their work into her tapestry style.
ts currently include painters Millard Sheets
Marquerite Fletcher.

tapestry technique employs weaving
ous yarns to create a three-dimensional
ured relief unique to her style. All yarns
custom dyed, lightfast and moth proof.
uction time runs approximately 6 months
6' x 8' tapestry.

ection of tapestries, portfolio, commission
edures, pricing and additional
mation are available upon request.

"Slipping Between the Worlds" 8' x 8' 1989 private collection of Jack + Bobbi Linkletter.

"French Landscape" 6' x 8' original painting by Millard Sheets woven by artist.

At a time when most interiors "cry out" for personalization, THE GUILD series of directories offer unique opportunities to identify new generations of craftsmen with skills in a wide range of media. These are leaders in fields as diverse as stained glass, basketry, and stone cutting—working in styles from avant garde to 19th century restoration.

Any of us would be pleased to see such a fine compilation of current work in so many idioms. The large page format and deluxe, full-color printing is impressive; so is the size and heft of the book—about 500 pages. The scales of the images, illustrating both major installations and actual scale details of surfaces, is both exhilarating and informative. So is the section showing the "stables" of artists sold through some of this country's leading galleries and dealers.

For the design professional, GUILD 6 will be that much more useful. Sequencing by such media titles as Lighting and Accessories, Painted Finishes, and Architectural Metalwork makes for easy access to a mountain of material. So does the cross-reference of artists listed by state. Quite honestly, it would take a resource librarian years to assemble such a compendium of talent.

The need for such work has never been greater. Whether for work, play, or living, most interiors built today are without a sense of materials or structure. Surfaces are monotonous, elements such as doors, windows and fixtures mass produced. Worse yet, these shoebox spaces tend to be look-alike and impersonal. It is the furnishings within that provide a sense of place, of materials and warmth, and, of identity. But of all furnishings, craft particular to site and client, best provides the quintessential antidote to mass production.

From my personal experience, the artist craftsman is the solution. I find they can read plans, analyze needs and provide solutions. Models and actual-scale samples are within their grasp. Since they know their materials so well through first-hand, and hands-on experience, they can predict patination and life expectancy. They know which surfaces will age gracefully and which are so delicate as to require protection. Thankfully, their media range has quickly expanded. Today's metalsmiths include those working in iron and bronze, aluminum and Coreten steel. Fiber now includes dozens of idioms in every new and old material.

Craftsmen are, by definition, problem solvers. They tend to grasp the "larger picture", including medium and processing, fabrication and installation, and performance through use and time. By and large, they want their work to become the appreciated art which will be collected when the building is pulled down.

However, this is still a relatively underground movement: the producers are found neither in the Yellow Pages or Sweet's catalogs. But they can be found in THE GUILD. Because the distribution channels are so direct, the costs are amazingly competitive. And the results endurably satisfying.

Jack Lenor Larsen
President Emeritus
American Craft Council

w York Tapestry Artists

Chelsea Station, P.O. Box 1747
York, NY 10113-0940
) 924-2478; fax (914) 225-0382

A is an international group of
emporary fiber artists whose tapestries
represented in corporate and private
ections. Portfolios and prices are available
request. Work by four of the artists is
n here (clockwise from top right): Rita R.
nt, Mary-Ann Sievert, Bojana H. Leznicki,
Betty Vera.

Julia Schloss

Handwoven Originals
6005 28th Street N.W.
Washington, DC 20015
(202) 363-4718

Award winning fiber artist Julia Schloss creates one-of-a-kind originally designed handwoven wall hangings for corporate, institutional and private spaces.

Her handwoven wall hangings are included in over fifty collections, and are installed in banks, hotel suites, conference rooms, lobbies, hospital meditation and recovery rooms, private offices and private residences.

Ms. Schloss accepts commissions and also has available a varied selection of completed work.

Retail prices range from $100–$150 per square foot. Slides and information are available upon request.

"Reflections IV" 56" x 104", wool on linen.

"Paths of Light" 56" x 104", wool on linen.

nor Steele

Weybridge Street
dlebury, VT 05753
) 388-6546

r Steele combines her strong sense of
phic design with meticulous craftsmanship
reate contemporary tapestries that are
ally exciting in large public spaces as well
timate home or office settings. She has
bited nationally since 1974. Collectors
de IBM and Prudential Insurance
pany.

missions of any size are invited and may
porate design elements from the
unding architecture and furnishings.
s per square foot range from $150–250
ending on size and complexity.

t) "Magic" 41" x 52"

w) "City at Dawn" 48" x 72"

Nancy Wines-DeWan

Contemporary Maine Textiles
P.O. Box 861, Sligo Road
Yarmouth, ME 04096
(207) 846-6058

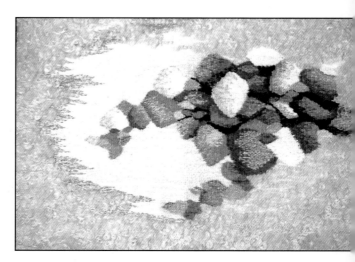

Nancy Wines-DeWan creates woven tapestries for public spaces, churches, and private residences. Her designs, inspired by the Maine landscape, are studies in texture and subtle colors. Natural fibers are featured in her work, especially mohair from her herd of Angora goats. The hand-spun and hand-dyed fiber can be dyed to match color samples provided by the client.

Her work is in the collection of the University of Nebraska's College of Nursing; Northwestern Bank, Omaha, Nebraska; and many other institutional and private collections throughout the country.

Prices start at $100 per square foot. Please contact the artist for additional information.

(Top right) "Rock Study," 20"w.x30"h.

(Middle & Bottom) Details of "Tidal Tryptich," 108"w.x48"h. Private Collection, Falmouth Foreside, Maine.

ART QUILTS

113 Teresa Barkley

114 Chris Bobin

115 D. Joyce Davies

116 Susana England

117 Pamela Hill

118 Jean Hoblitzell

119 K. H. Klein

120 Melba La Mountain

121 Dottie Moore

122 Therese May

123 Kathleen Sharp

124 Ann Trusty

eresa Barkley

40 27 Street
oria, NY 11102
8) 545-4281

esa Barkley creates art quilts that merge
rkmanship characteristic of the nineteenth
ntury with themes for the twenty-first
ntury. To achieve this, she frequently
ploys historic fabrics and the motif of a
stage stamp—a conventional means of
ghtening public awareness.

o) "Vietnam Veteran's Memorial," fiber,
w. x 16"h.

ttom) "Peacock Plaid," fiber, 53"w. x 69"h.
signed as part of a series of quilts based on
ostage stamp motif, the imagery
ployed in the quilt depicts levels of
rning. "Peacock Plaid" was commissioned
he Textiles, Design and Consumer
nomics Department in the College of
nan Resources, University of Delaware,
ere it is on permanent display in Alison Hall.

photos by: Stuart Bakal-Schwartzberg,

East 23 Street NYC 10010 (212) 254-2988.

Chris Bobin

5 East 17th Street
6th Floor
New York City, NY 10003
(212) 691-2821 (studio); (212) 475-7268 (home)

Chris Bobin's fabric assemblages are quilted appliques, rich in color, texture and humor. Many include dimentional objects.

Production time varies depending on size and complexity. An average completion time: one to two months. Commissions accepted; Ms. Bobin will work directly with clients on projects for public or private sites. Pieces can be stretched on frames and wired for easy hanging.

Prices range from $600. to $5000.

Slides of currently available work on request.

(Top) "Chinese Girls" - 4 1/2' x 5' x 6' x 7'.

(Bottom) "American Food" - 45 1/2" x 63".

Photos: Carl Picco.

Joyce Davies

Front Street East, Number 425
onto, Ontario M5E IT3
hada
5) 365-3250

ts by D. Joyce Davies are the products of
ve of bright colors and bold, creative
ign elements...combined with experience
oral photography, sculpture, painting and
ing.

work has been included in a number of
or exhibits and juried shows in the United
es and Canada, as well as magazines,
books and furniture catalogs.

es' quilted wall hangings are designed
esidential and specialized commercial
iors. All works are hand-appliqued and
d-quilted, with borders machine stitched.
erials are cottons, blends and silks. The
s can be drycleaned.

es range from $80 per sq. ft., depending
complexity of design. Additional
mation and slides available from the
on request.

Stampede at the Old Carousel, 27" x

om) *Bed of Roses*, 36" x 38".

Susana England

P.O. Box 20601
Oakland, CA 94620
(415) 235-4660

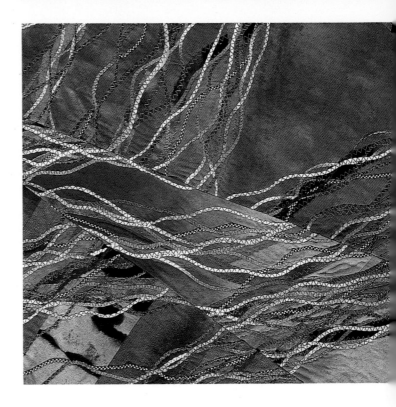

Susana England's wallhangings are paintings in cloth. Silk fabrics are hand dyed and pieced. Sections are then embellished with stitched yarns and ribbons. The diagonal movement of the stitching adds drama to the planes of color. The abstract images and the textural quality of cloth make these "fabric paintings" ideally suited for contemporary private, commercial and corporate settings.

Examples of England's work are included in the corporate collections of Kaiser Permanente, Petaluma, CA and the Kaiser Permanente Northern California Regional Facility in Oakland, CA.

Further information and slides are available upon request. Prices range from $60 to $110 a square foot.

(Top) Detail of "In Depth."

(Bottom) "In Depth" 54" x 55" Hand dyed raw silk fabric pieced and embellished with hand dyed yarns and ribbons.

Recently featured in *Metropolis*, June 1990

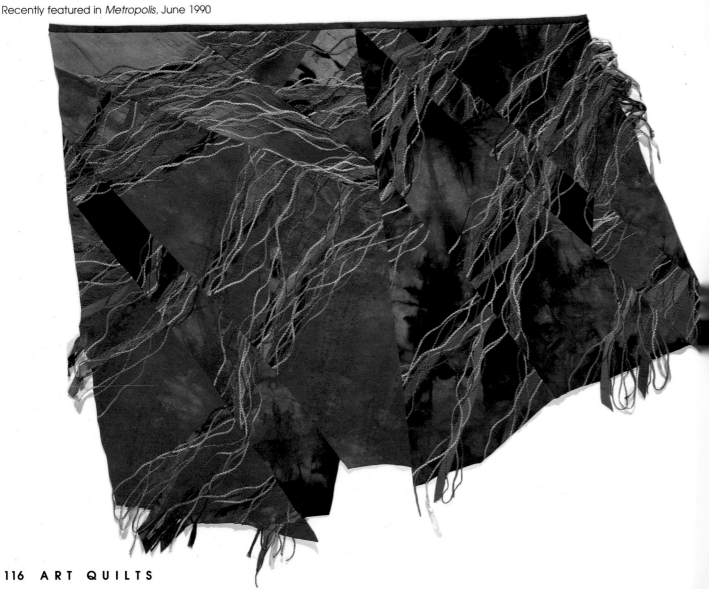

amela Hill

0 Lafayette
, Box 328
kelumne Hill, CA 95245
9) 286-1217

quilts of Pamela Hill combine the history
d tradition of the craft with her use of bold
tern and strong clear color. Although
quently used as wall pieces, the quilts are
gned and constructed to be durable for
ryday use as bedcovers. All are filled with
rguard and most are machine-washable.
quilts are available either as limited
on or one of a kind pieces.

es range from $900 – $2500.

) "Sasano," 96" x 108" - Machine pieced
quilted of pima cotton, satin and
allic fabrics.

tom) "Homeland," 100" x 115"- Machine
ed and quilted of 100% pima cotton.

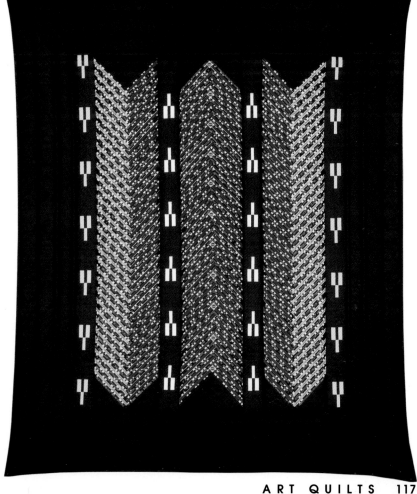

Jean Hoblitzell

The Storefront, Suite A
20 East Randall Street
Baltimore, MD 21230
(301) 332-8032

Jean Hoblitzell designs and creates
one-of-a-kind quilts for residential and
commercial spaces. Her architectural
background provides the inspiration for her
unique designs. She collaborates with each
client to create
a piece for their particular interior.

Her quilts are exhibited nationally and
included in corporate collections such as
Corestates and United Way.

Slides and resume available upon request.
Delivery time ranges from four to six months.

(Top) "In Truth There Is More Than One Face",
20" x 25".

(Bottom) "One Of Three" 74" x 74".

. H. Klein

5 Grandview Blvd.
ncaster, PA 17601
7) 293-9453

aberly Haldeman Klein specializes in custom
signed traditional wall quilts for residential
d commercial areas.

de of 100% cotton in deep Amish hues
d quilted by hand—these pieces add a
king accent to contemporary as well as
ditional spaces. Prices range from
00–$2000 depending on the size and
nplexity of the piece. Average delivery
e is 8–12 weeks.

Klein's work has been featured in House
d Garden, The New York Times, Country
ng, and Creative Ideas for Living. Slides
ailable upon request

p) Sunshine and Shadow 52" x 52" ©1990.
ttom) Log Cabin 50" x 50" ©1990.

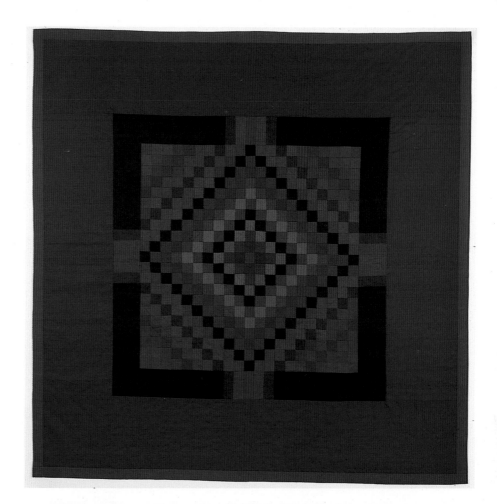

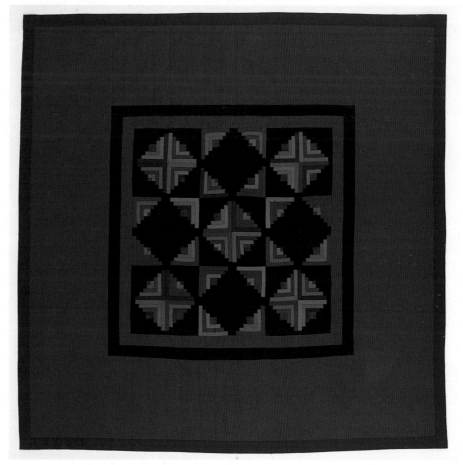

Melba La Mountain

The Quilt Connection
9014 Prairie Lane
Houston, TX 77064
(713) 466-0609

Recapture a time of beauty and day gone by with one of our heirlooms. We do yesterdays quilts, also the new arts of tomorrow. This is where ideas become reality! All quilts are hand-made with the finest quality of materials and workmanship.

Sizes range from king to twin, and prices vary according to quilter. Many quilts to choose from or select your own pattern and colors.

More than just a cover-up—refinement the country way!

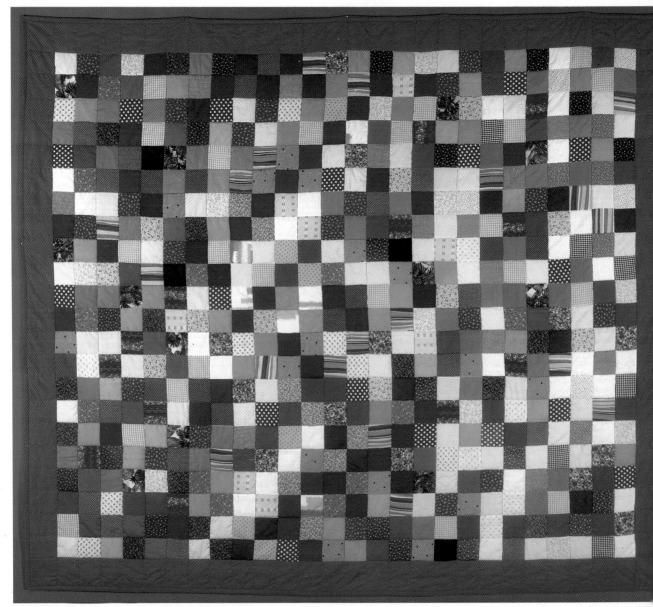

image 1

ottie Moore

4 Charlotte Avenue
k Hill, SC 29732
) 327-5088

rie Moore creates one-of-a-kind and
ed edition wall pieces. These are
liqued, embroidered, and quilted for both
vidual and corporate clients. Her work is
wn for its strong sense of color and the
ailed intricate quilting which produces a
ptural quality.

ent projects include: a 6' x 12'
ntennial commission for Tusculum College
reeneville, Tennessee, a 4' x 5' wall
ging of the barn and landholdings of
gs Industry, and a grant from the Rock
rts Council with funds through the South
olina Arts Commission and the National
owment For The Arts.

s and prices are available upon request.

w) "Windows", 70" x 44".

t) "Windows", (Detail).

Therese May

651 N. 4th Street
San Jose, CA 95112
(408) 292-3247

Therese May has been making quilts since 1965 and has degrees from the University of Wisconsin, Madison and San Jose State University, San Jose, Ca. Her work is included in many publications such as *America's Glorious Quilts* and *The Art Quilt*. She has exhibited throughout the U.S., Europe and Japan. Her current project is a 14' x 14' quilt to hang in the new San Jose convention center. Her work is also included in numerous private collections.

May's quilts are made up of playful fantasy animal and plant imagery and are all machine appliqued using straight stitch and satin stitch. Threads are left uncut and form a network of texture across the surface. Acrylic paint is added as a finishing touch. Prices range from $1000.00 for 2 ' x 2' to $36,000.00 for 14' x 14'

(Top) "Rose" 66" x 56".

(Bottom) "Rose (Detail).

athleen Sharp

60 Valley Oak
nte Sereno, CA 95030
3) 395-3014

Kathleen Sharp's distinctive use of large-scale
architectural images evokes the feeling of
timeless archetypal space. The finest materials
and careful attention to detail assures the
integrity and permanence of each piece.

Widely exhibited in museums and galleries,
her quilts are included in private and
corporate collections, the most recent being
Hewlett-Packard Corporation.

Commissioned work can be tailored to
individual or corporate color/space
requirements. Finished works are available for
purchase.

Further information available upon request.

"Vigil" 50"w x 82"h © 1990 Kathleen Sharp.

"Alcove" 64"w x 60"h © 1990 Kathleen Sharp.

Ann Trusty

Hulsey/Trusty
925 Maine
Lawrence, KS 66044
(913) 841-4242

Ann Trusty's art quilts are distinctive for their
brilliant and unexpected color and energy.
Her widely published work has been exhibited
in Paris, throughout France, Turkey, Japan
and in Boston, New York City and San Diego.
Please contact the artist for information on
commissions and slides of available work.

(Top) Twilight–The Mythology Quilt, 5' x 6'.

(Bottom) Window of Opportunity, 6' x 6'.

FIBER INSTALLATIONS

127 B.J. Adams

128 Sandy Askew

129 Barbara Barron

130 Nancy Boney

131 Jeanne Braen

132 Joyce Marquess Carey

133 Jeanne Dawson

134 Su Egen

135 Ann Epstein

136 Lucy G. Feller

137 Al Granek

138 Marcia Hammond

139 Janis Kanter

140 Janet Kuemmerlein

141 Nancy Lyon

142 LaVerne McLeod

143 Jennifer McLeod

144 Cynthia Nixon

145 Elizabeth Nordgren

146 Amanda Richardson

147 Amanda Richardson

149 Jude Russell

150 Carole Sabiston

151 Carole Sabiston

152 Sally Shore

153 Vincent Tolpo
     Carolyn Lee Tolpo

154 Pamela Twycross-Reed

155 Lydia Van Gelder

156 Judi Maureen White

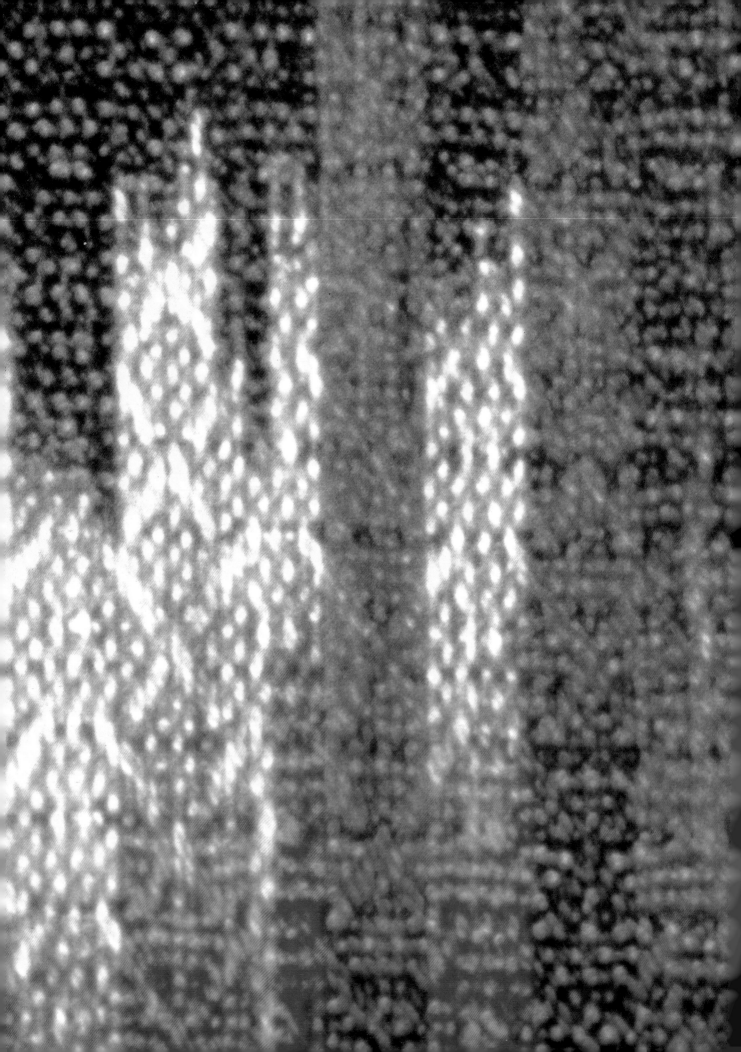

J. Adams

n Fiber

Arizona Terrace, N.W.
hington DC 20016
) 364-8404 (studio)
) 686-1042 (home)

Adams' art work can be bright or
dued, free-flowing or geometric, earthy or
ant, flat or highly textured. Single or
dular units are stretched over wood
es. These one-of-a-kind wall hangings are
gned for both commercial and residential
ors.

ns will collaborate with clients, art
ultants, interior designers, and architects
eet their specific design, scheduling and
get requirements.

work has been purchased or
missioned by individual collectors as well
usiness, medical, banking, hotel, and
ernment facilities.

ure and commission information is
able on request.

"Sequentially Random", 17" x 17"
ed and framed, machine stitchery over
us fabrics.

om) "Inexhaustable Network", 20" x 20",
ed and manipulated fabrics with
nine stitchery.

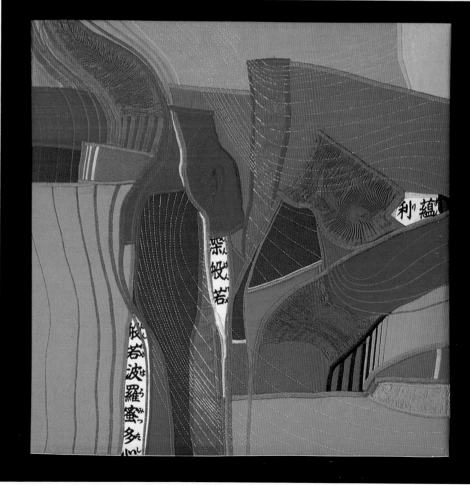

Sandy Askew

50951 Expressway
Belleville, MI 48111
(313) 483-5529

Working with clients, designers, consultants
and architects, Sandy Askew considers color,
design, space and cost when developing
wall hangings for home or office. Combining
enthusiasm for texture with interest and skill,
her pieces are woven on their own custom
framework and utilize a variety of fibers and
materials to compliment any decor.
Installation is simple and care requires only
occasional dusting as pieces have been
treated with a fabric protectant. Commissions
by phone or correspondence, delivery is
usually within 4 to 6 weeks. Prices generally
range from $35 to $75 per square foot. Some
commissioned works include Dow-Corning
Corporation, Van Buren Area Museum,
numerous Rutenberg model homes and
several midwestern galleries.

(Top) "Gallaxy" 45"dia.

(Bottom) "Rapsodie flamande" 3x5.

arbara Barron
3 New York Avenue
tington Station, NY 11746
) 549-4242
) 549-9122

Barbara Barron specializes in a full range of site-specific wall hangings for commercial and residential interiors. She has successfully used the medium of wrapped fibres to create dimensional one of a kind fibre sculptures world wide. Barron has been creating wall hangings for eighteen years, and is assisted by family members, Steven and Ruth Barron, exhibiting artists.

Pricing information, brochures, slides and color samples available upon request. Individual needs for size, color and budget considered. Gallery/workshop.

Delivery time: 2–8 weeks. Complete installation and maintenance services. Scotchguard and fireproofing available.

Collectors include: Burt Reynolds, Trump Plaza, A.T.&T., Shearson Lehman Hutton, Weight Watchers International, United Virginia Bank, Australian Film Institute.

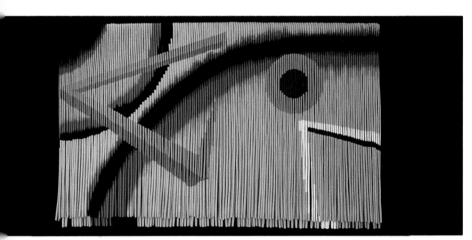

AR RAINBOW", 8' x 4¹/2' The Penn Central Corp., Cincinnati, OH.

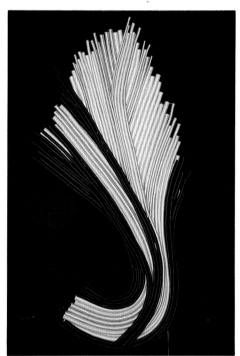

"FLAME", 8'x3', Private Residence.

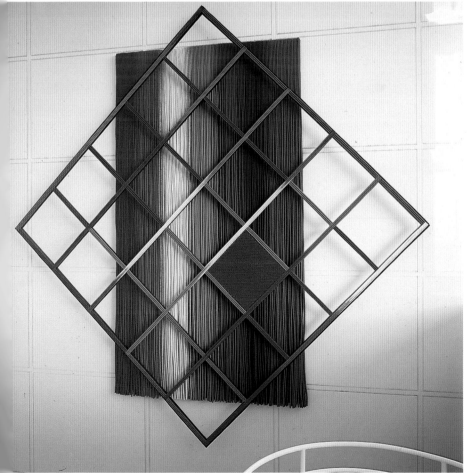

ADE", 24'x24', Hauppauge Corp. Center, Hauppauge, NY.

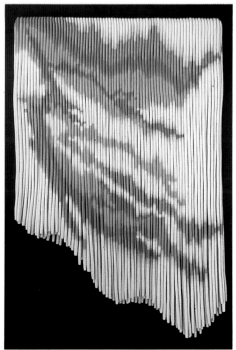

"EVOLUTION", 4'x6', Private Residence.

Nancy Boney

97 King Street
Fanwood, NJ 07023
(908) 889-8219

Vitality, strength of design, and richness of color are central to the appeal of the fabric wall hangings and wall sculptures of Nancy Boney. Her palette varies from soft and subdued to deep and luxurious. A diversity of fabrics and/or painted canvas are used to suggest the natural environment as well as abstract ideas.

Installations of Boney's work are found in professional and corporate offices, hospitals, churches, and private homes. Retail prices begin at $650 for sculptural wall pieces, and at $80 per square foot for wall hangings. Delivery is 4–6 weeks. Works are protected with scotchgard and are easily installed and maintained. Framing is optional. Commissions and collaborations are welcomed.

(Top) "Happy Tears", Applique and constructed fabric wall hanging, 44" x 44" x 1".

(Bottom left) "Moon Rose", Painted canvas and fabric, 22" x 22" x 5".

(Bottom right) "Satisfied", Painted canvas, 48" x 22" x 3".

Jeanne Braen

Rockhouse Road
lton, CT 06897
03) 834-9549

Jeanne Braen creates woven sculptural wall and ceiling hung works in both architectural and intimate scales for residential and corporate spaces.

She enjoys collaborating with designers, consultants, and architects to meet specific client and space requirements.

The artist's unique commissioned works hang in atriums, lobbies, conference rooms and numerous residences.

Prices are $80 to $100 per square foot. A proposal fee of 10% of the final price will provide the client with drawings and woven fabric samples of the artwork. Slide sheets, resumeé, information on commissioning procedures and on available completed wall hangings will be supplied upon request.

(Left) "In Her Honor", 6.5' x 11.5' x 4.5".

(Right) "Primrose Path", 82" x 44" x 3".

(Bottom) "Synergia", 9' x 12'.

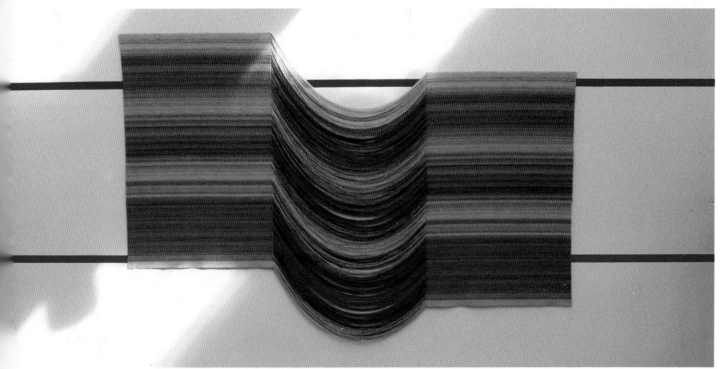

Joyce Marquess Carey
913 Harrison Street
Madison WI 53711
(608) 256-1537

Carey specializes in site-specific sewn wall pieces using luxury fabrics in varied textures that are durable, warm, fade-resistant and easily maintained. Clients include many public art programs, corporations and collectors. Her work is exhibited and published internationally. Carey works with architects, designers and clients to develop unique design proposals which include scale drawings and sewn samples. Works range from 10 to 200 square feet or larger, priced at $100–$200 per square foot. Prices, resume and slides available.

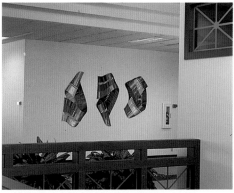

"Glad Rags," 4' x 10', Demco Corporation, Madison, WI.

"Sunburst," Auditor General Building, Tallahassee. FL.

"Earl Grey's Garden," 13' x 21', Dean Clinic, Madison, WI.

eanne Dawson
8 E. Las Olas Boulevard #101
t Lauderdale, FL 33301
05) 462-4347

ommissioned by designers, architects, art
nsultants, galleries, and individuals, Jeanne
ves to create original and dramatic fiber
ll pieces, which explore the myriad of
anipulations possible with fiber forms,
tures, and colors.

r unique pieces are done both on a large
r loom and on coil forms suspended from
s on ceilings or walls.

es range from $80–$150 a square foot.
-approval drawings or models, fireproofing,
allation available.

l or write for resumé, photos or slides.

Su Egen

2233 East Hawthorne Street
Tucson, AZ 85719
(602) 325-0009

Bold geometric and figurative tapestries and damasks characterize the works of Su Egen, known for her delicate intricate weavings and masterful color usage. Handwoven with the finest Scandinavian yarns, they are durable and practically maintenance free.

Su has been weaving for over twenty years and her work can be found in collections in the US and abroad.

All work is designed and woven by the artist in her Tucson studio on Swedish rug and drawlooms combining old techniques and new designs which integrate well in their surroundings.

Additional information, resume and color slides of work on hand are available upon request (refundable fee of $1 per slide). Prices begin at $200. Allow up to three months for custom work.

(Below) "Chinle" 19"w x 57"h - 100% linen.
(Right) "Serenity" 34"w x 65"h - linen and wool.

nn Epstein
6 N. Maple Road
 Arbor, MI 48105
3) 996-9019

Ann Epstein's painterly ikat-woven hangings integrate color and texture to express the interior landscape and universal emotional themes of our everyday lives. The one-of-a-kind multi-panel weavings are of fine, hand-dyed, cotton yarns in complex twill patterns.

Panels can be combined to meet any space requirement and the color range is unlimited. Prices are approximately $125 per square foot wholesale; drawings and installation costs are extra. Ready-made works are available and most commissioned pieces can be completed within several months.

Ann Epstein's work has been exhibited nationally, and has been featured in *Fiberarts* and *Surface Design Journal*. The artist accepts both residential and corporate commissions, and is pleased to work with architects, designers, art consultants, and gallery agents.

(Top left)"Parallel Processes", 46" x 69".

(Top right) "Fun-Loving But Not Anti-Intellectual" detail.

(Bottom) "Fun-Loving But Not Anti-Intellectual", 45" x 69".

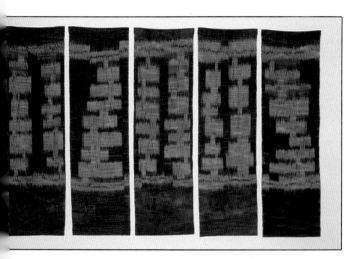

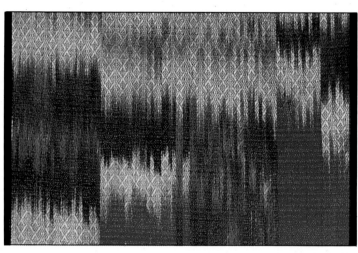

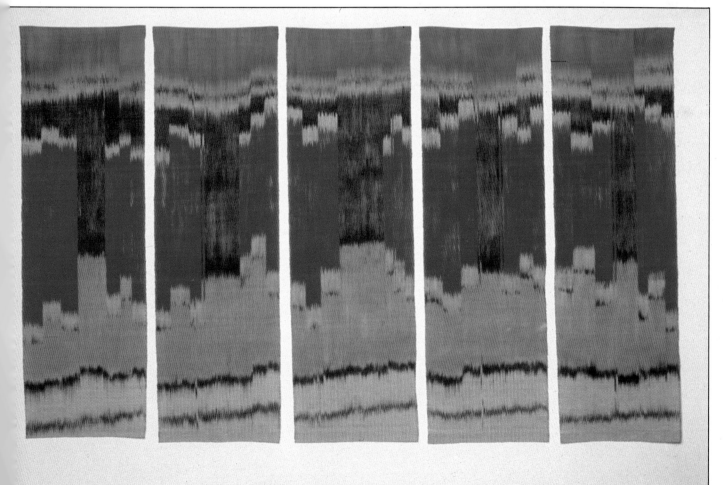

Lucy G. Feller

Photo Linens
941 Park Avenue
New York, NY 10028
(212) 628-1361

Lucy Feller will create a unique piece of art for your office or home. She calls these Photo Linens. The intent is to preserve important moments in time or chronicle a series of events. By manipulating photographs and using the Canon Laser these images are then transferred onto fabric. Stitching, embroidering and found objects add artistic accents.

There is no limit to the creative possibilities once a client's wishes are known. It can be as political as one client's dinner at the White House or as personal as a child's youth recaptured on her old favorite bath robe.

Feller's work is seriously humerous, detailed and precise. Prices range from $2,000 to $10,000 depending on size and intricacy.

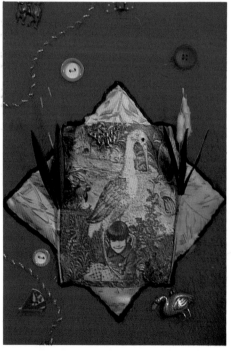

l Granek
r in Fiber
). Box 31257
Verde, AZ 85263
2) 471-7223

Al Granek has developed the technique—and designed the tools—for wrapping fine yarns, such as silk, linen, cotton, metallics and synthetic fibers. He uses fiber windings as the canvas and an array of colored yarns for the palette of his craft art.

The result: beautiful contemporary wall hangings for artistic focal points and important visual sites.

He has been commissioned by a number of notable clients, including AT&T, Marriot Hotel, Westinghouse and Kimberly Clark.

Granek's experience in interior design, woodworking and sculpture is appreciated by architects, interior designers and art consultants. Prices vary from $40 to $120 per sq. ft. Delivery is 4 to 12 weeks.

For additional information, photos and slides, please contact the artist.

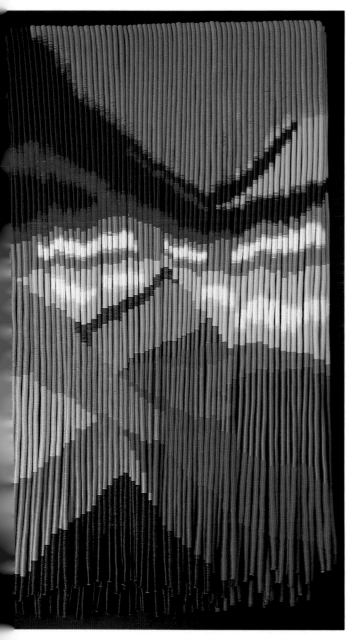

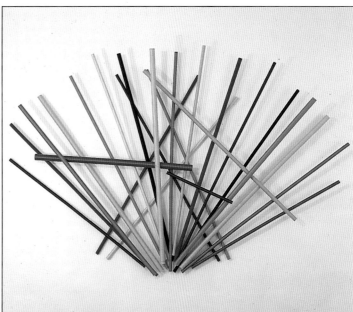

Marcia Hammond

Route 1 Box 898 Town Farm Road
Putney, VT 05346
(802) 387-2202

Marcia Hammond creates twice-woven wall
hangings and sculptural pieces from the
intensely layered colors of her previously
handwoven fabrics. These fabrics of cotton,
silk, rayon chenille, mohair and wool are
again woven to create landscape—like
paintings in fibre. Moving, fluid colors invite
the viewer to participate in her understanding
of the natural world. She has been weaving
and designing with color and fibre for 23
years.

Prices range from $80.00–120.00 /sq. ft.
Collaboration is acceptable and installation
can be included in the price.

She has exhibited her work in a wide range of
settings. Her most recent commission for a
corporate setting is IBM.

nis Kanter

West Dickens
ago, IL 60622
252-2119

orating mixed media, such as neon
g, with the use of varied fibrous materials,
impact and movement become the
t elements of Janis Kanter's fiber
ations.

only the finest quality wool, linen and
lic yarns, these contemporary art works,
asted through a traditional craft
um, are easy to maintain and are highly
ble for most interior spaces.

orations with architects, designers and
duals are welcome. Prices range from
200 per sq.ft. Recognizing that each
's needs are different, Kanter will meet
ly with the client to work out the details
commission.

ed works are also available.

"Summer Storm" 5'w x 7.5'h. Collection
al, Gerber and Eisenberg Law Firm.

om)"From Plight Comes Light" 7'w x 4'h.

Janet Kuemmerlein

Kuemmerlein Fiber Art Inc.
7701 Canterbury
Prairie Village, KS 66208
(816) 842-7049 (studio)
(913) 649-8292 (home)

Janet Kuemmerlein's fiber relief murals and fiber vessels range in size from 2'x3' to 10'x50'. Her original technique was developed over a period of twenty years. She uses fabrics and yarns in a combination of hand and machine stitching. Her work has won numerous Art in Architecture Awards, Religious Art Awards and Artist-Craftsman Awards.

Kuemmerlein studied at the Center of Creative Studies, Detroit, Michigan and Cranbrook Academy of Art, Bloomfield Hills, Michigan.

Her work is included in the permanent textile collection of the Chicago Art Institute; The Museum of Contemporary Crafts, New York, New York; The Smithsonian National Collection of Fine Arts, Washington, D.C.; The Rochester Institute of Technology; IBM Corporation; AT&T Building, Golden, Colorado.

Prices are available upon request. There is a 10% retainer for sketches. Supervision of installation by artist is available on request.

(Top) Rickel Grain Co., stitched fiber relief, 4'x7'.

(Bottom right) Lobby of J.C. Penney Offices, Kansas City, MO, 8'x20'.

(Bottom left) Baptist Memorial Chapel, 7'x10'.

ancy Lyon

Shaker Street
 London, NH 03257
) 526-6754

Nancy Lyon creates impressionistic landscapes in fiber. Her weaving techniques explore the many ways in which color, form and texture interact.

Wall hangings are available in different handwoven fabrics including brushed mohair, lustrous cotton and reflective metallic yarns.

Pieces are available in limited edition and by commission. Work ranges from $60–$90 per square foot, retail.

Recent commissions include: IBM, Price-Waterhouse, General Motors, and Hyatt Hotels.

(Upper right) "River's Edge," 17" x 24".

(Bottom center) "Hilly Landscape: Evening," 52" x 44".

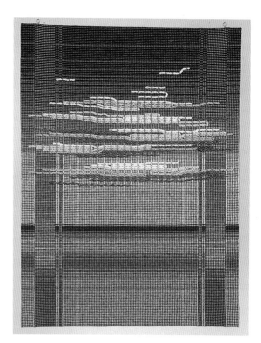

LaVerne McLeod

Big Sur Handwovens
The Village Shops #7
Big Sur, CA 93920
(408) 667-2589

These handwoven wall hangings are one-of-a kind designed by LaVerne McLeod. She incorporates natural fiber yarns with gems, feathers, and driftwood.

Designing for corporate and residential spaces, sizes vary from 2' to 10' in width or length. McLeod's contemporary wall hangings range from $400-8000 depending upon the size and complexity. Her weavings are shipped unframed or shadow box framed. Average delivery time is 6 to 10 weeks after color consultation and design acceptance.

(Top) On exhibit at Pacific Grove Art Center, Pacific Grove, Ca., 2' x 3'.

(Bottom) Commissioned by Esalen Institute, Big Sur, Ca., 30" x 40".

ennifer McLeod

W. 75th Street
w York, NY 10023
2) 362-8173

nnifer McLeod's unique sculptural work with
ther incorporates paint, padding and
er surface design techniques resulting in
ces of extraordinary color and texture.
se pieces are extremely durable and
ally maintenance-free. Pieces can be
ctly wall-mounted or fabric-mounted and
ditionally framed.

nifer has extensive experience in
aboration to ensure a site-specific piece
ch will enhance the aesthetic vision of the
gner or architect.

vell as wall pieces, Jennifer also makes
ens and floor or furniture coverings in
fabric and leather.

uired lead time averages three months
completed work and prices range from
to $150 per square foot. Call or write for
itional information, slides or photos or to
work in person.

) "In Flight" 28"x44"

om) Detail

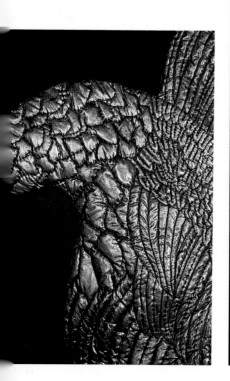

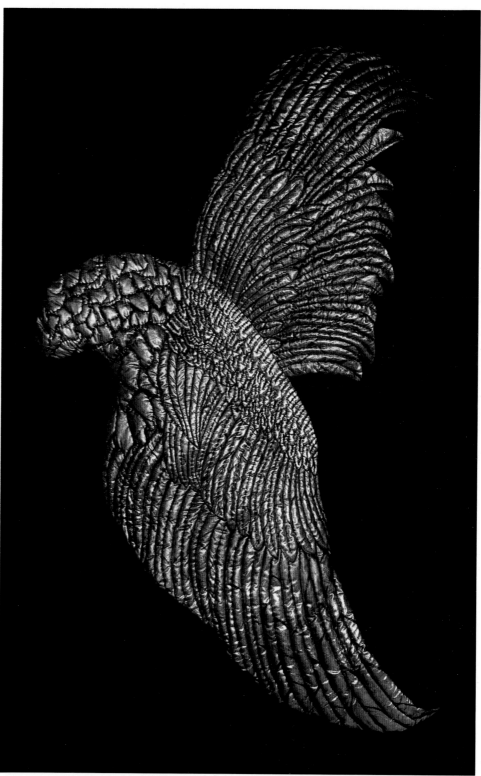

Cynthia Nixon

Cynthia Nixon Studio/Images In Fabric
P.O. Box 89
Pine Grove Mills, PA 16868
(814) 238-7251

Cynthia Nixon has designed quilt installations, known for their detailed imagery and rich colors, for public, corporate, and residential settings since 1978. Painted with permanent textile pigments on fine cottons, each multi-layered piece is meticulously machine-quilted for strength and texture. The quilts are displayed behind plexiglas inside enameled frames.

Exhibited nationally, Nixon's work is published in five books on contemporary quilting. Commissions include large quilts for the Baltimore Hilton (7' x 56'), Polyclinic Medical Center, Harrisburg, PA (4' x 14') and Dickinson College (10' x 20').

Prices for site-specific pieces begin at $100 per sq. ft. Proposal includes scale color renderings. Completed work requires three months.

Please call or write for slides, brochure and scheduling.

"Nittany Valley," United Federal Savings Bank, State College, PA, 30" x 84".

izabeth Nordgren

van Way
ham, NH 03824
) 868-2873

abeth Nordgren designs and weaves
temporary wall pieces. She uses textile
to create separate layers of colored
p which are then woven into a single
p-faced piece. Commissioned works are
ilable for both residential and commercial
allations, in single or multiple panels. They
y be either horizontal or vertical to
ommodate any size and developed to
color specifications. Pieces are available
scose, rayon-silk, or wool. Retail prices
in at 65 per square foot depending on
plexity of design. Please contact artist for
mation about commissions and for slides
urrent work.

right) Pastel swag 24" w. x 16"h.

tom right) "Enfolding" 29.5"w x 49"h. Both
es are woven of viscose yarns.

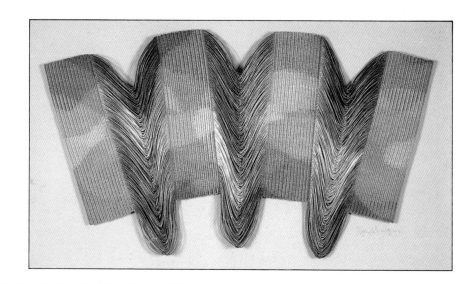

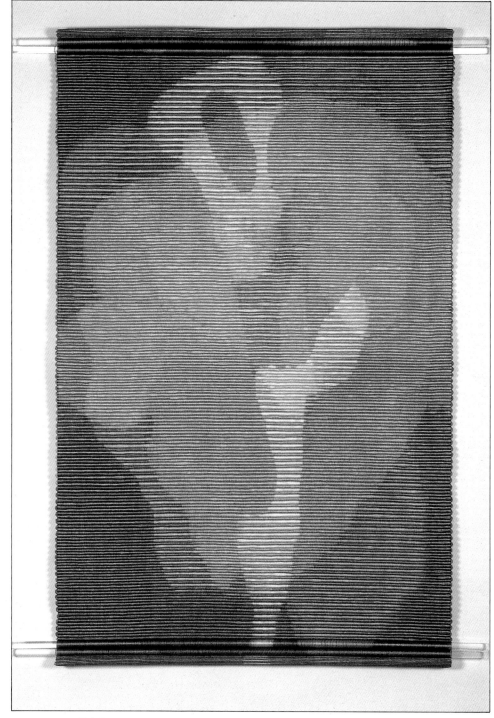

Amanda Richardson

Richardson Kirby
P.O. Box 2147
Friday Harbor, WA 98250
(206) 378-3224

The rich, light-reflective tapestries of Amanda Richardson respond to their environment, the image varying with the angle and intensity of light allowing the viewer to become actively involved in the artistic experience.

Richardson developed the technique of Richardson-tapestry in which fabrics are hand-dyed, cut into intricate forms, and bonded together, layer on layer, to build up a rich and complex final image. These images give the impression of great spatial depth, with a visual impact few art mediums can equal.

A graduate of Goldsmiths' College, London University, and a professional artist for thirteen years, Richardson has had numerous shows both in America and Europe. The majority of the artist's work is commissioned, including large tapestries for public places. Recent clients include Marriott Hotels, Hilton Hotels, The Rouse Co., The Oliver Carr Co. and the University of Alaska.

Price is $300 per square foot. Framing and supervision of installation are available. Proposal (10% fee deductible from final price) consists of detailed scale watercolour design and contract confirming date of delivery, price, terms and installation arrangements.

Colour brochure: $6.00.

"Evening Sunlight East Anglia" 6' x 12'.
Oliver Carr Co., Commercial National Bank Bldg., Washington D.C.

(Top right) "Granite Shore, Shuyak" 6'6" x 19'
University of Alaska, Juneau, A.K.

(Bottom right) "Golden Grasses" 5'6" x 6'6"

Julie Nudd

Nudd Ltd.
1338 W. Grand Avenue, 2nd Fl.
Chicago, IL 60622
(312) 243-2283

Julie Nudd's original and humorous way of viewing life is reflected in her appliqued fabric collages with handpainted frames. Each work is individually created with both flat and dimensional components. The inspiration for these collages comes from real places, people, photos and literature. Prices start at $250 and commissions for specific places, people and photos are welcome.

As for biography, Julie Nudd admits, "...there really isn't one. I went to college for four years (at least), but I never did graduate. As a philosophy major, I didn't take any art classes. And as far as sewing goes, I taught myself. My mom can't even sew on a button. She thinks the 'Buttoneer' is the greatest invention of the 20th century."

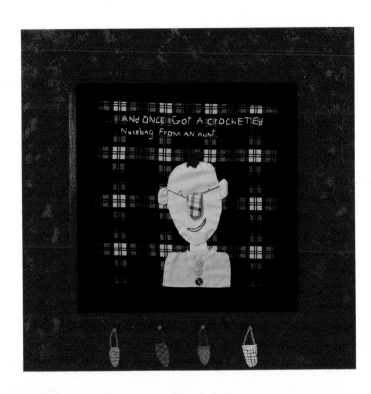

ude Russell

49 S.W. 43rd Avenue
rtland, OR 97221
03) 297-3546

Jude Russell challenges and expands the traditional concepts of textile arts in a rich and diverse body of work which includes fabric collage, multiple-layered transparencies, painted and layered textile pieces and three-dimensional aerial sculptures and banners.

Russell works in collaboration with architects and design firms on a regular basis and maintains professional standards from preliminary design to execution of all commissions.

Collectors include The Smithsonian Institution, NIKE, Inc., Nordstrom, The Boeing Company, and Kaiser Hospitals.

Price: $175–225/sq. ft.

Preliminary design fee: $350.00

Completion time after contract approval: six to twelve weeks.

Full brochure available on request.

(Top left) "Sunset Strip" (detail)

(Top right) "Ee-lectricity" 33" x 48"

(Bottom) "Sunset Strip" Mentor Graphics Corporation Portland Or. 3' x 12'

Carole Sabiston

1648 Rockland Avenue
Victoria, B.C.
Canada, V8S 1W7
(604) 598-8139

Carole Sabiston's texile wall hangings and 3D works are dramatic, vigorous, and magically ‹alive.› Her original technique, developed over 20 years is of multi-layered fabrics bonded together to create a strong, light-weight, easily maintained construction. With the restrained use of metallic fabrics, continual reflective light-plays and extraordinary spatial depths are realized. The works can be opaque or translucent, as in two-sided banners.

Sabiston's award-winning art is found in government, public, corporate, hotel and private collections including: Government of Canada, Cadillac-Fairview, Olympia & York, Expo 86 Vancouver, Westin Hotels.

Ruby Red Planet, 9' x 10'.

Blush Pink Planet, 18' x 15'.

arole Sabiston
8 Rockland Avenue
toria, B.C.
nada V8S 1W7
4) 598-8139

Carole Sabiston welcomes commissions and architectual collaborations, and is willing to supervise installations. Delivery time is 2 to 6 months after contractual approval. Prices range from $125 to $250 per sq. ft. depending on size and complexity. Brochure, photos and slides available for $10.

Into Delos, 21' x 5' 6".

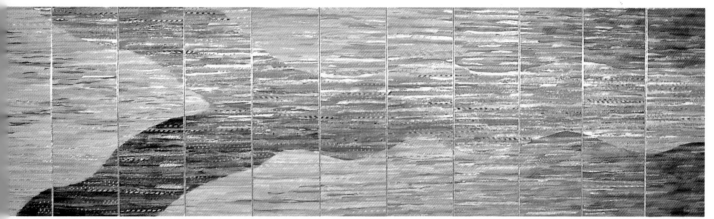

Reflecting Seasons, 23' x 6' 6" x 1".

e, 17' x 7'.

Fireworks Suite, 5' x 7.

Sally Shore

Ludlam Lane
Locust Valley, NY 11560
(516) 671-7276

Working through architects, designers and interior decorators over the past 20 years, Sally Shore has produced work for corporate offices, apartment lobbies and private homes. Her working techniques include traditional tapestry, rya and soumack knotting, loom-controlled fabric weaves and the combining of knitting with weaving.

Each commissioned piece is designed for its specific location and use with regard to size, colors, texture and content.

Prices range from $75 to $150/yard for fabrics, pillows or throws to $125 to $200/square foot for surface-manipulated techniques (including tapestry) all depending on materials and intricacy of design.

(Top) Window Tapestry with looped pile foilage and flowers, 42" x 48", stretched on wooden frame.

(Bottom) Monochrome textured hanging, 54" x 99", stretched on wooden frame.

incent Tolpo
arolyn Lee Tolpo

18 U.S. Highway 285, Box 134
wnee, CO 80475
3) 670-1733

Since 1981, Vincent and Carolyn Lee Tolpo have created site-specific wrapped fiberart for public, corporate, and residential spaces. Working with clients, designers, consultants, and architects, their collaborative fibers consider color, concept, space, and budget. Project art can be commissioned direct. The Tolpo's fiberwrapped art provides a lightweight, durable, cleanable, high-tech/high-touch, sound-absorbant, textural form for today's contemporary setting. Imagery ranges from landscape to abstract. Surfaces may be flat, bas-relief, three-dimensional, or combined structurally with metal, metallic mylar, acrylic prisms, or stoneware.

Prices, resume, references, photo/slide catalogue, delivery, installation available. Retail prices: $100–$250/square foot.

(Shown: Clockwise) "Chrystals," "Surfaces," "Turnasol," "Rose Ricochette."

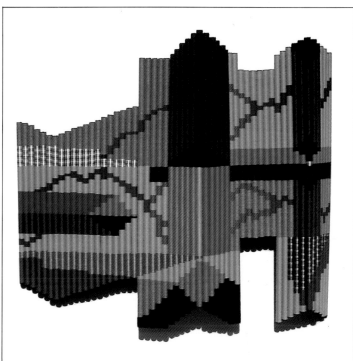

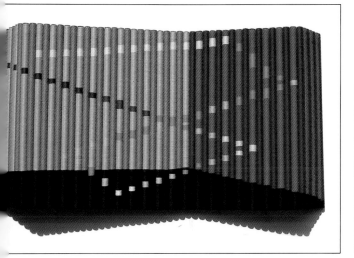

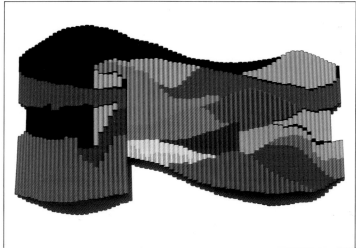

Pamela Twycross-Reed

117 Lamarck Drive
Snyder, NY 14226
(716) 839-2691

Weaver Pamela Twycross-Reed creates three-dimensional wall-hung or free-standing works featuring abstract landscape tapestries. After completion of the weaving process her tapestries are stretched on wood-laminated convex forms and framed in plexiglass and wood.

Working with designers and architects the artist has completed over 100 commissions for private and corporate installations.

Prices range from $85–$100 per sq. ft. plus cost of frame and shipping or installation.

(Top left) 5 piece tapestry, 8'w. x 6'h. "Tidele Gardens."

(Top right) Installation, Civic Center, Saratog Springs, NY, 15'w. x 5'h.

(Bottom) 4 piece tapestry, 8'w. x 5'h. "Fiesta

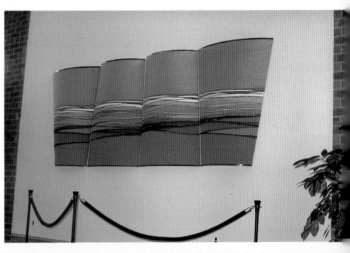

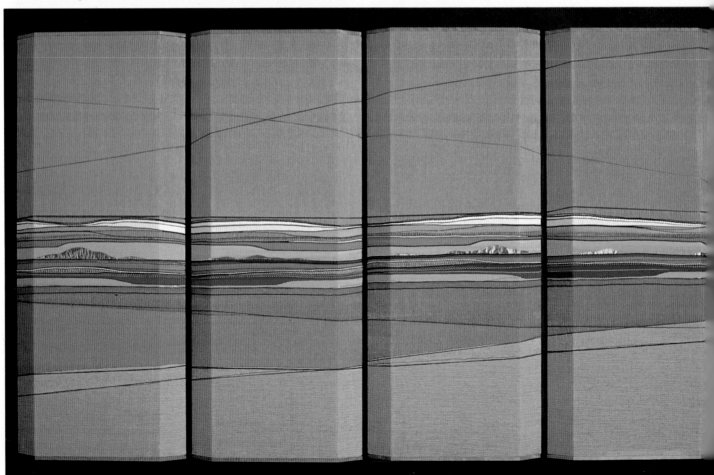

dia Van Gelder

Sucher Lane
a Rosa, CA 95401
) 546-4139

resist dye technique Ikat, loom woven
ces, is Van Gelders special interest in fiber
ression and large sculptural works in
ng, bobbin lace, tatting.

nor, IKAT, Watson-Guptill;
EMAKING/TATTING, Encyclopedia Crafts,
ls., Scribners.

national Textile Competition, '87, Kyoto.

International Textile Design Contest,
ion Foundation, Tokyo, 1988.

national Shibori City Exhibition Nagoya,
, purchased from show.

lation ready -
hangings, $300 sq ft.
otural works, $950 upwards, depending
ze.
4 weeks (small work) to 12 weeks.

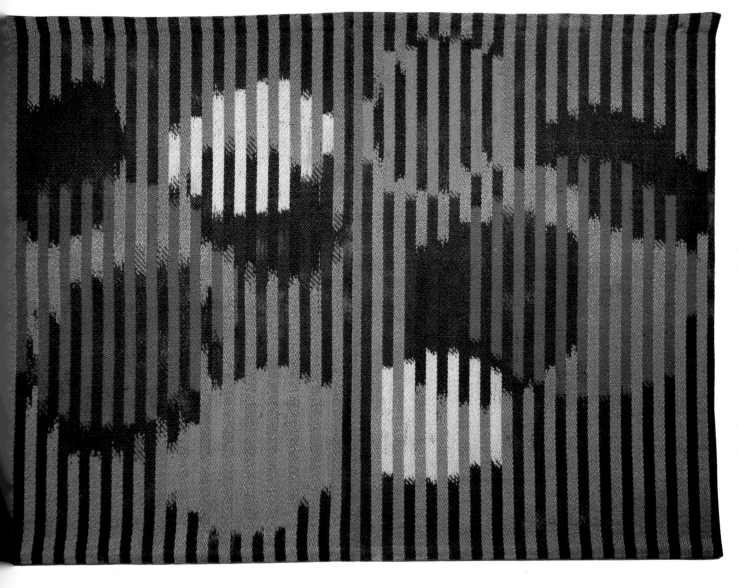

Judi Maureen White

Renaissance Fibres
2062 East Malibu Drive
Tempe, AZ 85282
(602) 838-0416

Artist Judi Maureen White, although not Native American, spent her youth on the Hopi and Navajo Indian reservations of northern Arizona and New Mexico. The vast space and timeless majesty of the land and it's people highly influenced the evolution of White's work, beginning as a tapestry weaver and moving toward her current fiber/mixed media constructions. Embellishment of the abstract imagry is achieved through stitching, weaving, felting and painting, thus creating rich reflective surfaces in the work.

The unique approach in White's one-of-a-kind creations has earned her numerous awards. Her work is included in public, private and corporate collections, as well as being published in *Fiberarts Design Book Three*, 19_ and *Cerulean Blue Ltd.*, 1988 catalog. Slide and prices available upon request

(Top Left) "Spirit Renaissance Series: Struggle," 48" x 77" x 3"

(Top Right) "Spirit Renaissance Series: Struggle," (detail).

(Bottom) "Spirit Renaissance Series: Migration," 90" x 104" x 3".

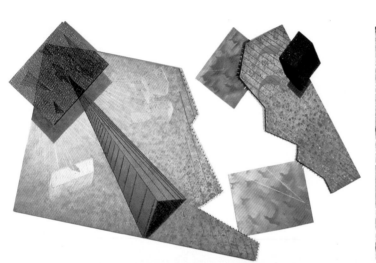

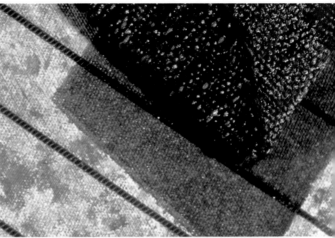

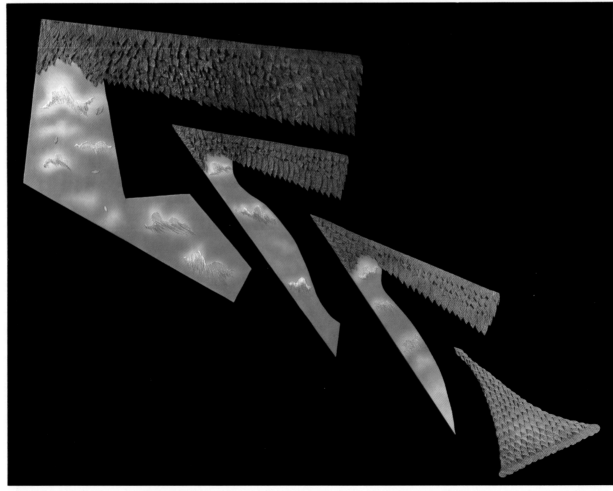

PAPER & MIXED MEDIA

159 Karen Adachi

161 Therese Bisceglia

162 Martha Chatelain

163 Martha Chatelain

164 Carolyn Cole

165 Beth Cunningham

166 Pamela Dalton

167 Joy DeNicola

168 Pamela Flanders

169 Barbara F. Fletcher

170 Wayne A. O. Fuerst

171 Harriet Hanson

172 Carol Herd

173 Joan Kopchik

174 Colette Laico

175 Wendy Lilienthal

177 Irene Maginniss

178 Marcella Morgese

179 Cyndi Mylynne

180 Faith O'Heron

181 Faith O'Heron

182 Carol Owen

183 Leroy Wheeler Parker

184 Beverly Plummer

185 Susan Singleton

186 Raymond D. Tomasso

187 Marjorie Tomchuk

188 Alice Van Leunen

189 S.M. Warren

190 Nancy J. Young

aren Adachi

Monarch Way
ta Cruz, CA 95060
3) 429-6192

en Adachi creates her three-dimensional
dmade paper pieces by using layers of
gularly shaped vacuum-cast paper. She
es free-standing two-sided sculptures
d wall-pieces for corporate, private and
dential interiors. Her work is shown
onally through major galleries and
esentatives.

pieces are richly-textured and
ellished with dyes, acrylics, metallics and
rlescents. Painted bamboo and sticks
used to create a dramatic statement of
ern and line. Three-dimensional sculptures
mounted on painted metal bases for
ility and strength.

s range from $250–5,000 depending on
Custom work in any size, shape and
r is available.

act artist for further information and
s.

AN OBJECT LESSON

Around my house, the women touched the clay and the paint. We men collected. Then in my teens I developed a love-fear relationship with the stage and left the world of objects altogether. Until one drizzly summer my sisters and I decided as a practical joke to build a metal collage (it was the year that fenders made their museum debut) and give it to our father-collector. We worked all day with machine shop parts and interwove them with beach treasures. Our giggles quieted to smiles which turned to sighs and deep breathing. We got serious about that object. Found a proper base for the thing and covered it with a sheet just prior to presentation. Well, the object was a fine success no matter what you had hoped for. Our mother choked with laughter and our father wanted to collect it.

You might say that taught me an object lesson. Not only could object manipulation be entertaining and even possibly humorous. It was arduous. And everything counted.

Years later now, we siblings play serious house. Adding screen porches and cellar studies to sensible New England homes. Punching holes in slate roofs for dormers or skylights. And we haven't forgotten that everything counts. Door handles especially count. And stairway railings. Things you touch a lot and things your eye naturally settles on.

I never knew the noun "finish" until I owned a place where there wasn't any. Sloppy corners and crude taping. It's the same with boats but more obvious, since you can be impaled on their sloppy corners.

Conversely, there's something nurturing about careful finish and thoughtful design. Surfaces and objects can exude the love and thought which bore them. Perhaps that's it. A finely finished object has lineage. Distinction.

Quite different from the cookie cutter world of mass design. And when you combine fine finish with custom finish, then the eye is arrested. You have just seen the floor breathe. That lamp has a grandfather.

Some folks want a chalk line between art and craft. They like to know which side they're stepping on. The same thing with art and architecture. It drives them crazy when the one-percent-for-art funds get spent on something they can't unhang. For me what matters is that someone thought about the object with an apt mixture of deep caring and playfulness. Charles Eames liked the word "appropriate."

Now all of us in the family collect. And my palms still sweat on stage. We siblings haven't made an object worthy of unveiling in a while. But thank heavens for those of you who do.

David Rockefeller, Jr.
*Trustee, Museum of
Modern Art
(Reprinted from THE GUILD,
1986)*

erese Bisceglia

e 19, Box 90–KS
a Fe, NM 87505
) 982-5914

ese Bisceglia creates two and three
ensional works in handmade paper that
ct her humor and embrace her sense of
n. Her dynamic images for corporate and
ential spaces use abaca fibers,
escent pigments, embossing, monotype,
ng, sheet forming, painting, collage,
ush and drawing.

orate and residential commissions are
omed.

talog is available on request.

s retail from $80.00–$200.00 per square

eft) Time Zone 48" x 14" x 4"
) 41"pot, 18"pot.

m (left) Vista 44" x 20"
) Nindii 22" x 30".

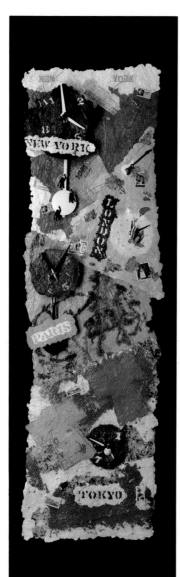

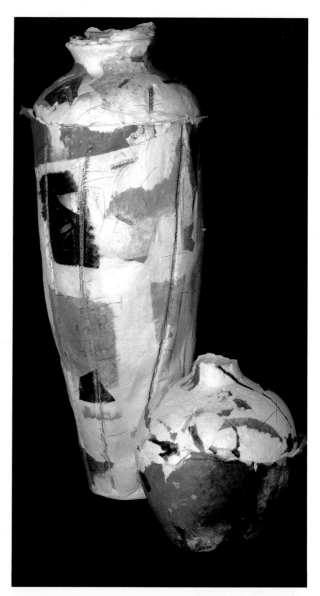

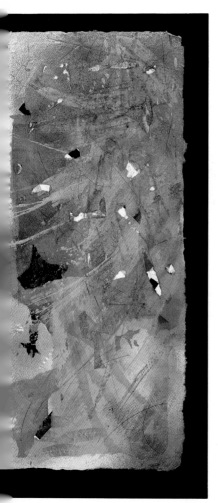

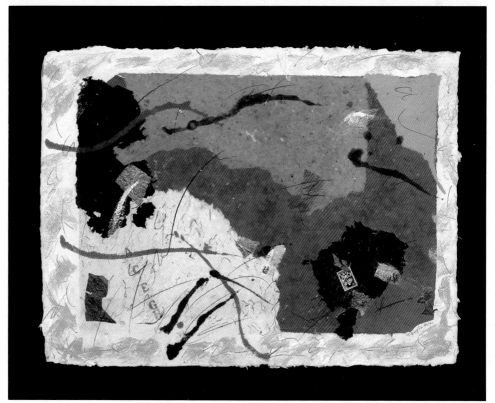

Martha Chatelain

Artfocus, Ltd..
833 "G" Street
P.O. Box 127238
San Diego, CA 92112
(619) 234-0749

Martha Chatelain creates richly textured three-dimensional handmade paper and mixed media wall sculptures. With vibrant or subtle colors from fiber dyes, accented by iridescent mica powders, her artworks can be enhanced with fiber optics if desired.

Prices, from $800–$5000, depend on size and complexity. Allow 4–6 weeks for delivery following design approval and price contract.

Chatelain welcomes site-specific commissions. Call for consultation on design specifications and client environment: public, corporate, and residential.

Selected collections:
Bank of America
Hilton Hotels
IBM
International Paper
Nordstrom
Potlatch Corporation
Price-Waterhouse
Sheraton Hotels
Upjohn Corporation
Xerox Corporation

(Top) "Northern Lights", 21" x 66" x 3", pape sculpture with fiber optics.

(Bottom left) "Terra Nova", 76" x 40" x 5".

(Bottom right) Detail, "Northern Lights".

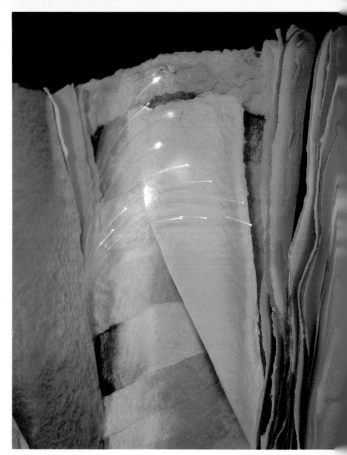

Martha Chatelain

tfocus, Ltd.
3 "G" Street
. Box 127238
n Diego, CA 92112
9) 234-0749

artha Chatelain creates richly textured
ee-dimensional handmade paper and
xed media wall sculptures. With vibrant or
tle colors from fiber dyes, accented by
escent mica powders, her artworks can be
hanced with fiber optics if desired.

es, from $800–$5000, depend on size and
mplexity. Allow 4–6 weeks for delivery
owing design approval and price contract.

atelain welcomes site-specific
mmissions. Call for consultation on design
ecifications and client environment: public,
porate, and residential.

ected collections:
nk of America
on Hotels

rnational Paper
dstrom
atch Corporation
e Waterhouse
raton Hotels
ohn Corporation
ox Corporation

) "Free Flight", 15' x 11' x 3".

tom) "Mt. Fuji Kimono", 60" x 52" x 4".

Carolyn Cole

Carolyn Cole Studios
3614 S.W. Canby Street
Portland, OR 97219
(503) 244-6770

Carolyn Cole meticulously paints her textured handmade paper so that each artwork looks just like a traditional quilt. Choose from many patterns and a wide variety of sizes, up to eight feet. They are durable and hand-cast from the finest 100% cotton fiber and color-fast acrylic paint. Cole's paintings have been featured in Country Living, Women's Day Country Decorating, and Child Mazagine.

Selected collections: Bankers Trust; IBM; Manufacturers Hanover Trust; TRW Corporation; Heinz Corporation; Campbell Soup Company; Zale Corporation.

Prices range from $600–4,000. Special installations and collaborations welcomed. Paintings shipped unframed or in custom plexiglass box frames. Allow 4–6 weeks for delivery.

(Left) Log Cabin 34" x 34".

(Middle) Wild Goose Chase 32" x 32".

(Right) Double Wedding Ring 45" x 45".

(Bottom) Triangles 28" x 34".

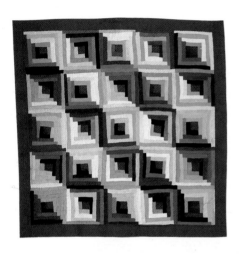

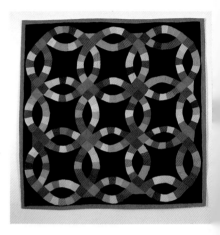

Beth Cunningham

2 Sweetcake Mountain Road
New Fairfield, CT 06812
(203) 746-5160

Beth Cunningham produces one-of-a-kind wall pieces by layering airbrushed canvas with a surface overlay of squares, strips or a woven grid constructed of muslin, silk tissue paper and pigment, and adhered and sealed with acrylic polymer. These compositions are durable and require little maintenance. Imagery is derived from abstractions and reflections of land, water and sky. Ms. Cunningham is experienced in working with the requirements of the clients and can produce both large and small scale work.

Wall pieces are designed and executed by her with collaborative work considered. Prices range from $100–$150 per sq. ft. depending on surface construction selected. Average construction time is 4–6 weeks. Completed works and information available upon request.

Collections of Heinz Corporation, NYC; Computer Craft, St. Luke's Methodist Hospital, Prudential, Sagestone, and Foley's, Texas include her work.

(Top right) Strip overlay.

(Top left) Detail of woven grid overlay.

(Bottom) Woven grid overlay.

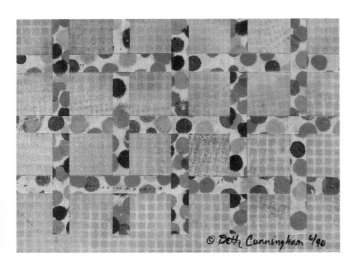

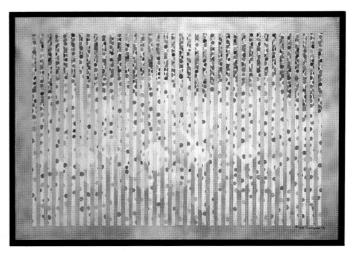

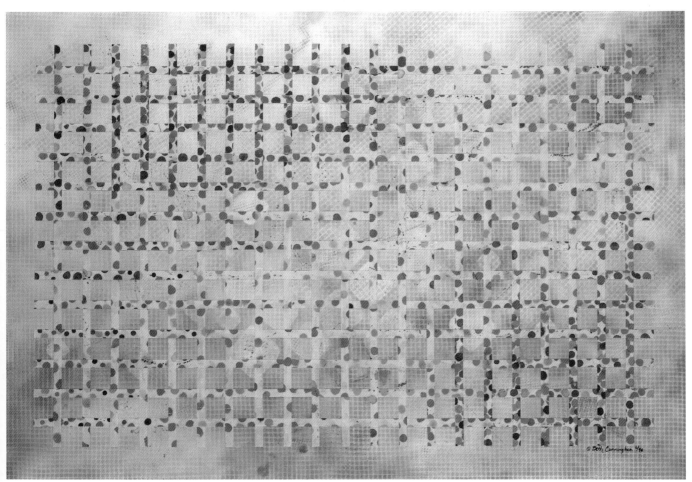

Pamela Dalton

Scherenschnitte
RD 2 Box 226A
Harlemville
Ghent, NY 12075
(518) 672-4841

Pamela Dalton's Scherenschnitte are created in the tradition of early nineteenth century American paper cutting. Biblical motifs and themes focusing on rural life are frequently used. Each piece is cut from a single sheet of paper and then water colored. Pieces cut from solid black silhouette paper and antiqued white paper are also available. Work is framed in wood which is false grained in the traditional vinegar/pigment method by the artist.

Prices for standard designs range from $60 to $1,000. Custom and personalized work is also available. Prices on commissions are determined by size and intricacy of the piece. Inquiries are welcome.

(Below) "Anniversary" 26"h.x32"w.

by DeNicola

6 South 16th Street
vaukee, WI 53221
4) 384-0456

DeNicola's elegant wall sculptures and
efs are inspired by the organic forms in
ure, and reveal an ethereal, abstract
gery of the earth's surface as seen from
aerial perspective. Each dramatic work
kes a strong reference to environmental
ervation and natural beauty.

structed in 100% cotton handmade
er with inner supports, each sculpture is
risingly durable yet lightweight. Sealed
an acrylic medium allows for the work to
displayed framed or unframed. However,
iglas boxes make a strong and
histicated statement.

University of Wisconsin—Milwaukee.
erous Private and corporate
nmissions. Exhibited and published
onally.

om commissions welcome. All artwork is
vrighted.

il Prices: $90–$175 per square foot.

kwise:

ashiku Chikyu" 29"x52"x5".

am of Gaia" 42"x72"x6".

urning to Pangaea" 42"x52"x7".

ve the Sonoran" 53"x28"x1¹/₂".

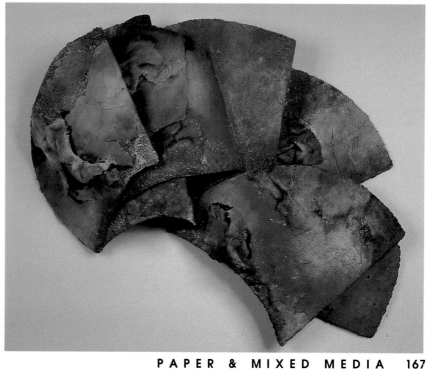

Pamela Flanders

Flanders Fine Art
31 Union Street
San Jose, CA 95110
(408) 578-3251

Pamela Flanders creates handmade paper collages with specific moods and settings in mind. She describes her work as "textural planes of interacting color, transparency, tension, and balance."

Texture is a key element in this artwork. The medium is cotton paper which she makes herself. The purposeful raw edges and integrity of her hand-pulled papers allow for interesting combinations of transparency and finishes married with other papers, acrylics, and pastels. The abstract sculptural effects are enhanced by layering and spraying the paper to play upon the textural and tonal subtleties.

Pamela's work is displayed extensively in both private and corporate collections. She invites commissions and proposals and will create any size piece for a specific environment. Installation and framing optional.

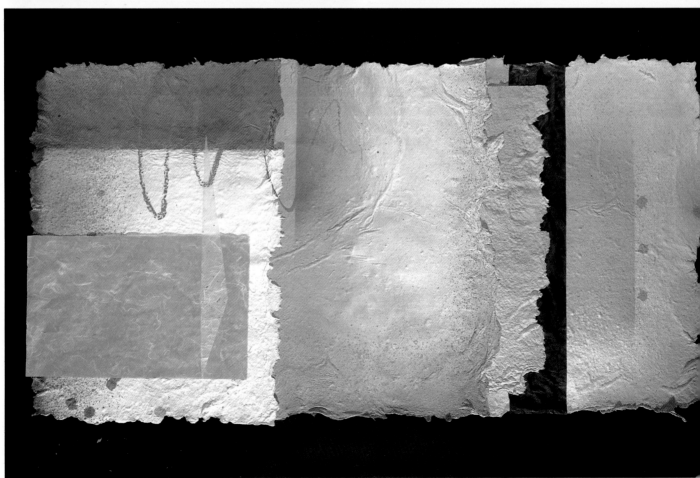

Photography by Dallas C.

arbara F. Fletcher

Beals Street
okline, MA 02146
17) 277-3019

rbara Fletcher creates cast paper wall and edestal pieces. Wet paper pulp is air dried in aster casts which are made from clay rms. One of a kinds or multiples can be ade with this process. The pieces are inted with procion dyes to give a onderful luminosity. The paper is made many layers

durability and then coated with a otective acrylic making it appropriate for mmercial as well as residential space. tcher's pieces are unique for their intense lor, texture and whimsicality. Her work has en exhibited nationally and is included in any private collections including writer phen King.

ces range from $200–1000. Slides are ailable upon request. Commissions are cepted.

p) "DesertScene," 51" circumference, 9" pth

ttom) "Birds on the Desert," 23" x 55" x 4" pth, Private Collection.

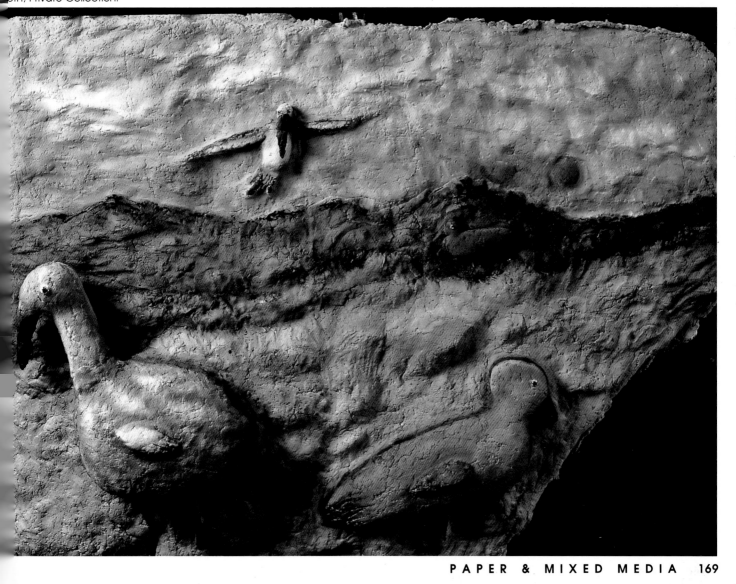

Wayne A. O. Fuerst

Orchid Studio 5
40 Woodland Road
Ashland, MA 01721
(508) 881-2525

Wayne Fuerst is a landscape painter, working exclusively in handmade paper, who has a love and concern for wetlands, and wilderness areas. His statement is subtly embedded in and between the layers of paper.

The combination of his imagery and his infatuation with color and texture produce pieces of paper that show an incredible sensitivity and attentiveness to details.

From a distance you see trees and depth—a unity of land, sky and water. As you move closer you see the explosion of color created by: opaque and translucent layers of fiber and hand placed areas of paper pulp. Layer by layer the surface is built in a wet state. Throughout the layering other materials are added to effect the final texture and make reference to issues concerning the destiny of the landscape still existing.

Wayne exhibits in galleries throughout the country.

Resumé samples and slide by request. Works on commission basis ⅓ downpayment.

Photo credit David Caras.

rriet Hanson

tudiospace
W. Hubbard Street
ago, IL 60622
) 243-4144

et Hanson is a nationally celebrated
made paper artist. She is recognized for
te specific artwork, and for numerous
es currently on display nationwide.

iverse approach of this prolific artist is
plified in the various series she creates.
series is a monochromatic study of
, citylike, architectural shapes with
atic contrasts in light and shadow.
er series resembles woven tapestries
old imagery and vivid color.

oming collaborations with architects and
ners, Hanson has studied in the United
and Japan. She deftly combines the
European and sensitive oriental
iques of this versatile media.

ed near Chicago's Merchandise Mart,
n invites interested parties to tour The
space.

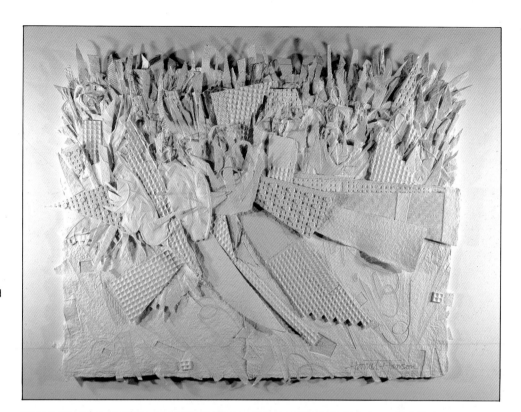

Carol Herd

1101 North HighCross Road
Urbana, IL 61801
(217) 328-0118
(217) 328-4864 Fax

With pigmented pulps and sophisticated techniques, Carol Herd layers pulp washes to create an enchanting composition that is a single sheet of fine handmade paper. Herd's work directly shares with the viewer her experience in nature, recording subtleties of mood, season, moment, and character. Her mastery of the material in her creative expression transcends craft.

Herd received her baccalaureate and master's degrees for her work in paper and teaches paper at the University of Illinois. She is internationally active lecturing, leading workshops, and exhibiting her work. Select collections: I BM, The Beckman Institute, The Technical Association of Pulp and Paper Industries.

Contact the artist for further information, slides, price list and resume. Commissions accepted. Companion works are available.

"Hedge Row #4", 18" x 24".

"Forest Series #22", 34" x 29".

"Autumn Dawn", 18" x 24".

"Impression of the Shawnee"; Forest Series #68", 26" x 38" each.

n Kopchik

ephen Way
mpton, PA 18966
22-1862

naker Joan Kopchik specializes in
g wall pieces of jewel-like tonality using
made with traditional mould and
. Abaca paper, pH balanced,
nted and sized is used in the
ctions.

vall piece utilizes a broad range of
and textures which may be custom
ed to meet client specifications. The
ctions are machine sewn together for
ity. Applications of decorative
nts complete the work which is hand
nto a cast paper surface.

ed commissions and collections:
es Incorporated, Johnson & Higgins,
, Chemical Bank, Fidelity Bank,
gton Trust, McNeil Consumer Products.

prices: $850–$3500. Information and
vailable upon request

Purple Bunting", 40"h x 52"w x 2.5"d.

n right) "Zebra Crossing", 60"h x 40"w x

n left) "Zebra Crossing", (detail).

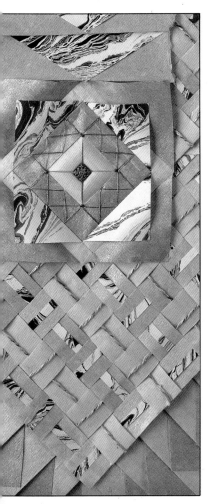

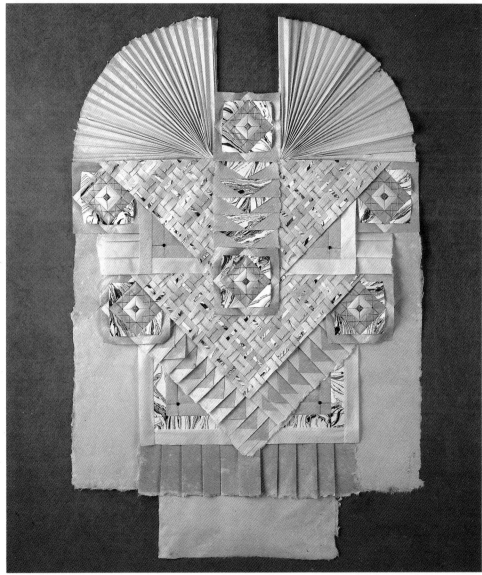

Colette Laico

21 Saxonwood Park Drive
White Plains, NY 10605
(914) 946-2632

Colette Laico creates one of a kind mixed media/collage/handmade paper wall pieces for corporate and home environments, from cotton/linen fibers.

Her sensibility is almost mosiac rather than collage; a composition of form, texture and color with visual and tactile responses.

The artist has exhibited nationally and is the recipient of many awards. She is represented in extensive private and corporate collections. Among the corporate are: Great Northern Nekoosa Paper Corp., Readers Digest, Aetna Life Insurance, Apple Computer, Seidman and Seidman BDO, and American International Life Assurance.

Available works are priced from $300 to $2000. Commissioned pieces are priced according to complexity and size.

Slides are available upon request, from the artist.

(Bottom) Magenta Angles, 27 x 37 x 3.

(Top right) Magenta Angles, detail.

(Top left) Euclidian Series, 40 x 49 x 3.

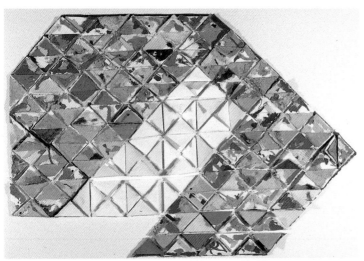

endy Lilienthal
Butterfield Road
Anselmo, CA 94960
453-1019

Combining elements of sculpture, painting, and collage with her own handmade paper, Wendy Lilienthal employs a refined sense of compositional awareness to assemble her multi-layered, three dimensional works.

Her pieces reflect many cultures and span a range of imagery from ancient to contemporary, creating dramatic moods for private, commercial and corporate settings.

Lilienthal appeared on national PBS, exhibiting and demonstrating handmade paper. She was featured in San Francisco Magazine, completed one of a kind 6' commissions for Metro Plaza, a 4' piece for Kaiser Hospital and Synetics, Inc.

Pieces are ready for hanging in plexiglass boxes, and are of durable, colorfast paper.

This internationally acclaimed artist invites commissions. Slides available. Delivery four to eight weeks. Prices from $800–$4,000.

As we move into the '90s, it is clear that to be competitive, interior designers, like others in the marketplace, need to be on the cutting edge. Today's client is more sophisticated and knowledgeable, and to remain competitive, designers must be sensitive to demands that even two or three years ago seemed negligible. For example, environmental concerns are not simply fashionable, they are becoming an integral part of the way today's consumers think.) That's good news for artisans who specialize in area rugs—be they machine-loomed or hand-woven, primitive designs or rich Oriental imports—and bad news for the wall-to-wall crowd. Why? Savvy homeowners have learned that many wall-to-wall carpets can produce toxic fumes because of both the adhesives that secure them to the floor and the synthetic fiber they are made of.

The interior designer or architect on the cutting edge is one who can provide his or her clientele with advice about where to go to find one-of-a-kind pieces, not just manufactured goods from Sweet's Catalog. In a very real sense, this helps to expand the designer's artistic vocabulary, suggesting new ways to be creative, new ways to make truly unique statements. It's equally rewarding for the artist to have his or her work represented in widely varied contexts. And most of all, it's rewarding for the individuals who end up owning works that they might never have thought of without the advice of an informed interior designer.

What this all amounts to is information, or perhaps more accurately, the sharing of valuable information. And with the demographics of the United States shifting as dramatically as they have in the last decade, what we all need to know to be up to date is changing and changing fast. Finding out what the best artisans are up to in today's volatile marketplace is one way to stay on the cutting edge. It might just make the difference between being current or obsolete.

Douglas Greenwood
Director of Public Relations
American Institute of
Architects

ne Maginniss

Andover Road South
nsfield, OH 44907
) 756-2841

handmade paper collage works of Irene
ginniss are unique and innovative, each
mplex design using cotton, pigment
red (for light fastness), poured and
ossed pulps. Metallic threads and
hing can further embellish the works.

accomplished artist, Maginniss has
bited nationally and internationally, and
works in numerous private and corporate
ections.

es start at $75 a square foot with framing
e arranged by the client. Acrylic coating
ailable.

missions are accepted and delivery time
es depending on size and complexity of

tact the artist for slides and additional
mation.

) 28" x 28" unframed.

om) 42" x 26" unframed.

Marcella Morgese

516 East Second Street
South Boston, MA 02127
(617) 269-5579

Papermaker and sculptor Marcella Morgese creates art work inspired by abstract geometric concepts.

The work is strongly influenced by remnant architectural structures and structures in progress. Textures, markings and forms created by nature, and humankind, reflect upon the development of Morgese's motifs.

Marcella is interested in one-of-a-kind commission and site specific projects, with an average work completion time of eight to ten weeks. Pricing depends on the size and complexity of the desired work, pieces begin at $800.00.

Further information is available upon request and work may also be viewed by appointment.

All pieces listed are handmade paper.

(Top Right) "Looking Through", 34" x 23".

(Top Left) "Transition," 84" x 20" x 14".

(Bottom) "Elements II", 23" x 39".

Cyndi Mylynne

Double Vision Studio
P.O. Box 965037
Marietta, GA 30066
(404) 977-4298

Like all fine paper artists, Cyndi Mylynne produces all her own paper. Her unique handmade paper wall sculptures are created using a variety of cellulose fibers. All chosen for their respective strengths, textures and flexibility. By using one or a combination of fibers Ms. Mylynne achieves a form that has a life within itself. To enhance each piece she uses pure pigments, acrylics, and iridescent powders. Her works can be created in many sizes, shapes and colors to fit corporate and private spaces.

Prices range from $250.00–$5,000.00 depending on the size and complexity of the design. Average delivery is 8–12 weeks after design and contract approval.

Collectors: TAPPI, Cadillac Fairview-Galleria Mall.

(top) "Shadows of Light," 27" x 35" x 2".

(bottom) "Crossroads," 32" x 40" x 3".

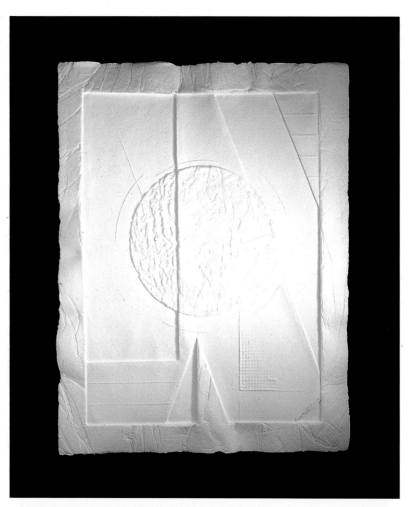

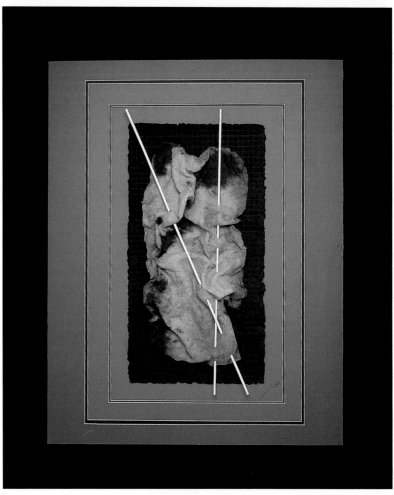

Faith O'Heron

P.O. Box 4303
Thousand Oaks, CA 91359
(805) 379-4155

Faith O'Heron is fascinated with the mythical world. Her knowledge and experience with handmade paper and leafing techniques has produced an outstanding collection of historical cats.

Each image originates from a different country with its own legend and is made by applying imported gold and rare color leafs to a very unique handmade rice paper.

Artist will accept commissions for custom pieces and quote prices accordingly.

Her work is in numerous private collections and Aetna and The Associates Corporation of North America are among her many corporate clients.

"Mayan Jaguar," 31 x 31.

"Leopards of Nigeria," 32 x 40.

aith O'Heron

. Box 4303
ousand Oaks, CA 91359
5) 379-4155

e artist's extensive design background in
e apparel and needlework industry lends a
que touch to her imaginative and colorful
llages. Created with combinations of
ndmade papers and natural textured
ers, she has produced a series of twelve
sical images. Imported gold and color
fs, fabrics, beads, sequins and paints are
e of the materials used to create these
isual works of art.

mmissioned work is available on
dscapes, Oriental themes, florals or other
ject matter and will be quoted
cordingly.

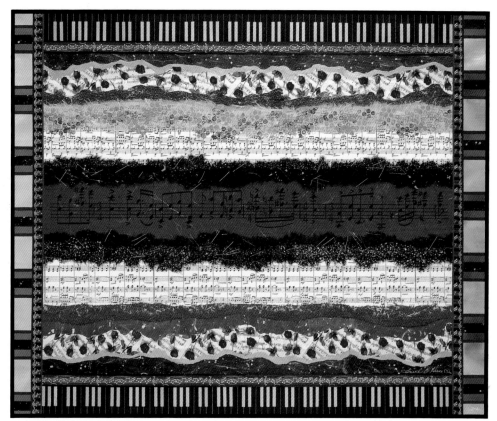

"Spring Sonata" 32 x 40 Collage.

"Crescendo" 32 x 40 Collage.

Carol Owen

3424 Cormorant Cove Court
Jacksonville, FL 32223
(904) 260-4867

Richly textured and colored, Carol Owen's quilt inspired paper pieces are of archival quality. Her work is in numerous private and corporate collections, including Vistana Corporation, Champion Paper Company, and Acceleration Insurance Company; it has been featured in Country Living magazine and Fiberarts Design Book III.

Delivery on commissions in eight weeks; retail prices range from $100 - $150 per sq. ft.

(Top) Crosscurrents (detail).

(Bottom) Dawn Shadows 30" x 40".

eroy Wheeler Parker

Meek Place
ayette, CA 94549
5) 937-7336

Iti-media artist Leroy W. Parker is very
ductive. He creates hundreds of large
tercolors, ceramic vases and columns,
rmanent installations in concrete and
amics, large colorful handmade paper
ces (8'x4' and larger) and marbleized
rics.

ker received an M.F.A. from the California
llege of Arts and Crafts in Oakland. He has
n creating an extensive assortment of art
ns for 20 years, continually producing new
exciting work which is exhibited
onally. Parker is currently a professor of
art at San Jose State University.

uild 3, 4 and 5, Parker continues to show
many varieties of his work. He is available
nstallations.

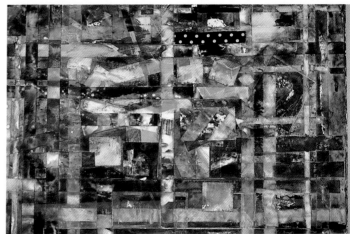

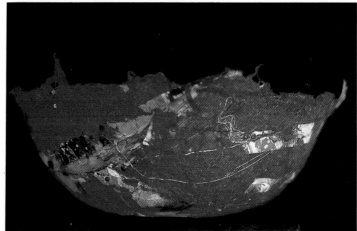

Beverly Plummer

2720 White Oak, Left
Burnsville, NC 28714
(704) 675-5208

Beverly Plummer designs colorful images that evoke the aura of playful innocence associated with childhood.

The images appear in and on heavily textured archival paper that has been hand-formed from cotton fibers and light-fast pigments. Many pieces also glisten from the addition of luster pigments. After framing, the pieces require no further care. Pieces measure roughly 30" x 30". Prices for available work start at $250.00.

Plummer welcomes commissions and can create work of any size, color or design. Custom designs require four to eight weeks after design approval and deposit. They are priced according to size and complexity.

Work is represented in galleries and collections internationally.

(Top) "Four and Seven"

(Bottom right) "Lulu Loves Her Trampoline"

(Bottom left) "Imaginary Bird Dreams of Real Worms"

Susan Singleton

...D Inc.
...1 E Pike Street
...ttle, WA 98122
...) 322-0390 or (800) 344-0390

...o Moon Bay" is from Susan Singleton's
...st recent series of work. The pieces
...orporate paper and fabric collage,
...nting, rubbings and drawings that are
...nse with rich color reminiscent of
...diterranean walls. Prices range from
...).00 to $2500.00 according to size. For this,
...ny other available work; paintings,
...missions and atrium sculptures or AZO
...er prints please call.

Raymond D. Tomasso

Inter-Ocean Curiosity Studio
2998 South Bannock
Englewood, CO 80110
(303) 789-0282

A definitive statement in corporate, hospitality or private collections, the three-dimensional cast handmade rag paper wall sculptures of Raymond D. Tomasso integrate dynamic, sharp edged elements with a palette of subdued, natural hues to create timeless archaeological images. For 16 years Tomasso has focused his talents on developing a distinctive technique based on his in depth understanding of the age-old craft of papermaking through history and around the world. Each piece of the artist's work is composed of hand formed sheets of 100 percent cotton rag paper for a durability that ensures a 100-year life expectancy. Tomasso's subtle color range is derived from a combination of pure pigment, colored pencil and latex paint, which is protected by a finish of clear flat lacquer. The artist will design his work to fit custom architectural specifications. Selected corporate collections; AT&T, Century 21, Citicorp, Coca Cola Co., Emory University, Hallmark Cards, Hyatt Regency, IBM, Knoxville Museum of Art, Mountain Bell, Munich Marriott Hotel, Prudential-Bache Securities, Sheraton Hotel, University of Arizona, University of Nebraska at Omaha

A Time To Think of Other Things, 21" x 27", 1990.

In an Ancient Cumbrian Dream, The Search Continued, 40" x 64", 1990.

arjorie Tomchuk

Horton Lane
w Canaan, CT 06840
) 972-0137

a professional artist for 28 years, Marjorie
chuk has art placed in more than 50
or corporations, including IBM, Xerox,
orp, AT&T, GE, and also in museums
uding the Library of Congress. She
cializes in limited edition embossings on
-made paper, the style is semi-abstract.

embossings are editions of 100, retail for
. Available immediately. A 16 page color
hure packet can be obtained for
ence, price: $4.ppd. Commissioned art:
up to 4' x 6', retail $2000.–$3400. per
el. Maquette fee $150., delivery: 4–6
ks. Also available: a hard cover book "M.
chuk Graphic Work 1962–1989," 143
es, $32.ppd.

right) "Summer Hills," painting on
-made paper, 25" x 34" ea.
missioned by GE, Stamford, CT

w) "Sounding," original print, embossed,
d colored, 25" x 36", edition 100, retail

Alice Van Leunen

P.O. Box 408
Lake Oswego, OR 97034
(503) 636-0787

Alice Van Leunen specializes in mixed-media wall treatments and aerial installations. Many of the works are site-specific, and the artist has extensive experience collaborating with designers as well as with other artists. Works range in size from small intimate pieces up to major architectural installations. Materials include folded or woven paper or plastic, loom-woven fibers, silk fabric, acrylic rod, and, especially in public works, durable industrial materials which require minimum maintenance. Surface treatments include watercolor, airbrush, pastel, collage, needlework, and reflective metallic foil.

Works are represented in numerous private, corporate, and public collections. Commissions are welcomed, and the artist available to supervise installations of major works. Prices, slides, and further information furnished on request.

(Top) "The Invention of Music: The Rattle, Th Cithera, Panpipes," triptych, 1989.
(Left) "The Rattle", (Center) "The Cithera", (Right) "Panpipes", handmade paper with mixed media, triptych with overall dimensio 27" x 136". Commissioned by the Hillman Corporation for Kruse Woods I, Lake Osweg OR.

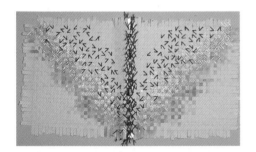
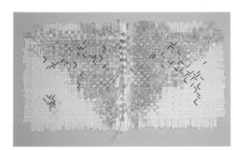
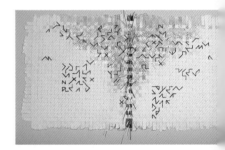

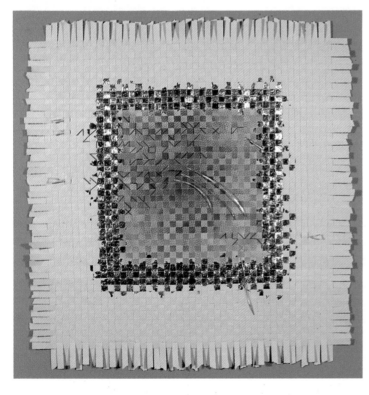

M. Warren

nont Paperworks
7, Middletown Road
fton, VT 05146
) 843-2369

se seductively textured, organically
ed handmade paper pieces are suitable
vallhangings, atrium mobiles, pedestal
esktop pieces. Sizes range from 6"H.
otures to 15-foot wall-pieces and mobiles.
work has been exhibited across the
ntry in juried shows as well as private
eries.

en's 13 years of experience as a
ermaker insures excellent workmanship.
olors (custom tailored) are lightfast. An
asional dusting is the only maintenance
ired.

s range from $400–$4,000 for
missioned works.

ce list, resume, and slices of sample work
available upon request. Allow 6–8 weeks
elivery after the contract is signed.
om plexiglass cases available.

"Sunrise Basket"; handmade paper;
x 6 1/2"h x 8"d.

om) "Turquoise Fountain"; handmade
er 16 1/2"w x 6"h x 10"d.

Nancy J. Young

11416 Brussels Avenue, N.E.
Albuquerque, NM 87111
(505) 299-6108

Young designs and produces unique two-and three-dimensional works in handmade paper. These durable works are available in a variety of sizes, textures, and colors. Commissions accepted.

Prices from $100–$2000 retail depending on size and complexity. Allow 4–8 weeks from design approval and contract. Shipping FOB Albuquerque.

Selected collections include: AT&T; Atari; American Express; Burlington Northern.

(Top) Wood and cast paper figures: 6' high x 5' wide x 21 over 2 1/2' deep.

(Bottom) Cast paper panel: 20" high x 5'6" long by 4" deep: Vessels: 6" high x 7" diameter; 9" high x 11" diameter.

ALL INSTALLATIONS/OTHER MEDIA

193 Carol Adams

194 Susan Bach

195 Bruce Smith Designs

196 Janis Colella
Linda Fisher

197 Nancy Weeks Dudchenko

198 Lisa Harris

199 Georgina Holt

200 Margie Hughto

201 J.E. Jasen

202 Pamela Joseph

203 Rip Kastaris

204 Vivian Kline

205 Bonny Lhotka

206 Joyce Lopez

207 Joyce Lopez

208 Elizabeth MacDonald

209 Richard Mann

210 J. Wade Meeker

211 Andrew Moritz

212 Louise Pappageorge

213 Arline Peartree

214 Dean Petaja

215 Michael Rocco Pinciotti

216 Tom Radca

217 Carl Schmitt

218 Victoria Schuh

219 Kenneth Sedberry

220 Ned Souder

221 Robert Sullivan

222 Jackque Warren

223 Bill Wheeler

224 Claudia Zeber

225 Len Zeoli

226 Dale Zheutlin

arol Adams
ensional Works of Art
5 Main Street
insula, OH 44264
) 657-2681

To enhance the interior of a building, office, or home, Carol Adams' designs create rich visual textures which unite a space. They reflect the landscapes, images, and theatrical influences experienced in her extensive travels. Her work incorporates weaving, handmade felt, metals, enamels, stitchery, carved wood, neon, or stage lighting.

Her recent explorations are light related. The translucent fabric within these objects creates an elegant light receptor which is decorated with reflection, glittered and colorful areas. Their outer edges are made of metal and are three-dimensional. A light show is then created using neon, stage lights, and possibly lasers. The result is a "painting" of the walls or ceiling with light.

"Aerial Garden I" includes five light switches with dimmers which allow the clients the power to create their own sculpture. Since this piece is in a physical rehabilitation facility, it also involves the healing effect of color and light. These sculptures are ideal for atriums.

(Top right) "Aerial Garden II: Alliances," fabric, mylar, paints, metal, lights 4' x 4' x 12'

(All others) "Aerial Garden I: Fantasy," fabric, mylar, paints, wood, metal, chrome, neon, lights, 9 objects within 18' x 27' x 9'

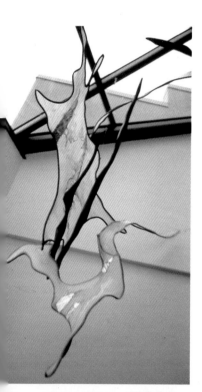

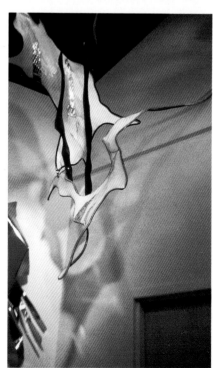

Susan Bach

2423 McRae Avenue
Orlando, FL 32803
(407) 896-6350 (407) 898-7272

Susan Bach's work is a unique blend of natural forms and distinctive design. Referring to these pieces as "Future Artifacts," Bach treats each endeavor as a possible archaeological "find." Terra cotta segments that incorporate 22K gold leaf, glazes and overglazes are presented in a custom framed format.

Her award winning designs are exhibited in galleries and museums throughout the United States as well as private and corporate collections.

Retail prices begin at $250. Please contact the artist for resumé, slides of available work or information regarding commissions.

(Top) "Ibis and Frogs," 20" x 20".

(Bottom) "Orchids and Trout," 18" x 20".

~~B~~ruce Smith Designs

~~Br~~uce F. Smith
~~P.~~O. Box 868
~~Rid~~gefield, CT. 06877
~~(2~~03) 431-0948
~~fax~~ (203) 438-0568

~~Bru~~ce Smith innovative designs focus on the
~~livin~~g environment. Often using found or
~~prev~~iously used objects, Smith creates works
~~of ar~~t, lighting systems as well as vibrant new
~~sur~~face textures.

~~Oft~~en Mr. Smith uses unusual methods to
~~prod~~uce remarkable patinas, textures and
~~surf~~aces that are entirely unique. Using an
~~arra~~y of talented craftspeople, Bruce Smith
~~Des~~igns works with the individual as well as
~~corp~~orate clients traveling throughout the
~~cou~~ntry and abroad.

~~Price~~es begin at a few hundred dollars for
~~sma~~ll light fixtures and sculptures.
~~Awa~~rds include:
~~Th~~e Creative Glass Center of America
~~   ~~Fellowship.
~~Th~~e Djerassi Foundation Residency.

Janis Colella
Linda Fisher

632 Center Avenue
Mamaroneck, NY 10543
(914) 698-7727

Working closely with the client to harmonize practical and aesthetic considerations, Janis Colella and Linda Fisher call upon years of excellence in wood and fiber to evolve highly innovative wall reliefs and free standing sculptures for homes and public spaces.

Selected commissions include Mercy Medical Center, Baltimore, MD; Royal Ontario Museum, Toronto, Canada; Fireman's Fund Insurance Company, Greenwich, CT.

Pricing available upon request.

(Top) "Odyssey in Harmony" 15' x 2' x 14'.

(Bottom left) "Amazon Argus" 13" x 4 1/2" x 22".

(Bottom right) "Molten Spirit" 15" x 5 1/2" x 19".

Photographs by Rick Albert.

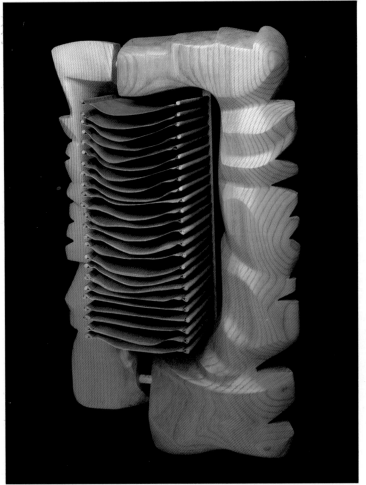

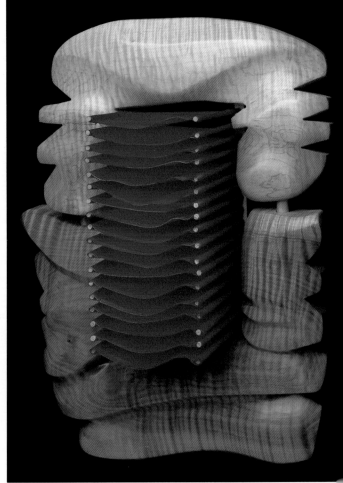

Nancy Weeks Dudchenko

Dudchenko Studios
C. Weeks Bldg.
15 Ridge Pike
Collegeville, P.A. 19426
(215) 489-7231

Nancy Dudchenko has been a full time producing artist since 1968. Her works are one-of-a-kind glazed and painted ceramic sculptures for the wall.

She has nationally exhibited in one person exhibitions, invitationals and juried competitions throughout the United States. Her sculptures hang in over 200 corporate collections and numerous museums and private collections.

These multi-sectional unique works are high fired stoneware using oil paint and stains over parts of glazed surfaces.

Prices range from $250–$350 (retail) per sq. ft. Most commissions can be completed within several months. Many finished works are available.

Unlimited size restriction.

Please write or phone for further information.

(Top left) "It's A Symphony", 74"w. x 39"h.

(Bottom left) "Fleur-de-Lis", 34"w. x 47"h.

(Bottom right) "Angel Falls", 39"w. x 88" h.

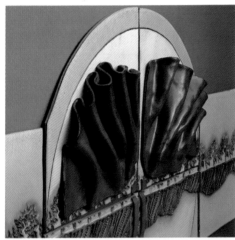

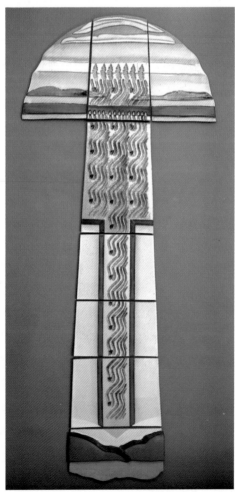

Lisa Harris

Lill Street Studios
1021 W. Lill Street
Chicago, IL 60614
(312) 477-1256
(312) 871-4151–Home

Lisa Harris' architectural wall constructions are inspired by dramatic urban vistas. Incorporating clay, sheet rock, acrylic paints, wood and other media, she creates highly textured and evocative surfaces.

Pieces are durable and easily mounted in component parts. Prices range from $900–$2500 depending on size and complexity. Collaborations and commissions are welcome.

The artist has exhibited widely and is included in private and corporate collections.

(Top) "Urban Remnant" 45"w.x33"h.

(Bottom) Composite View/Cityscape.

eorgina Holt
nd Built Porcelain
7 Cove Court
ksonville, FL 32211
4) 744 4985

orgina Holt creates intriguing porcelain
l installations. Her work is in private,
seum, and corporate collections
ughout Florida and the southeast.

h artwork is individually designed for its site
g hand-built, high-fired porcelain tiles,
ch are light weight, fade proof, and
emely durable.

installation shown here featured two
nal wall panels each consisting of 12"
are tiles. The tiles have been formed from
y rolled and folded porcelain, with
erglazed painting. The result is a visual
ression of fabric, a subtle oriental tone,
calligraphic directional strokes.

kon Inc., a Johnson and Johnson
npany, commissioned the work. The wall
a reflection of the firm's corporate
ge of progress and sophistication.

) Untitled Wall Relief.

om) Installation in lobby of the new
kon building, Jacksonville, Florida.

Margie Hughto

6970 Henderson Road
Jamesville, NY 13078
(315) 469-8775

Margie Hughto is nationally recognized for her ceramic paintings and collages. These elegant wall reliefs are made of stoneware clays, slips and glazes, and are constructed of beautifully colored and textured elements. The works range in size from small intimate pieces up to installations of architectural scale. Commissions are welcome and existing works are available. Prices, slides and further information are furnished upon request.

Works are represented in numerous museum, corporate and private collections including: Museum of Fine Arts, Boston; Everson Museum, Syracuse, NY; IBM, Kodak, NYNEX, Mayo Clinic, Port Authority, NYC; NFTA, Buffalo; Connecticut State University.

(Top) "Summer Shimmer," 1990, 35"h. x 108"w., ceramic, corporate commission for lobby entrance.

(Bottom) "Spring Blooming," 1990, 35"h. x 108"w., ceramic, corporate commission for conference room.

ndrew Moritz
ecial Creations in Metal
). Box 7126
nd, OR 97708
3) 389-1107

Andrew Moritz has been creating sculptures in bronze and steel for private collections (as shown in guild 5) as well as corporate and public installations since 1971.

Using no molds or patterns each of his sculptures is an original in the truest sense helping insure the investment quality of every piece he creates.

The care in planning and detail of execution is reflected in every commission accepted and has helped gain Moritz an international following.

As well as satisfying the aesthetic requirements, practical aspects such as

shipping, installation and lighting are always considered and discussed before work begins.

• Client satisfaction guaranteed.

• Prices begin at $1500.00.

• Please call or write for further information.

(Left) "Proud Stand", welded steel trees w/gold plated mountains—10'x10'x12".

(Right) "In Memory Of", welded steel, and hand poured glass—5'x4'x8".

Louise Pappageorge

1627 North Burling
Chicago, IL 60614
(312) 787-9106
(312) 944-4522

Combining traditional weaving techniques with non-traditional material, wire, Louise Pappageorge creates two and three dimensional sculpture. Her surfaces retain the elemental sensibilities of cloth while incorporating the luminescence and sculptural capacities of metals.

Pappageorge holds a BFA from the School of the Art Institute of Chicago, where she studied traditional and non-traditional fiber/fabric techniques.

Recent acquisitions/commissions include the City of Chicago, Homart Development Co, IL., Ana Kanazawa Hotel, Tokyo, Japan.

"Emerging Form" 40" x 63" x 10"

"Gale" 89" x 38" x 10"

Michael Rocco Pinciotti

Neon Art
John St. #1108
New York, NY 10038
(2) 285-0959

...cky Pinciotti's neonized "temples" focus on ...e concept of man-made structures as ...vered objects reflecting the poetry of ...ace. Here in these holy, harmonious and ...agical temples, neon's sacred glow brings ...into a place of comfort and at the same ...e energizes us.

...cky has been creating one-of-a-kind and ...ted edition neon pieces since 1979. He ...s an MFA from Pratt Institute and exhibits ...d lectures extensively in the USA and ...ernationally. His work is featured in the ...oks, *The Magic of Neon* and *The New Let ...re Be Neon.*

...se neon and mixed media temples are ...ntweight and handled and hung as any ...med artwork. Prices range from $1,000 to ...000. Additional information available.

...p) "Temple of the Heart" 35"h x 28"w x 6"d

...ttom right) "Greek Temple" 30"h x 36"w x

...ttom left) "Miami Deco" 39"h x 30"w x 5"d

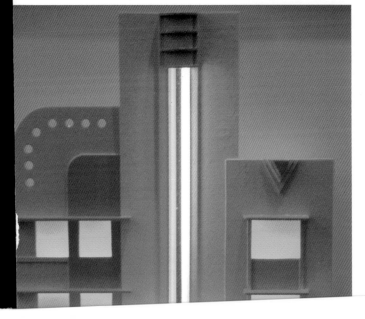

Tom Radca

Route 2, Box 340B
Port Washington, OH 43837
(614) 498-4303

Frequently large in scale, the work of Tom Radca incorporates marvelous depth of color. By using special techniques in his kiln, pieces frequently develop a luster highlight.

Tile pieces, vessels and plates can be used for interior or exterior applications. Individually hand made tiles are mounted on sectional recessed wooden bases for ease in shipping.

Completed installations include fifteen Saks Fifth Avenue stores. Work is available from designers, showrooms and galleries throughout the Eastern United States. Inquires and commissions are welcomed; resume and slides depicting additional work are available upon request.

Prices range from $350 for 21" plates to $1500 for 36" x 40" tile pieces.

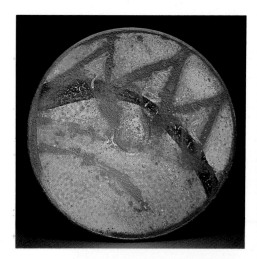

Carl Schmitt

New Expressions In Clay
5 East Clinton
Fresno, CA 93704
(209) 229-1246

Carl Schmitt's wall murals depict dynamic
rippling sand dune patterns; contemporary
abstract landscapes in three dimensional
surfaces with soft or intense colors. Waterfall
sculpture features include the subtle and
refreshing sound of cascading water.

Ceramic wall murals are durabile for interior
or exterior locations. Mural sections are
constructed for simplified installation. Allow 6
to 12 weeks for completion.

Costs: Murals $100 to $140 per square foot
and $500 per unit for waterfalls. Call or write
for more information.

Waterfall, 20" x 18", Interior or Exterior.

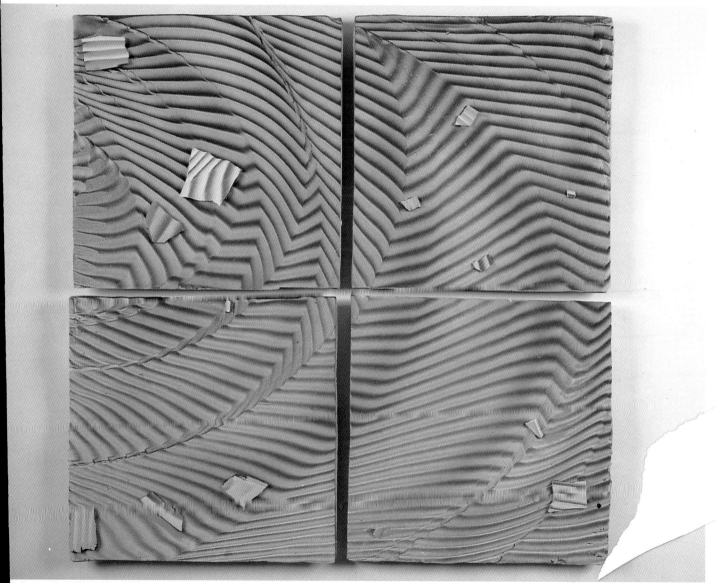

Classic Rippling Sand Dune, 4' x 4', Wall Mural.

Victoria Schuh

GrayWing Arts
31 Washington Street, Suite 2A
Brooklyn, NY 11201
(718) 855-5816

Schuh's murals and painted finishes refresh the urban eye. Her scenes, decorated ceilings and free-standing painted panels can be seen in corporate and residential collections in the U.S. and Europe.

After receiving her M.F.A. at Ohio University, she began working professionally. She encourages client interaction. Scale drawings and color maquettes precede the final execution on canvas, masonite, wood or wallboard. Work is produced directly on site or in studio.

Prices start at $2500. Estimates and production schedules are furnished to client specifications. Collaborations and commissions welcomed.

Below:

(Left) Details from residential piece, oil on canvas, Southampton, NY.

(Right) Painted panel, private collection, Paris

(Center) 4' x 7' mural, corporate installation, NYC.

enneth Sedberry

n Sedberry Studio
x 47 Mine Creek Road
kersville, NC 28705
04) 688-3386

n Sedberry, MFA from the Rhode Island
hool of Design, has been working in clay,
marily wood-fired clay, for 18 years. His
rk is represented in private collections, and
hibited in galleries throughout the country.

presented here are works from a series of
uardians". They are approximately four feet
height, wood-fired terra cotta and are
able for interior or exterior installations in
dential, corporate or public spaces.
cessed alcoves, entryways or other vertical
ces are excellent frameworks for individual
allations, while multiples are striking on
ge wall surfaces.

ividual works begin at $800. Slides and
ume available upon request.

otos were taken at the Penland School in
th Carolina by Bart Kasten.

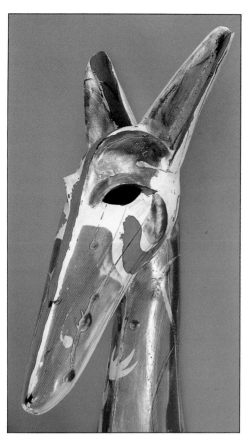

Ned Souder

Studio: (612) 439-2266

Art Resources
494 Jackson Street
St. Paul, MN 55101
(612) 222-8686

Site specific, client specific works by Ned Souder, utilize the finest materials in glass, fibers, metal and stone. Ned works from blue prints or on site observations. He collaborates with other professionals on the job, and personally installs each commission. Clear instructions of each work are given. Ned Souder has accomplished over 80 commissions. His work is represented in many corporate and private collections.

Personally scaled works begin at $2000., photo example range - $6000. to $12000., and major installations are priced accordingly. Detailed proposals communicate concept, image, color and materials, along with installation technique, time frame and budget schedules.

Current projects include a 15' x 23' suspended glass "Veil of Glows" for Sioux Valley Hospital, Sioux Falls, S.D., Ellerbe Becket Architects.

"Air Over La Spezia", 5' x 8', 1989 detail and residence

Robert Sullivan

sed Glass Studio
715 Goodrich Drive, N.W.
g Harbor, WA 98335
06) 857-4605

Known for his imagery and rich colors, Robert Sullivan is commissioned for large paintings of high-fire fused glass wall reliefs and architectural installations. Sullivan custom designs individual works for the public, corporate, and residential settings. He is exhibited nationally and internationally and is in numerous collections.

Prices start at $150.00 per square foot. Design fee is 10 percent of proposal budget. Allow 6–8 weeks for delivery and installation. Commissions and collaborations are welcome. Further information is available upon request.

Exhibited regularly are his highly decorative, stylized portraits of contemporary women titled the 'Urban Women Series'.

(Top left) "Jessie, Urban Women Series", 20 x 20"

(Lower left) "Tokido Banners", 6' x 4'.

Residential Installation.

(Below) "Color Currents", 12' x 12'.

Corporate installation.

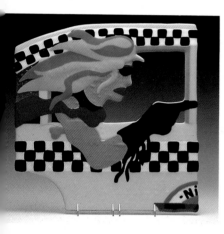

Jackque Warren

Stevens Design Associates
P.O.B. 183020
Fort Worth, TX 76118
(817) 589-7101

Jackque Warren combines abstract, geometric and lyrical images for a dramatic statement in any Architectural environment. Her painted surfaces present beautifully executed shapes and forms thoughtfully integrated in each facility.

Based in fine arts education and experience, Jackque's national and regional exhibits reflect her commitment to Art. Collaboration with Interior Designers and Architects refect her commitment to the Built Environment.

Her work range includes Corporate, Institutional and Residential. For Futher information contact Patricia Stevens at Stevens Design Associates.

TILES & MOSAICS

229 Christine Belfor

230 Design Works, Inc.

231 Design Works, Inc.

232 Firebird Inc.

233 Franz Mayer of Munich, Inc.

234 Marion Grebow

235 Nancy Heller

236 Elle Terry Leonard

237 Paul Lewing

238 William Palanza

239 Mathers Rowley

240 Siglinda Scarpa

241 Karen Singer

242 Irene Wittig

Christine Belfor

Christine Belfor Design Ltd.
East 87 Street Studio 402
New York, NY 10128
(212) 722-5410

Christine Belfor Design Ltd. is a unique company that specializes in large scale "Art on Ceramic Tile" with architectural appointments. The artistic aptitude of the studio extends beyond tile for decoration. Entire rooms can be clad in tile in order to define the shape, from Baroque to Post-Modern styles.

Established in 1986, Christine Belfor Design Ltd. has a well known designer and architect clientele. Her installation venues stretch across the continental United States as well as the Caribbean and the Middle East.

(right) Polychrome tile niche.

(far top) Entire room clad in tile features architectural elements.

(far bottom) Frost free exterior tile for gazebo floor.

Design Works, Inc.

David Wright
P.O. Box 163
Murfreesboro, TN 37133
(615) 895-1645
(615) 890-0934

Design Works offers handmade vitreous porcelain tile for kitchens, baths, tabletops, and exterior signs. David provides custom colors, designs, and installation. Each project is approached with the client's needs in mind. Photos and prices are available upon request.

(Right) Bathroom vanity and mirror with stoneware sink 30"x70".

esign Works, Inc.
vid Wright
. Box 163
rfreesboro, TN 37133
5) 895-1645
5) 890-0934

Bar 66"x40" with stoneware sink.

Firebird Inc.

Cynthia Berek
335 Snyder Avenue
Berkeley Heights, NJ 07922
(201) 464-4613, FAX (201) 464-4615

Meticulous, handcrafted, handpainted ceramic tiles.

Select from a wide range of murals. Motifs include florals, fruits, vegetables, herbs, animals and land and sea scapes.

Our continually expanding design line includes individual decorative tiles, many with a subtle, raised, embossed surface.

Field tiles, trim pieces and borders are also available.

Custom work is a specialty - both in theme and color. Some of this work graces kitchens bathrooms, pools, cabanas, fireplaces and furniture.

With a well earned reputation for service, reliability and originality, Firebird is now in its 10th year, offering professional services to architects, designers, builders, and individual clients throughout the country.

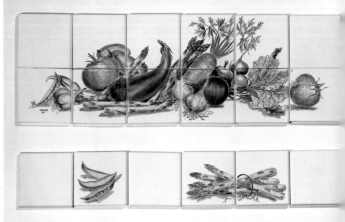

anz Mayer of
unich, Inc.
osaic Studio

stic Mosaic/Stained Glass
Passaic Avenue
field, NJ 07004
1) 575-4777/FAX: (201) 575-5588

nz Mayer of Munich/USA is a professional,
dern mosaic studio to the service of the
ependent artist/designer.

A staff of European trained craftsmen offers thorough knowledge of the craft, experience in contemporary mosaic concepts and sensibility for the artist's wishes. More than 50 tons of mosaic materials are on stock and 'state-of-the-art' equipment is at hand. Mayer of Munich offers consultation, submission of designs and estimates, execution, delivery and installation throughout the USA, Canada and the world.

The German Studio, "Franz Mayer'sche Hofkunstanstalt", established in 1845, is one of the oldest, largest and foremost international studios for stained glass and mosaic.

Reference: thousands of stained glass windows and mosaics for buildings all over the world, including 42 Cathedral Churches in North America or the spectacular artistic glazing of Frei Otto's Heart Tent in Rhiadh.

The pictures show: (Upper row, from left): Valerie Jaudon's 12' x 72' mural 'Freestyle' for the Equitable Center, NYC (1988/9); Thomas Holzer's mosaic sculptures for Ogden, UT (1989); craftsmen working on the large mosaic panels for the new Convention Center in Tampa, FL (1989/90); (Below) Robert Kushner's 18" x 36" mosaic piece in the work process.

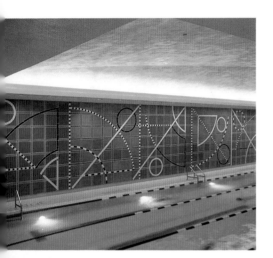

Marion Grebow

784 Columbus Avenue, Suite 7A
New York, NY 10025
(212) 866-5034

Marion Grebow specializes in hand painted tile installations. She has 20 years of experience in ceramics and fine arts. She combines these skills in her tile painting.

Grebow works closely with designers, architects and individual clients. She has exhibited internationally in museums and galleries, and has been featured in numerous publications. Her commissions have been for private homes and public buildings.

Prices vary according to size and detail. Designs can be adjusted to fit budget requirements.

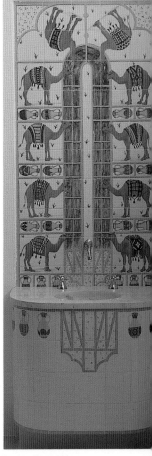

Design: David Moss.

Photos: Allen R

Nancy Heller

Nancy Heller Design Originals
01 Melvin Drive
ghland Park, IL 60305
08) 432-0425

aster ceramicist, Nancy Heller, is an artist
d designer specializing in the production of
ndmade ceramic tiles for both corporate
d residential sites. Her work is either
presentational or abstract, and ranges from
t or relief wall and floor surfaces to
ctional furnishings. Her tiles are durable,
quiring no maintenance and are used for
erior or exterior purposes.

llaborative work is accepted and
signed in close cooperation with the client.
es start at $1,500 for furniture and
–$125/sq. ft. for wall and floor surfaces, but
y depending on size and detail of subject.

ler's work is presently shown in corporate
ces and galleries throughout the country,
d is actively sought by interior designers,
hitects, and private collectors.

Tile-mirror table: 16" x 16" x 21"h.

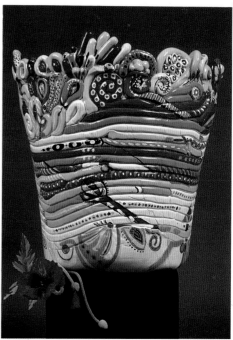

Ceramic vessel: 18" diameter, 21"h.

Photos by Sharon Goodman.

Elle Terry Leonard

Architectural Ceramics
P.O. Box 49645
Sarasota, FL 34230
(813) 951-0947

Architectural Ceramics, Inc. specializes in site-specific commissions in clay for corporate and residential clients.

Leonard produces originally designed, handbuilt ceramics for architectural application.

Studio specialties include fireplace, wall and floor treatment, with emphasis on relief murals. Accessories are also available.

Complete studio services range from concept and consultation through production, shipping and installation.

Recent commissions include The City of Venice, Venice, FL.; The Worldgate Marriott Hotel and Worldgate Athletic Club, Reston, Va.

Prices range from $36–150 per sq. ft.

A portfolio is available on request.

(Below) "Swimmer", 24' x 3' x 8', The Worldgate Athletic Club, Reston, VA.

aren Singer
West Washington Lane
adelphia PA 19144
5) 844-1767

en Singer is a sculptor as well as a ceramic
maker—complementary talents evident in
work. She creates colorful pieces that
ve rich textures, almost a stained glass
pearance, combining bold designs and
eful details.

work has won national honors for
ovative design, and she has had
ntinuous representation in individual and
up exhibits in museums and galleries.

created by Singer lend themselves to
ide range of interior and exterior
plications. She is an effective collaborator
o likes to incorporate imagery that is
aningful to the client. Recent commissions
e included specific building portraits
duced as collectibles.

views her art as a "visual prompter" that
llenges others to expand their perceptions
e familiar.

ail prices are from $25 per tile. Commission
es range from $100 to $300 per square
. Contact the artist for additional
rmation.

Irene Wittig

1619 South Quincy Street
Arlington, VA 22204
(703) 521-8184

Irene Wittig specializes in custom designed, handpainted ceramics: slipcast and hand-thrown dinnerware, accessories, tiles and
murals. She welcomes collaboration with clients, designers and architects to develop original and individualized designs that coordinate with clients' fabric or wallpaper; or incorporate unique personal elements: house portraits, genealogy, favorite places, animals, flowers etc.

The artist's fresh, colorful, European-naif style especially suited for home and restaurant settings. Unique accessories include tiled tables and letter boxes, lampbases and doc plaques.

Price list available upon request.

Irene Wittig is the author of the book *The Cl Canvas: Creative Painting on Functional Ceramics* (Chilton Books, 1990), and placed first in a recent international design competition at SURTEX.

LIGHTING & ACCESSORIES

245 Kerri L. Buxton

246 Penelope Fleming

247 Rob Johnson

248 Mesolini Glass Studio

249 Modern Objects

250 Lois Sattler

251 Hank Saxe and
     Cynthia Patterson

252 Fred Searls

253 Society of American Silversmiths

254 Judy Stone

255 Michelle Svoboda

256 Larry White

erri L. Buxton

xton/Taylor Design
3 West Pierpont, #2
t Lake City, UT 84101
1) 531-7515

Kerri Buxton specializes in handbuilt ceramic vessels with an emphasis on bold form and intimate detail. Originally trained as a metalsmith, the forms of her slab-constructed vessels are influenced by both holloware and sculpture.

The artist welcomes commissions. Prices to $3000 retail. Coffee services start at $1100, Urns at $400.

Permanent collections include the Nora Eccles Harrison Museum Collection, and the State of Utah Fine Arts Collection.

Additional information available by written request.

(Top) Urns—"Aquatic" Glaze, Height 32".

(Bottom) Coffee and Tea Service—Height 20".

Penelope Fleming

7740 Washington Lane
Elkins Park, PA 19117
(215) 576-6830

Mirrors, shelves and sculptural wall pieces artistically designed for the wall. A variety of colors, shapes and sizes are available. Mirrors and shelves can be purchased as a set or individually. Custom orders are honored.

The primary material is black and white modulated clay with additions of anodized (colored) aluminum, slate, stained glass and collective other materials.

Fleming has worked with many designers, art consultants and galleries to meet the criteria of design integrity, budget and completion deadlines. Commissioned wall pieces have been done for corporations such as Smith Kline Beckman, Reichhold Chemical Incorporated and Ragu' Food Incorporated as well as private individuals across the USA.

Call or write for a catalog, prices and the availability of completed pieces.

(Right) Mirror 35" x 20" x 3".
Wall shelf 10" x 23" x 10":

(Left) Detail view of wall piece.

ob Johnson

o Johnson Furniture
Amsterdam Avenue
v York, NY 10025
2) 865-6027

elf-taught artist with no formal design
ning, Rob Johnson both designs and
cutes his line of contemporary furniture.
Johnson's seating, tables and lighting are
ilable in galleries and stores in New York
. Matte Black and Grinded Steel, plate
s and industrial rubber materials ensure
ngth and durability. Rob Johnson
aborates with glass artist Jerry Morrell and
her artist Toshiki to expand his own skills
to showcase the work of others in his
neworks of steel. Commissions are done
nptly and correctly. Retail prices available
equest.

nt) Warrior Lamps—Telescope to 11 ft. tall.

ow) Adult seating at Soho Gallery location.

M E T A L   F U R N I T U R E

Mesolini Glass Studio

Gregg S. Mesmer
Diane A. Bonciolini
13291 Madison Avenue NE
Bainbridge Island, WA 98110
(206) 842-7133

Mesmer and Bonciolini combine extensive backgrounds in art glass production to create award-winning dishware that is both beautiful and practical (i.e. dishwasher safe). Each signed and dated piece is created from hand-rolled iridescent, transparent, or opalescent glass that is "slumped" into molds during a kiln firing.

Their limited edition filigrana bowls (top photo), available in a variety of color combinations, are constructed entirely of imported Italian glass rods. Two Mesolini hall-marks are evident in their production dishware (bottom photo): the glass caning and bead motifs, and the distinctive "cut off" edges, which result from using ruffled edges of the raw glass as design elements.

For additional examples of their work see The Guild 5, page 99. Call or write for prices.

odern Objects

hael Aguero
hael Sarti
Aarshall Street
h Norwalk, CT 06854
)334   Fax 866-9469

cumulative knowledge and experience
phases of design have had innovative
ts for Michael Aguero and Michael Sarti
the introduction of Modern Objects an
dable addition to the 9art9 furniture and
e accessories market.

criteria are pure use of materials, simple
gn and engineering, beauty and strength.
choice of materials such as wood,
, steel and marble is derived from an
itectural aesthetic. They are crafted so
the natural beauty and textures are
anced and then combined with such
ents as unusual patinaes, exotic papers,
er hinges and natural fibers.

initial concept of designing a line of
ucts inspired by architectural form has
olished this team as a major contributing
e to a trend that has become the
gest influence in the design of home
hings today. A brochure is available
request.

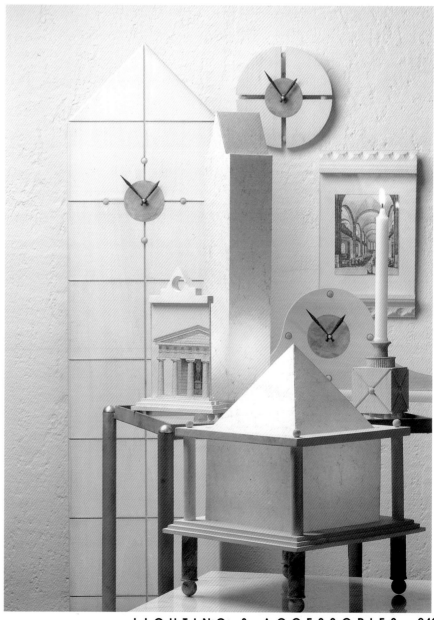

Lois Sattler

3620 Pacific Avenue
Venice, CA 90291
(213) 821-7055

Lois Sattler has had a life long love of Art. Her work is influenced by her love of nature, combined with her interest in ethnic cultures.

Each piece is one of a kind. She will work custom orders to client specifications. Her work can be seen in galleries and showrooms throughout this country and Canada, as well as in the 1987 and 1988 editions of *THE GUILD*. A price list of her work is available upon request.

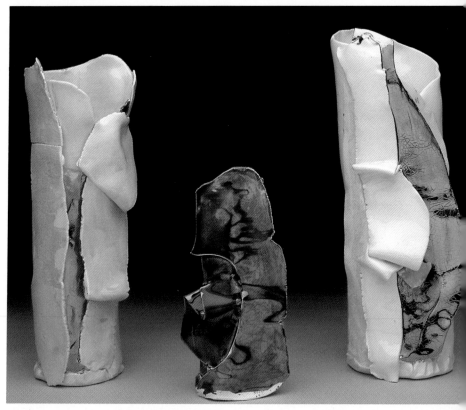

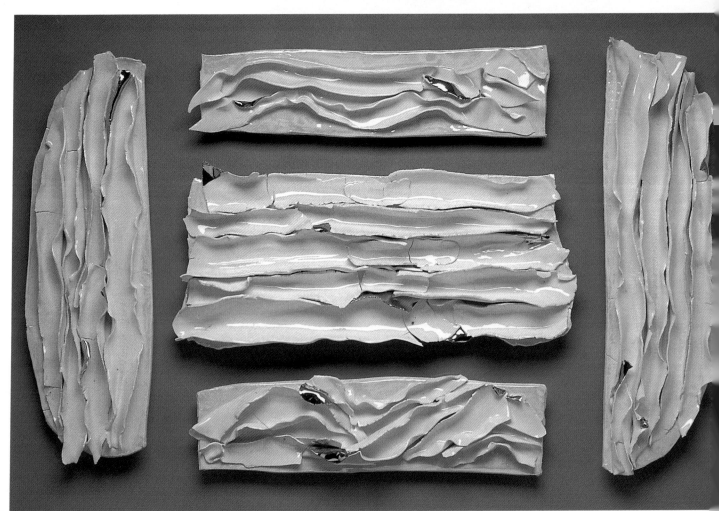

ank Saxe and
ynthia Patterson

e-Patterson
Box 15
, NM 87571
) 758-4336   (505) 758-9513

k Saxe and Cynthia Patterson produce
itectural work in high-fire ceramic.

produce custom lighting such as the
Paper Lights (pictured bottom),
mbling torn and textured porcelain
ers in dynamic juxtaposition. They also
duce the Ziggurat series of wall sconces
ured top) in a variety of sizes,
igurations, and finishes.

collaborate with other designers to
luce custom lighting incorporating stone,
, metal, and other materials as well as
mic.

lighting production is listed by
erwriter's Laboratory. Various lamping
ns are available and they work to
ommodate new or unusual lighting
nologies.

Saxe and Cynthia Patterson also design
produce geometric tile installations in
ed stoneware tile.

Fred Searls

Searls Design Group
285 Scenic Road
Fairfax, CA 94930
(415) 485-6888

Mr. Searls creates his work in various media including marble, plastics, metal and clay using internal illumination to dramatize residential and commercial interior designs.

Styles span primitive through High Technology and create vivid impressions in any setting. The forms are freestanding abstract, table and floor illumination, and built-in surfaces.

His work can be seen in executive offices, corporate boardrooms, restaurants, major hotel chains and private residences.

Creation and installation are personally composed with the client, and range in price from $550.00 to $60,000.00.

All photographs by Allen Lott © 1990.

Society of American Silversmiths

Box 3599
[Cra]nston, RI 02910
( ) 461-3156

The Society of American Silversmiths is an [org]anization comprised of America's finest [prof]essional silversmiths who handcraft [one-]of-a-kind and limited production [holl]oware and flatware. To receive a [com]plete list of names, addresses, and [pho]ne numbers of those silversmiths whose [wor]k is pictured here, contact the Society.

HAROLD ROGOVIN, NJ, sterling candelabrum & centerpiece, 9" ht.

[ ]EWING, OH, sterling "Penetrated Sphere Teapot," 17" ht.

CURTIS K. LAFOLLETTE, MA, sterling & copper teapot, 7" ht.

Judy Stone

25 A Mirabel Avenue
San Francisco, CA 94110
(415) 285-0572

Judy Stone's enamels are stylistically unique, designed to enhance the exterior or interior spaces around them. During multiple firings on carefully formed copper she creates texture over subtle colors to evoke the spirit of New Mexico, where she grew up.

Stone's one-of-a-kind enameled switch covers (bottom left) can fit any electrical configuration. They cost $65–$85 depending on their size, number of interior openings, and detail. Her production line of covers, $39–$60, fit most common American switches and outlets. All covers come with copper-plated screws.

Stone's enameled house numbers (approximately 4" x 6 1/2") are $40 each and are made to the customer's color specifications. Her bowls vary in shape and size, the largest being 10". Prices range from $45 to $200.

Brochure available.

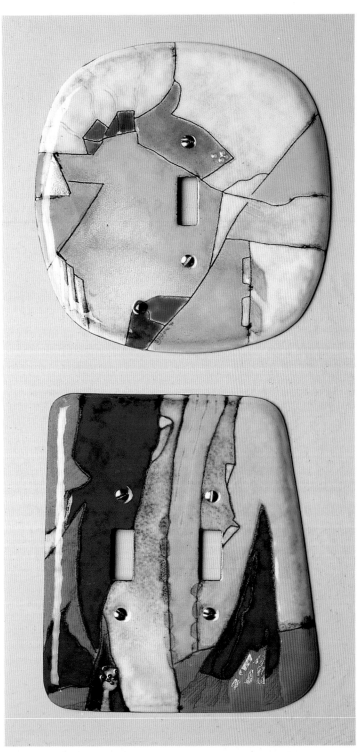

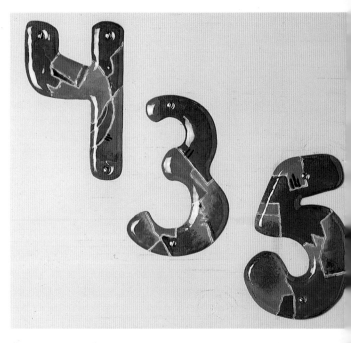

ichelle Svoboda

Top Design
Box 213
una Beach, CA 92652
) 494-6151

helle Svoboda produces hand-built
henware dinnerware and larger
-of-a-kind pieces. Many coats of glaze
e an appearance of intensely colored
bossing.

nerware varies in shapes, colors and
erns. Sets can be complimented with
accessory pieces.

helle's ceramics have been featured in
eries nationally, Ceramics Monthly, Bon
etit, and collections including
cDonald's Corporation and President
's.

s and prices available upon request.
nissions welcome.

Fruit and Vegetable Bowls.

om) Checker Nude and Geometric
e Dinnerware.

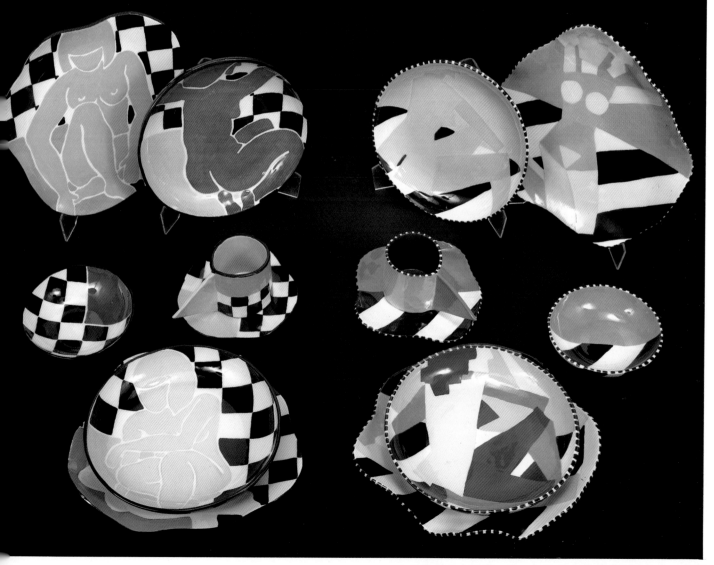

Larry White

664 South Coast Hwy.
Laguna Beach, CA 92651
(714) 494-4117

Larry White's furniture and architectural
accessories have earned him the respect of
both clients and peers.

A seven year apprenticeship with preeminent
woodworker Sam Maloof influenced Whites
background in fine arts.

His work has been exhibited nationally and is
included in both private and public
collections.

Contact Katherine White, Garrett/White
Gallery, (714) 494-4117.

(Top) 'Night Light,' Illuminated Objects Series,
16"w. x 35"h. x 6"d., aluminum, maple.

(Bottom) Night Table, 16"w. x 20"h. x 16"d.,
wenge, satine.

SCULPTURAL OBJECTS

259 Dina Angel-Wing

260 Shawn Athari

261 Shawn Athari

262 Nancy Moore Bess

263 Logan Fry

264 Judith E. Goldstein

265 Mark Grychczynski

266 Glenn J. Hill

267 Christine B. Knox

268 Pamela Laurence

269 Anne Mayer Meier

270 Jacque Parsley

271 Sandy Richert

272 Kerry Vesper

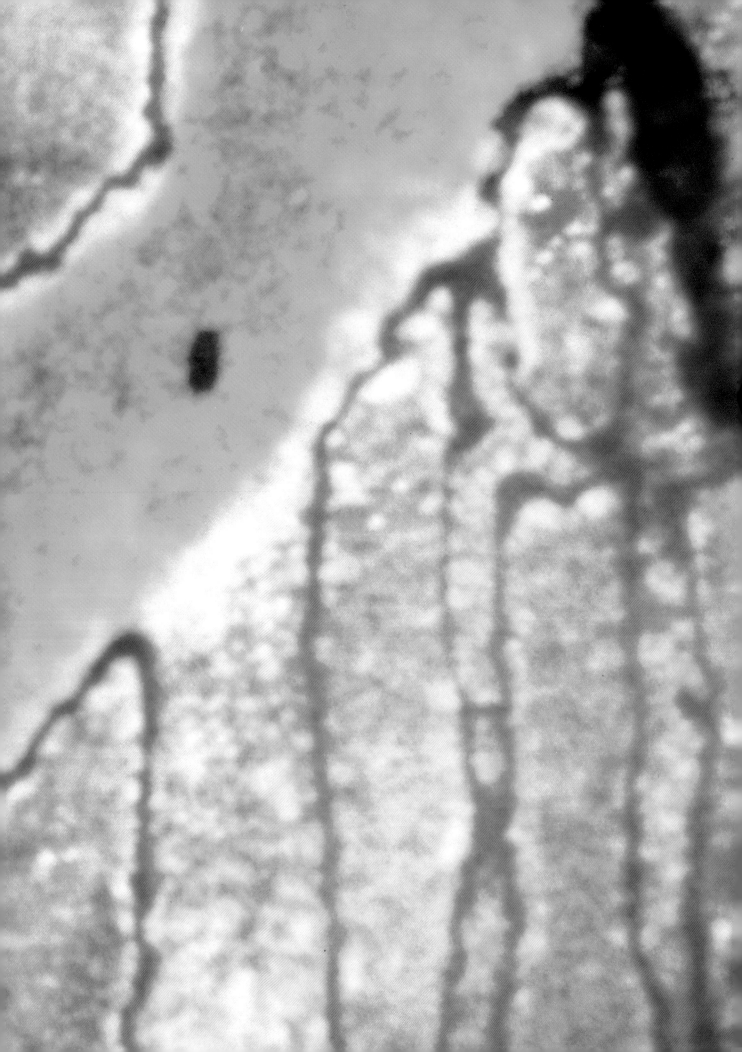

ina Angel-Wing

4 Cragmont Avenue
keley, CA 94708
) 526-3006

Dina Angel-Wing produces mixed media sculptures featuring clay forms and incorporating hand made paper, natural woods and found objects. Her on-going "Dream Box" series began over six years ago.

Recent experiments with larger sizes and new materials resulted in a new series of environment pieces which suspend found elements in a controled spatial environment.

Angel-Wing's sculptures are shown around the country including Gallery Eight in La Jolla, the Clay Pot in New York, PR Coonley in Carmel and Palo Alto. Her work has been exhibited internationally at the Biennale International de Ceramique D'Art in Valleuris, France and the Istituto Statale d'Arte per la Ceramica in Castelli, Italy.

Sizes: from 12" to 4 feet high or larger.

Prices: from $500 to $5000.

Wall pieces available, commissions and collaborations for designers accepted.

(Below) Ocean Secrets, 22" x 12" x 8".

(Left) Marine Archeology, 18" x 14" x 8".

Frank Wing.

Shawn Athari

Shawn Athari's, Inc
13450 Cantara Street
Van Nuys, CA 91402
(818) 988-3105
Fax (818) 787-Mask

Shawn Athari combines a knowledge and appreciation of ancient and foreign cultures with sixteen years of glass experience to create her glass sculptures.

In doing so she produces works evocative of cultures long since diminished or extinct.

Shawn Athari's work is in private and corporate collections throughout the US and Canada, has appeared in a wide range of publications and has won many awards.

Galleries: Elaine Horwitch, Santa Fe, NM; 2112 Design Studio, Minn. MN; Esther Frank, W. Bloomfield, MI; K.O. Galleries—Boca Rato FL.

(Bottom left) "Fishman," from a Pacific Northwest Indian Artifact, 21" x 43".

(Bottom right) "Shabti of Sati," Egyptian sculpture from reign of Amunhotep, 21" x 43

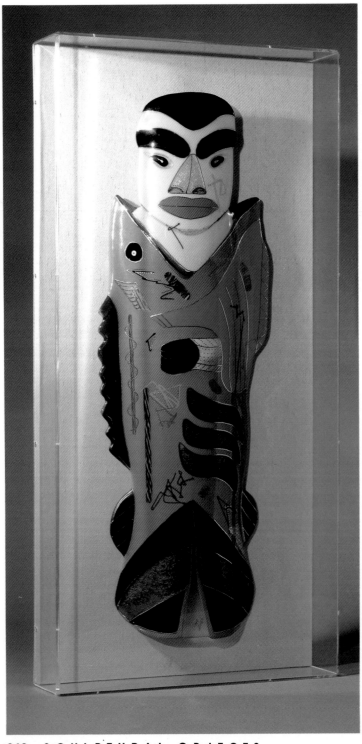

Shawn Athari

Shawn Athari's, Inc
50 Cantara Street
Nuys, CA 91402
988-3105
(818) 787-Mask

Shawn Athari reaches beyond her art to
cultural preservation in her contemporary
glass sculpture

(Bottom left) "Kachina Dolls," Originals
excavated from a cave in Southwest NM and
traced to 13th century. Each 14" x 34".

(Top right) "Twins," Gelede mask from
Yoruba, Nigeria, 17" x 29".

(Middle right) "Raven," Hamatsa Raven Mask,
23" x 24".

(Lower right) "Haida" portrait mask from the
Queen Charlotte Islands, 14" x 22".

Nancy Moore Bess

5 East 17th Street 6th floor
New York, NY 10003
(212) 691-2821

Utilizing traditional techniques associated with basket weaving, fencing and thatching, Nancy Bess combines raffia, cords and linen with accent elements to create a selection of basket forms and fiber constructions. Some pieces are mounted in custom lucite boxes, others rest on Japanese river stones or bamboo. A wide range of related wall pieces are available and are mounted in lucite boxes to ensure easy maintenance and installation.

Wholesale prices for these one-of-a-kind and limited edition basket forms start at $100; prices for fiber constructions begin at $190.

Special orders for larger work and multiples are welcome. Additional information is available upon request.

(Top left) "Package from Two Cultures", 5"h.

(Top right) "Reference to Kenya", grouping, 4 1/2"h.

(Bottom center) "Changing Perceptions", 9"

Christine B. Knox

Ceramic Sculptor
Mount Road
mmington, MA 01026
(3) 527-6390

Uplifting creativity with a flair for exuberance, the sculptural works of Christine B. Knox bring vitality and life to every setting. Working with high temperature stoneware and durable acrylic paints, the artist creates one of a kind and limited edition works of art. Free-standing, or in wall presentation, these sensual creations range from necessarily functional to purely visual.

Christine holds an MFA from Ohio University in Ceramics. Her work is represented in fine galleries in England, Canada, and throughout the United States. She has collaborated with both corporate and private clients in creating site specific works. Retail prices range from $400 to $5,000. Further information is available upon request.

(Top) Mantle, 9" x 42" x 4".
(Left) Mirror, 25" x 26" x 7"; Succulence #133, 21" x 16" x 14".
(Right) Table, 26 " x 24" x 24".

Pamela Laurence

508 Oakwood Road
Huntington, NY 11743
(516) 673-9768

From a piece that's only one foot square to a design that covers an entire wall, Pamela Laurence's work is created to serve a use or make an imaginative statement beautifully.

Her craft includes sculptural and functional pieces for tables, walls and floors, in interior and outdoor settings.

She has worked closely with designers and architects on commissions for homes, schools, offices and churches. Site evaluation has often been an important aspect of the collaboration in creativity.

Laurence's craft art has been featured in a number of galleries and exhibitions. Each original sculpture is signed and dated.

Prices range from $50 to $5000. Delivery is within four to eight weeks. For additional information, please contact the artist.

ne Mayer Meier

tive Textures
andalwood Way
wood FL 32750
332-6713

Meier has been a successful and
ular fiber artist for thirteen years. Her
ets and woven vessels are in collections
ss the country. (See Guild IV and Guild V
rther basketry information.)

r's current work is a series of figures
ing man's primitive past as well as being
emporary in design and fabrication.
e "Alter Egos©" offer spontaneity and
dom to age-old mystical concepts of
uality. They are carriers of culture,
ern memory keepers. Sizes begin at 24"
get larger. Prices start at $160.00. Please
act the artist for further information.

Jacque Parsley

2005 Indian Chute
Louisville, KY 40207
(502) 893-2092

Shells, rocks, crystals, fossils, old photographs, found objects, memorabilia....this is the stuff that these unique collage/assemblages by Jacque Parsley are made of. Works commissioned by using an individual's personal objects start at $800 wholesale.

Parsley earned a BFA from the Louisville School of Art and a MA from the University of Louisville. She has exhibited professionally since 1976 and her work has been published in *American Craft* and *Fiberarts* magazines.

Her work is included in the collection of the Evansville Museum of Art and Sciences, Evansville, In., Alabama Power and Light, Huntsville, Alabama, and Hilliard Lyons, Louisville, Kentucky.

(Top) "Dubl-Handi Washboard" 1990, 21" x 9" x 3", Found object collage/assemblage.

(Bottom) "Fossil Box" 1990, 9" x 12" x 14", Found object collage/assemblage.

ndy Richert
Kenbridge Drive
land Heights, OH 44143
) 449-5133

dy Richert's one-of-a-kind vitreous glass
mel on copper sculptures are small in
e but large in impact. Imagery is based
n landscape of real or fantasy places,
l interpretations, and color study
ractions.

e unit sculptures, like the pictured
ngrila," and multiple-pieced works, like
halla," also pictured, are meant for
ere or credenza. Multiple-pieced
tures are designed in several
igurations, allowing the owner to
ange at will.

e for photos/slides of completed work;
range is $225 to $800. Inquiry on
missions and proposals for collaboration
vited.

ert's enamels have been seen in The
eland Museum of Art May Show and
mithsonian's National Air and Space
eum; detailed exhibition list available
equest.

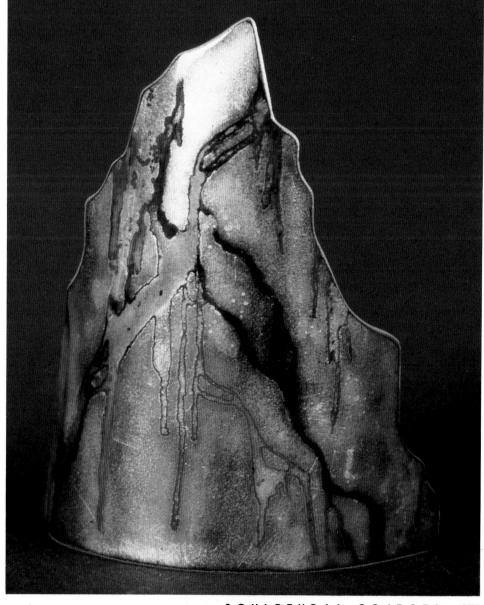

Kerry Vesper
Sculpture and Design Studio
116 East Ellis Drive
Tempe, AZ 85282
(602) 839-5376

Kerry Vesper uses solid woods and plywoods to create one-of-a-kind sculptural forms and functional vessels. He achieves a variety of finishes from smooth sanded, natural surfaces, to heavily wire-brush textured and stained layers.

Vesper works with his clients to create pieces for specific settings in homes and business environments. His work may be seen in galleries throughout the United States. Contact the artist for additional information.

Prices of vessels begin at $600.

Sculptural pieces begin at $1,000.

(Top left) "La Ola," Birch plywood and Africa Paduak, 8 1/2"h x 17" x 14".

(Top right) "Quetzal," Birch plywood and African Paduak, 17"h x 9" x 3"

(Bottom) "Rock Pot," 16"h x 18" x 18", "Caja Alta," 20"h x 16" x 11", "Cannister," 14"h x 12" x 12", Fir plywood.

VESSELS & BASKETS

275 Rosemary Aiello

276 Ruth E. Allan

277 Tim Bissétt

278 Allester Dillon

279 Ron Fleming

280 Michael K. Hansen
Nina Paladino

281 Valarie Lee James
Liz Cunningham

282 Eric L. Jensen

283 Will Johnson

284 Linda Brendler Studios

285 Bobby Medford

286 Gordon Middleton

287 Susan M. Oaks

288 Orient & Flume Art Glass

289 Kevin Osborn

290 Charles Pearson
Timothy Roeder

291 Robin Renner

292 Betsy Ross

293 Toar Schell

294 David Van Noppen

295 Eva S. Walsh

296 Timothy Weber

297 Westcote Bell Ceramics

298 Lee Zimmerman

n Bissétt

Bissétt Designs
2A Street, N.E.
ary, Alberta
ada T2E 4R5
247-3800

ptuous surface, opulent luster and refined
is the signature of Tim Bissétt's Raku fired
elain.

fine art pieces are uniquely presented in
dmade Baltic Birch boxes on a bed of
lsior.

e vessel art works are cherished by
te and corporate collections in Japan
Grand Kabuki Theatre), Canada, United
s of America, Finland, Britain, Africa,
nany, New Zealand and Belguim.

varies with size and presentation. A
hure is available. Corporate gift inquiries
nvited.

Allester Dillon

Clay and Fiber
1565 Vendola Drive #11
San Rafael, CA 94903
(415) 491-4037

Using coils of clay, Allester Dillon produces a variety of objects from woven baskets, seven inches high, to sculptures as tall as seven feet. Her forms are loosely tied to basic geometric shapes: triangles, pyramids, squares, rectangles, ovals and circles. She uses a rough sculptural clay and her methods of construction are always visible in the finished piece.

Her most recent work involves cutting openings into the clay to show the inside structure, while adding tied and twined reeds. The work is not functional. The clay is low fired and washed with ceramic stains in soft colors. The reeds may be dyed or left natural. The height of these objects varies from 15" to 44". Prices range from $500 to $2500 retail.

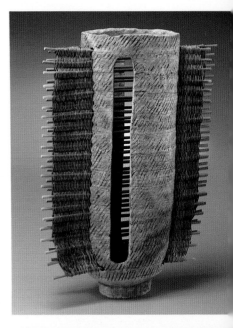

on Fleming

arthstone Studios
1 North Evanston
a, OK 74130
8) 425-9873

n Fleming's wooden vessels are distinctive
their flowing form, and sensual
nd-carved or painted designs.

ning's pieces have exhibited
rnationally and are represented in
eries, private collections and museums
oughout the United States.

Right) "Datura," Bass wood/Acrylic,
/2"-h, 17"-w

ttom left) "Kingwood Flora," Mexican
gwood, 10"-h, 5 1/2"-w

ttom Right) Detail of "Kingwood Flora"

Michael K. Hansen & Nina Paladino

California Glass Studio
P.O. Box 215786
Sacramento, CA 95821
(916) 925-9322 Fax (916) 925-9370

Michael and Nina have been working together for 14 years. Their glass is represented internationally in galleries and private and corporate collections

Pictured are handblown vessels and a roundel (plate), from the limited edition and one of a kind series.

A complete catalog is available upon request.

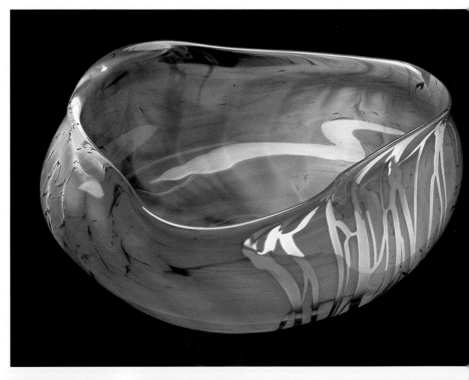

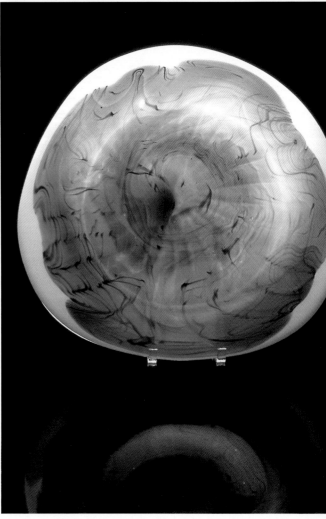

Valarie Lee James
Liz Cunningham

The Art of Calabash
P.O. Box 302
Healdsburg, CA 95448
(707) 431-0609

Valarie Lee James and Liz Cunningham merge the ancient and contemporary when transforming American Calabash into sculpture, vessels, and instruments.

Recipients of a National Endowment for the Arts multi-cultural arts grant, the Art of Calabash can be found in private and public collections across the United States.

Brochure/price list available upon request.

(Top) Inlaid Calabash.

(Bottom) Calabash grouping.

Eric L. Jensen

Lill Street Studios
1021 W. Lill Street
Chicago, IL 60614
(312) 477-1256

Incorporating landscape elements alongside references to primitive and modern architecture, Eric Jensen creates a series of one-of-a-kind vases. The work is done in high-fired porcelain and stoneware with porcelain slips, stains, and china paint, prices range from $150-$400 retail. Consignment inquiries are invited.

Eric Jensen received his M.F.A. from Cranbrook Academy of Art and has seventeen years experience as a ceramic artist. His work is collected and exhibited nationally.

(Top left) Vase 24"h. x 8"w. x 4"d.

(Top right) Vase 24"h. x 10"w. x 4"d.

(Bottom) Vase 8"h. x 26"w. x 4"d.

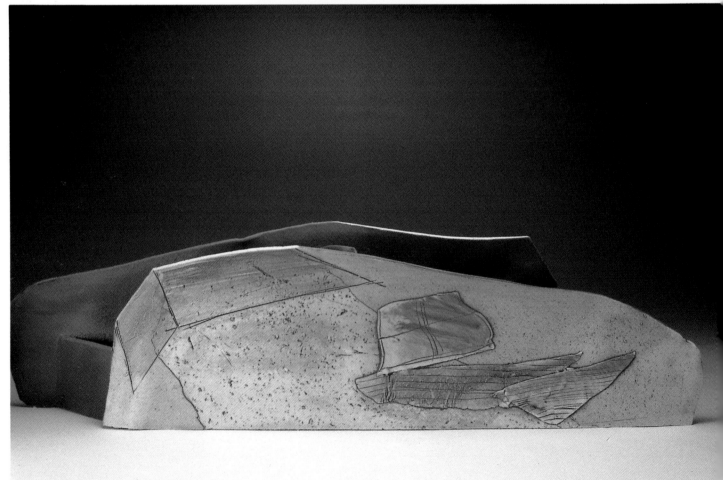

Eric L. Jensen
Lill Street Studios
1021 W. Lill Street

Vill Johnson
320 Doris Avenue
n Jose, CA 95127
08) 259-0472

Will Johnson's Sawdust Fired Work represents an attempt to express his appreciation for ancient and primitive hand built ceramics on a nonfunctional basis.

Each piece is one of a kind with the surfaces of some pieces burnished and hand tooled designed while others are unburnished. Johnson's work has been shown nationally and is in numerous private collections and is part of the permanent collection of Norma Eccles Harrison Museum of Art, Logan Utah.

Slides and additional information is available upon request. Prices range from $175.00–$900.00.

Piece below; 12″ x 17 1/2″ w.

Linda Brendler Studios

P.O. Box 4615
Modesto, CA 95352
(209) 522-3534

Working in the area of crystalline glazed porcelain for 18 years Linda Brendler has focused on the challenge of developing rare, unusual colors. The process is difficult, requiring a delicate balance of time and temperature with results varying. Crystals are actually grown in the glaze at high temperatures held for an extended period of time.

Possessing a timeless quality her one-of-a-kind work is unique in its beauty and intensity. Pieces are exhibited and sold in selected galleries and museums nationally and are also in many collections. They vary in height from 8 to 15 inches.

Linda Brendler holds an M.F.A. degree in Ceramics, having studied with Carlton Ball and Dr. Herbert Sanders.

Slides and resumé are available upon reque

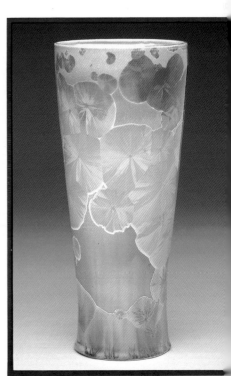

obby J. Medford

66 W. Bopp Road
cson, AZ 85746
02) 883-7453

bby Medford makes ceramic vessels and
all pieces utilizing both sculptural techniques
d throwing on the wheel. He is known for
use of color, creating designs of pastel
uthwestern urbanity as well as vibrant
mitive images executed with a
ntemporary flare. His work is in major retail,
rporate and resort collections. Medford is
presented by galleries in 15 states and in
nada.

all plates range in size from 16" to 40" in
ameter. Height of thrown or sculptured
ssels ranges from 20" to 60".

mmissions may specify color, size, and type
design. Six to eight weeks are required for
mpletion of most orders. Retail prices range
m $300 to $4,000.

es and a resumé are available upon
quest.

Gordon Middleton

9615 Palm Beach Lane
San Diego, CA 92129
(619) 484-4971

The majority of Gordon's wheel-thrown vessels are raku, incorporating incising, hand-made additions and metalic leaf to enhance the earthy texture and coloring of his pieces. These vessels are extremely versatile as decorative elements and work well with many types of decor. The other process incorporates high-contrast, black and white glazes to create interesting patterns and textures for a more contemporary look. Allow 6–8 weeks for delivery following signed contract. Price range: $150–1,500. Size range: 6–26".

usan M. Oaks

31 Fox Run
n Antonio, TX 78233-4706
2) 656-8440

Susan M. Oaks has been working with the coiled vessel form for several years. She uses fine materials—silk, wool, linen, cotton, and top-quality man-made fibers. The one-of-a-kind objects present well under plexi-glass. They work well on shelves with ceramic pieces, too. The vessels can be brushed lightly to removed dust or even shaken lightly.

Susan's vessels have been in exhibits in CT, IL, LA, NM, TN, TX, and UT. Her work is owned by collectors in several states and range in price from $100.00–$800.00. For more info—send $6.00 for a slide packet.

(Top left) "The Survivor," 4"h.x9$^{1}/_{2}$"d.

(Top right) "Empowerment," 3"h.x6$^{1}/_{2}$"d.

(Bottom) "Maybe," 3$^{1}/_{2}$"h.x10"w.

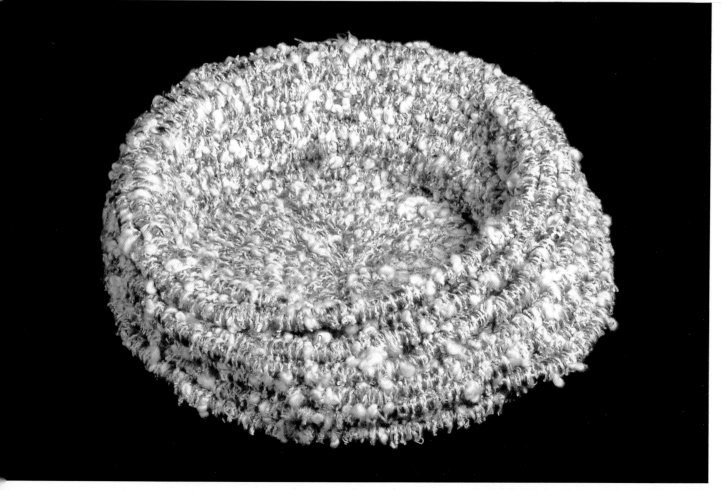

Orient & Flume
Art Glass

2161 Park Avenue
Chico, CA 95928
(916) 893-0373
FAX (916) 893-2743
Attn: Douglas Boyd

Internationally acclaimed, the artists of Orient & Flume specialize in one-of-a-kind, handblown vases, perfumes, and paper-weights. Using only "off-hand" blowing techniques, each piece is individually designed and created. Motifs range from traditional to contemporary.

Orient & Flume Art Glass can be found in the permanent collections of most major museums, including The Metropolitan Museum, The Smithsonian Museum, The Chrysler Museum, The Steuben Glass Museum, and the Chicago Art Institute.

Descriptions & retail prices: Rhino $60.00, Chrysanthemum $1300.00, Cased Cabinet Magnolia $280.00, Cased Cabinet Wisteria $330.00, Cased Cabinet Cymbidium Orchid/Bamboo $330.00, Cased Cabinet Daisy $330.00, Cased Vase Lily of the Valley $990.00, Cased Vase Tulip $570.00, Lapis Vases: Bowl $490.00, Round Vase $450.00, Lidded Vase $590.00, Tall Vase $550.00.

-vin Osborn

outh Stone Avenue, Suite A
n, AZ 85701
624-2756

Classical shapes. Contemporary designs.
Evocations of function and celebrations of
form. Tactile surfaces with vibrating visual
dimensions. Interlocking, geometric forms
captured at play, like a freeze-frame from an
abstract animated film.

Large-scale vessels. Vigorous and interactive
in public places. Sculptural and harmonious
at home. Tailored to personal desires.
$600.00-$10,000.00

Charles Pearson
Timothy Roeder

Whitehead Street Pottery
1011 Whitehead Street
Key West, FL 33040
(305) 294-5067

Charles Pearson and Timothy Roeder collaborate to produce these large hand thrown Raku fired vessels.

The forms have a visual strength that demand a response while maintaining the traditional subtleties of color by reducing in a post-firing of seaweed.

Prices start at $450.

Slides ($3 refundable) and additional information can be obtained by writing directly to their studio.

(Top) Raku fired 15" h. x 13" diameter.

(Bottom) Raku fired 16"h. x 13"diameter

Represented by:
The Signature Shop and Gallery
Atlanta, GA

Kahale Kai Trading Co.
Kauai, HI

Acropolis Now
Santa Monica, CA

The Adam Whitney Gallery
Omaha, NE

Photography: Merle Tabor Stern

bin Renner
ner Clay & Beadwork
Road 5474 NBU 3040
nington, NM 87401
) 632-0182

Award winning clay works may be seen at fine art galleries in Los Angeles, Chicago, Sedona, Durango, and Santa Fe. Collaborations or Commissions are encouraged.

Renner received her M.A. from Cal. State at Los Angeles; and studied at the Academy of Fine Arts in Florence, Italy.

Pictured above, pit fired cover jar from "Arch Series" 19" x 9" x 9". Below, "Guardian" pit fired with beadwork, 20" x 11" x 11"; and American Craft Awards winner "Shard Series-Mesa Verde" heights 14" to 18"

Prices from $75.00 to $1200.00. Resume and slides upon request.

Betsy Ross

1160 Fifth Avenue
New York, NY 10029
(212) 722-5535

Betsy Ross' earthenware vessels are an amalgam of wheel-thrown and hand built components. Her works are hand painted and embellished with lustres, creating metallic-like qualities. By virtue of being hand crafted, each piece is assured individuality and is signed by the artist.

Her works are exhibited in prominent galleries, represented in private collections and major publications.

Ms. Ross enjoys collaborating with architects and designers. Commissions accepted. Prices from $300 to $900 retail.

Vessels featured on this page range from 11" to 26".

oar Schell

pper-Pot Pottery, Inc.
1, Box 209
:Kinney, TX 75070
4) 347-2011

rnished porcelain, by Toar Schell, is
signed to suit a variety of decors and
tings. These beautifully handcrafted
corative art pieces are at home in
chitectural settings, as well as homes and
ices.

ch vessel is one-of-a-kind, and is individually
signed to each customer's requirements.
e works are comprised of large vases, urns,
d lidded storage jars. Sizes range from 18"
30" high, with varing widths. Prices start at
00. to $4000. and up. Custom colors are
ailable, and yearly production is limited.

sels consist of a central design panel (s),
ounded by an all-around handcarved
nch, bird, and flower motif. Shown at right,
two panel storage jar. Second panel
etail) pictured below.

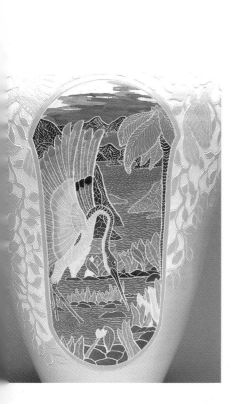

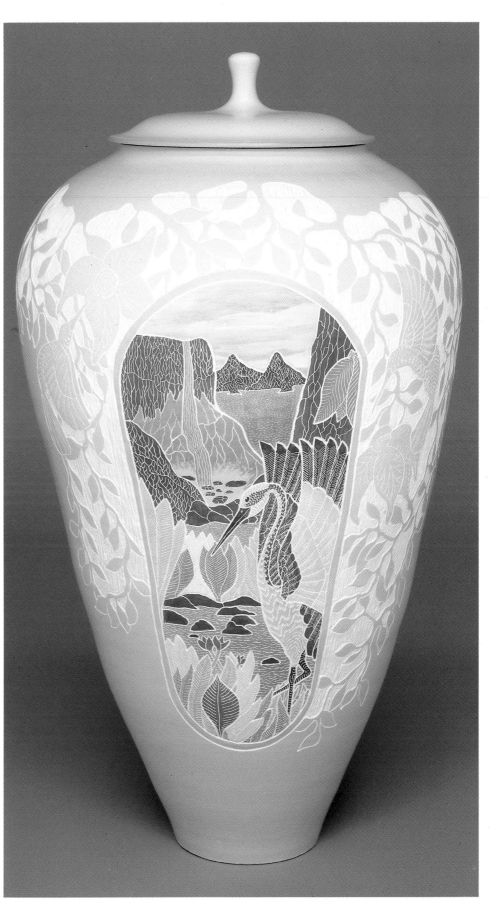

David Van Noppen

Van Noppen Glass, Inc.
69 Tingley Street
Providence, RI 02903
(401) 351-6770

David Van Noppen creates innovative hand blown glass vessels that are both utilitarian and decorative. His "silverwrap" vases reflect the artist's appreciation of the versatility found in working with glass. Transparent colors enveloped by a chord of metal based glass captures the brilliance and radiance inherent in this medium.

After completing his undergraduate studies at Appalachian State University, North Carolina, David Studied glass at Penland School of Crafts, Penland, N.C. and at the Pilchuk School, Seattle, Washington. His works are exhibited nationally.

Silverwrap vases vary from four to eighteen inches in height. A broad spectrum of colors is available. Prices range from $70–$400. Sculptural vessels (bottom left) begin at $120.

R E S O U R C E S

The following Resources
Section provides a wealth
of information to the interior
designer, artist, or individual
collector seeking some of
the finest sources of American arts and crafts. Included
in this section is an educa-
tional piece on how to work
with galleries followed by a
state by state listing of over
400 galleries and retail stores
throughout the United States.
In addition, this listing high-
lights contact information,
address, and phone, as well
as the type of work sold to
assist the innovative buyer in
tracking down the unique,
one-of-a-kind pieces of fine
craft artists.

An Orientation for Designers

*By Deborah Farber-Isaacson
and Ron Isaacson
Co-owners, Mindscape
Gallery, Evanston, Illinois*

Buying craft objects from a gallery for the first time can be a confusing experience for designers and architects. Certainly it's very unlike dealing with design showrooms in merchandise marts around the country, or with manufacturers at trade shows. Not only are galleries and showrooms different historically in philosophical intent and in their approaches to marketing, but their cost structures and business practices are different as well. When it comes to crafts, you must think in terms of quality rather than quantity.

Quality — A Richness of Spirit, Not Perfection

Quality implies exceptional craftsmanship and high-grade materials, but there's quite a bit more to it. Quality also refers to the originality of design — to an intellectually and visually intriguing problem solved with style and ingenuity. It means excellence in terms of form and composition and imaginative use of color, an innovative use of materials, and frequently a breakthrough technical achievement as well. Perhaps most of all, quality refers to a richness of spirit, a depth or fullness capable of reaching the viewer on a variety of levels —and engaging him for a long time to come.

Quality, however, is not synonymous with perfection in the craft field, or at least not with the kind of machine-honed perfection that you may be accustomed to. The most brilliantly conceived artforms in America may have air bubbles (seeds) in the glass or glitches in the clay. A matched set of goblets may vary in height or in diameter; if standard dimensions aren't among an artist's goals, then they're simply not a viable measure of quality. Rather, such variations — and the marks that some might view as flaws — are the evidence of individual effort, or the process by which the objects are made. Sophisticated collectors don't simply forgive such things; they enjoy them.

Cost Structures

Quantity is often related to quality, in the sense that the number of objects available from an artist is based on the uniqueness of his or her work. If each piece produced is totally unique or one-of-a-kind, then the number of pieces one can make is necessarily limited by the amount of time spent on design and execution. Limited production means restricted availability, and of course, a price structure that's substantially different from mass-produced objects.

The price of an artwork depends upon a variety of factors: the time involved in design and production; the de-

gree of difficulty of the process used; the cost of materials and studio overhead; how well known an artist is, and the price he or she can command for current work. Most people are surprised to discover just how enormous the range of prices is for works they consider comparably attractive. You should definitely ask gallery personnel to explain what you're looking at and the reasons for the price; you're likely to get a terrific education in hand-crafted work. Do tell them, also, if your priority is staying within a certain budget. That should simplify your search.

One-Of-A-Kind Works

Artists tend to consider one-of-a-kind pieces their most important or most innovative work. Naturally, these are more expensive than works produced in multiples.

Craft artists who make things in the one-of-a-kind category generally will not repeat a design, but might be willing to create a variation of it on commission to your specifications. Some craftspeople, most notably furniture makers, fiber artists, and sculptors, really enjoy the commission process and view each project as a unique design challenge.

Limited Editions

Another category of craft production is the limited edition group, which means that a small number of pieces (6? 12? 30? 100?) are made in a series. There are usually at least slight variations between limited edition objects created by an artist or small studio. Sometimes the variations are much more than slight. A piece that you order may be similar to a sample, but not identical. If your client understands that these variations are not only unavoidable, but are really quite interesting and desirable, then chances are

excellent that you will both be pleased with the results.

Mass Production

The mass production category of crafts is much more limited in quantity than to the types of mass production with which most people are familiar. Remember, we're talking about the number of pieces that a craft artist can make per year in his or her studio in Massachusetts, as opposed to what an automated factory can produce in Italy or Mexico or Taiwan.

Production craft objects (multiples) tend to be items like wooden desk accessories, ceramic dishes, hand-painted pillows and such. If you order a multiple production piece from a gallery, you should still expect variations within a series, although the piece you get will pretty much resemble the sample.

Commissions vs. Existing Pieces

Although we coordinate a number of commissions every year at Mindscape Gallery, we almost always find it more rewarding to sell a client on an existing piece, which they don't have to visualize, and which they can try out in their space on an approval basis. There is less left to chance for the designer and the client. With so many fascinating media and alternative looks to consider, we've found that very few environments actually require site-specific designs.

The Danger of Waiting

When you see a piece you want to purchase for a client in a design showroom, generally all you have to do is order it. It takes a few weeks or a few months, but what you'll get is exactly like the sample you saw. That's not necessarily so in the craft field.

When you walk into a gallery like Mindscape, the pieces you spot are quite often one-of-a-kind. If a specific, exact look is important to you, then you should probably buy the piece you want when you see it.

There's another good reason to purchase major or focal works especially at the time you see them — or to try them on approval, or place a deposit if the space isn't ready. Know that if you wait for another day, or until all the furniture arrives, a one-of-a-kind artform will probably be gone. All too often, customers (a.k.a. clients and collectors) will spot a piece, pass it up and then remember it longingly. What they envisage, unfortunately, is not necessarily accurate and tends to become idealized. A mental image can become so altered, that future works will never compare favorably, regardless of how strong they are, or how well they might work in the space. It's frustrating for all of us, this mild delusion.

A craft object of any form — clay, glass, fiber, paper, metal, wood or whatever else — is, above all, the product of an ever-changing inspiration, talented hands, and a quicksilver imagination. Beautiful as it is, whether one-of-a-kind or one of a series, it's a totally transient expression of creativity. Pay attention when you see it; if you blink, it may be gone.

Mindscape Gallery is one of the nation's largest and oldest galleries for contemporary American crafts and sculpture, representing over 350 artists.

A Listing of Galleries and Retail Stores

ALABAMA

MARALYN WILSON GALLERY
2010 Cahaba Road
Birmingham, AL 35223
(205) 879-0582

Pottery, glass, textiles and fine art

NEW DIRECTIONS GALLERY
111 B First Street N.E.
Cullman, AL 35055
Contact:
Diana Douglass Jones
(205) 737-9933

Contemporary crafts, sculpture and paintings by Southern artists

ARIZONA

GIFTED HANDS GALLERY
Tlaquepaque Village
P.O. Box 1388
Sedona, AZ 86336
Contacts:
Byron and Deanne McKeown
(602) 282-4822

Fine arts and crafts

MIND'S EYE CRAFT GALLERY
4200 N. Marshall Way
Scottdale, AZ 85251
Contact:
Jane Welsh
(602) 941-2494

Hand-made American crafts: ceramics, jewelry, wood and metal

OBSIDIAN GALLERY
4340 N. Campbell, #90
Tucson, AZ 85718
Contact:
Elouise Rusk
(602) 577-3598

Fine contemporary crafts: ceramics, fiber, metal, jewlery, glass and wood; paintings and sculpture

CALIFORNIA

ACROPOLIS NOW
2510 Main Street
Santa Monica, CA 90405
Contact:
Michelle Stein, Owner
(213) 396-7611

Contemporary crafts and architectural furniture

THE AESTHETICS COLLECTION, INC.
1060 17th Street
San Diego, CA 92101
Contact:
Annette Ridenour
(619) 238-1860

Fine crafts, furniture and signage

THE ALLRICH GALLERY
251 Post Street, 4th floor
San Francisco, CA 94108
Contacts:
Louise Allrich, President
Michelle Bello, Director
(415) 398-8896

Contemporary paintings, sculpture, works on paper, glass and tapestries

APPALACHIA
14440 Big Basin Way
Saratoga, CA 95070
Contacts:
Wendy and Owen Nagler, Owners
(408) 741-0999

Traditional hand-crafts and folk art from Southern Appalachian region

ART OPTIONS
2507 Main Street
Santa Monica, CA 90405
Contacts:
Fran Cey
Marlene Riceberg
(213) 392-9099

Ceramics, glass, art dinnerware, art jewelry and art furniture

ARTIFACTS
3024 Fillmore Street
San Francisco, CA 94123
Contact:
Patricia Blume
(415) 922-8465

Ceramics, glass, wood, metal, fiber, jewelry and paintings

ARTWORKS GALLERY
15 Helena Avenue
Santa Barbara, CA 93101
Contacts:
Richard & Pamela Mann,
Owners
(805) 966-9832

Contemporary fine arts in all
media: paintings, sculpture and
functional art

BRENDAN WALTER GALLERY
1001 Colorado Avenue
Santa Monica, CA 90401
Contact:
Brendan Walter
(213) 395-1155

CEDANNA GALLERY AND STORE
1925 Fillmore Street
San Francisco, CA 94115
Contact:
Cedric Koloseus, Partner
Mimi Haas, Partner
Zoe Koloseus, Partner
(415) 474-7152

Furniture, ceramics, wood,
metal, glass and fiber;
functional and decorative

CLAUDIA CHAPLINE GALLERY
3445 Shoreline Highway
P.O. Box 946
Stinson Beach, CA 94970
(415) 868-2308

Contemporary paintings and
sculpture

COMPOSITIONS GALLERY
2801 Leavenworth (The
Cannery)
San Francisco, CA 94133
Contact:
Siegfried Ehrmann, Director
(415) 441-0629

Contemporary glass art and
designs in wood

COUTURIER GALLERY
166 North La Brea Avenue
Los Angeles, CA 90036
Contact:
Darrel Couturier
(213) 933-5557

Paintings, sculpture and
ceramics

THE CRAFT AND FOLK ART
MUSEUM SHOP
5800 Wilshire Blvd.
Los Angeles, CA 90036
Contact:
Sally Shishmanian, Manager
(213) 937-9099

Ceramics, jewelry, textiles,
wood and leather

CROCK-R-BOX
73425 El Paseo
Palm Desert, CA 92260
Contacts:
John Wenzell
Joann Becker
(619) 568-6688

All crafts by American artists

DEL MANO GALLERY
11981 San Vincente Blvd.
Los Angeles, CA 90049
Contacts:
Jan Peters, Owner/Director
Ray Leier, Owner/Director
(213) 476-8508

Wood, glass, ceramics, fiber,
jewelry, and fine crafts

DEL MANO GALLERY
33 E. Colorado Blvd.
Pasadena, CA 91105
Contacts:
Jan Peters, Owner/Director
Ray Leier, Owner/Director
(818) 793-6648

Wood, glass, ceramics, fiber,
jewelry and fine crafts

DOROTHY WEISS GALLERY
256 Sutter Street
San Francisco, CA 94108
Contact:
Dorothy Weiss, Owner/Director
(415) 397-3611

Ceramic and glass sculpture,
drawings and mixed media
here

EILEEN KREMEN GALLERY
619 N. Harbor Blvd.
Fullerton, CA 92632
Contact:
Eileen Kremen, Director
(714) 879-1391

Contemporary glass art,
kaleidoscopes, ceramics,
wood, wearable art, sculpture
and mixed media

ELIZABETH FORTNER GALLERY
1114 State Street, #9
Santa Barbara, CA 93101
Contact:
Theil Morgan
(805) 966-2613

Contemporary fine crafts

GALLERY EIGHT
7464 Girard Avenue
La Jolla, CA 92037
Contact:
Ruth Newmark
(619) 454-9781

Fine crafts

GALLERY JAPONESQUE
824 Montgomery Street
San Francisco, CA 94133
Contact:
Federico de Vera
(415) 398-8577

GARRETT WHITE GALLERY
664 S. Coast Highway
Laguna Beach, CA 92651
Contacts:
Sally Garrett, Owner
Katherine White, Owner
(714) 494-4117

Hand-blown glass, jewelry and
home accessories from over
100 American artists

GUMP'S GALLERY
250 Post Street
San Francisco, CA 94108
Contact:
Michelene Stankus, Director
(415) 982-1616

Fine arts and crafts

HENLEY'S GALLERY ON THE SEA
RANCH
1000 Annapolis Road
The Sea Ranch, CA 95497
Contact:
Marion H. Gates
(707) 785-2951

Fine art and crafts

IMAGES OF THE NORTH
1782 Union Street
San Francisco, CA 94123
Contact:
Lesley Leonhardt
(415) 673-1273

Native North American art

INTERNATIONAL GALLERY
643 G Street
San Diego, CA 92101
Contact:
Stephen Ross
(619) 235-8255

Contemporary crafts, folk and
primitive art

JUDITH LITVICH
CONTEMPORARY FINE ARTS
2 Henry Adams Street, M-18
San Francisco, CA 94103
Contact:
Judith Litvich
(415) 863-3329

Major dealer of fine art prints,
monotypes, and other works on
paper; corded silk, weavings,
reliefs, screens, metal sculpture.
Bay Area artists and beyond: in
fine museum, private and
corporate collections.

KURLAND/SUMMERS GALLERY
8742A Melrose Avenue
Los Angeles, CA 90069
Contact:
Ruth Summers
(213) 659-7098

Contemporary decorative arts
and sculptural glass

LAISE ADZER
Beverly Center
131 N. La Cienega Blvd.
Los Angeles, CA 90069
(213) 659-2813

Clothing, handicrafts, books
and jewelry

MICHAEL HIMOVITZ GALLERY
1020 10th Street
Sacramento, CA 95814
(916) 448-8723

Fine art and fine craft

MODERN LIFE DESIGNS
682 Post Street
San Francisco, CA 94109
Contacts:
Douglas and Kathleen Brett
(415) 441-7118

Fine jewelry and sculpture

NEW STONE AGE
8407 W. 3rd Street
Los Angeles, CA 90048
Contacts:
Fran Ayres
Susan Skinner
(213) 658-5969

OLIVE HYDE ART GALLERY
123 Washington Blvd.
P.O. Box 5006
Fremont, CA 94537
Contact:
Cynthia Raap
(415) 791-4357

Invitational, juried fine art,
contemporary arts and crafts

OUT OF HAND
1303 Castro Street
San Francisco, CA 94114
(415) 826-3885

All hand-made contemporary
American crafts

PLUMS CONTEMPORARY ARTS
2405 Capitol Street
Fresno, CA 93721
Contact:
Polly Brewer
(202) 237-1822

Paintings, sculpture and fine
craft Plums Contemporary Arts
is both a gallery and a
discovery shop. It provides one
of Central California's finest
collections of Valley artists'
paintings and a wide range of
carefully selected national
decorative artists in glass,
ceramics, jewelry and fiber.

POTTERY PLUS
189 S. Washington Street
Sonora, CA 95370
Contact:
Virginia Seibert, Owner
(209) 533-1309

Quality hand-crafted pottery,
etched glass, jewelry and wood

ROOKIE-TO GALLERY
14300 Highway 128
P.O. Box 606
Boonville, CA 95415
Contact:
Bob Altaras
(707) 895-2204

Bronze and stone sculpture,
blown glass, leaded glass,
wood sculpture, ceramic
sculpture and functional pottery

SCULPTURE TO WEAR
8441 Melrose Avenue
Los Angeles, CA 90069
Contact:
Jan Ehrenworth
(213) 651-2205

Gallery of contemporary art
jewelry

SEEKERS
4090 Burton Drive
P.O. Box 521
Cambria, CA 93428
Contact:
Lynda Adelson
(805) 927-8626

Contemporary American
studio glass, ceramics, wood,
metal and jewelry

SUSAN CUMMINS GALLERY
32 Miller Avenue
Mill Valley, CA 94941
(415) 383-1512

Contemporary American
jewelry and figurative ceramic
sculpture

TAPESTRIES
447 Cambridge Avenue
Palo Alto, CA 94306
Contact:
Jacqueline W. Stewart
Betty Denebeim Watkins
(415) 324-1908

Tapestries

TARBOX GALLERY
1202 Kettner Blvd.
San Diego, CA 92101
Contact:
Ruth Tarbox
(619) 234-5020

TIDEPOOL GALLERY
22762 Pacific Coast Highway
Malibu, CA 90265
Contact:
Jan Greenberg, Owner
(213) 456-2551

Ocean-related art and fine
crafts

TOPS
23410 Civic Center Way
Malibu, CA 90265
Contacts:
Judy and Robert Walker
(213) 456-8677

TOPS caters largely to the
entertainment industry
featuring and ecclectic
assortment of imaginative
functional American crafts.
Humor prevails. The gallery
features jewelry, furniture,
ceramics and great things.

VIEWPOINT GALLERY
224 Crossroads Blvd.
Carmel, CA 93923
Contact:
Chris Winfield, Director
(408) 624-3369

Emerging California artists,
primarily sculpture and high
color

VIEWPOINT GALLERY
2124 Fashion Island Blvd.
San Mateo, CA 94404
Contact:
Linda Braz, Director
(415) 571-0414

Emerging California artists,
primarily sculpture and high
color

VIRGINIA BREIER GALLERY
3091 Sacramento Street
San Francisco, CA 94115
(415) 929-7173

WALTER WHITE FINE ARTS
107 Capitola Avenue
Capitola, CA 95010
Contact:
Amy Essick
(404) 476-7001

Glass art and jewelry

WILD BLUE
7220 Melrose Avenue
Los Angeles, CA 90046
Contacts:
Sherry Kaine
Vesna Breznikar
(213) 939-8434

Contemporary ceramics, glass
and jewelry

WILDER PLACE
7975 1/2 Melrose Avenue
Los Angeles, CA 90046
Contact:
Jo Wilder
(213) 655-9072

CONCEPT:
PLEASURE/FUNCTION High style
design, artist created objects,
jewelry and acccessories.
"Visual candy" — Esquire
Magazine

ZOLA FINE ART
8163 Melrose Avenue
Los Angeles, CA 90046
(213) 655-6060

Contemporary art and custom
framing

COLORADO

APPLAUSE
1141 Pearl Street
Boulder, CO 80302
(303) 442-7426

Furniture, paintings, jewelry,
clothing and gifts

APPLAUSE
2820 E. 3rd Street
Denver, CO 80206
Contacts:
Jody Hunker
Pauline Olson
(303) 442-7729

Furniture, paintings, jewelry,
clothing and gifts

THE CLAY PIGEON
601 Ogden Street
Denver, CO 80224
Contacts:
Tom and Peggy Forte, Owners
(303) 832-5538

All hand-made pottery

COMMONWHEEL ARTIST CO-OP
102 Canon Avenue
Manitou Springs, CO 80829
Contact:
Ann Wardlow Rodgers
(719) 685-1008

Original work by local artists:
pottery, fiber, glass, wearable
art, wood, paintings and
sculpture

HIBBERD MCGRATH GALLERY
101 N. Main Street
P.O. Box 7638
Breckenridge, CO 80424
Contacts:
Terry McGrath
Martha Hibberd
(303) 453-6391

Ceramics, paper, wearables,
folk art and silver

J. COTTER GALLERY
234 Wall Street
Vail, CO 81657
Contact:
Jim Cotter, Proprietor
(303) 476-3131

Jewelry, glass art, painting,
sculpture and ceramics

JOAN ROBEY GALLERY
939 Broadway
Denver, CO 80203
Contact:
Joan Robey
(303) 892-9600

Contemporary crafts

PANACHE CRAFT GALLERY
315 Columbine
Denver, CO 80206
Contact:
Judy Kerr
(303) 321-8069

Contemporary art in the fine
craft media: ceramics, glass,
fiber and jewelry

**RACHAEL COLLECTION
201 S. Galena
Aspen, CO 81611
Contacts:
Charles T. Knight
Sandy Hagopian
(303) 920-1313**

Specializing in contemporary
glass art, featuring over 200
leading artists. On display is a
whole range of lighting (table
floor and ceiling) architectural
(stained and beveled glass
doors, windows and ceilings)
glass furniture, sculpture and
vases. Custom work created
for residential and commercial
installations.

**SHOW OF HANDS
2440 E. 3rd Avenue
Denver, CO 80206
Contact:
Sharill Hawkins, Buyer
(303) 399-0201**

High quality American crafts:
glass, wood, metal, ceramics
and fiber

THE TAVELLI GALLERY
620 E. Hyman Avenue
Aspen, CO 81611
(303) 920-3071

Folk art

TELLURIDE GALLERY OF FINE ART
130 E. Colorado
Box 1900
Telluride, CO 81435
Contacts:
Will and Hilary Thompson,
Owners
(303) 728-3300

Fine art, fine American crafts
and art jewelry

THE AMERICAN HAND
125 Post Road E.
Westport, CT 06880
Contact:
Susan Hirsch
(203) 226-8883

High quality functional and
decorative American crafts:
pottery, glass, jewelry, wood,
metal and fiber

ATELIER STUDIO/GALLERY
27 East Street
New Milford, CT 06776
Contact:
Beth Collings
(203) 354-7792

Contemporary American art
and crafts

BROOKFIELD CRAFT GALLERY
P.O. Box 122, Route 25
Brookfield, CT 06804
(203) 775-4526

Exclusively hand-made
American work

BROOKFIELD/SONO CRAFT
CENTER
127 Washington Street
South Norwalk, CT 06854
(203) 853-6155

Exclusively hand-made
American work

_____

THE COMPANY OF CRAFTSMEN
43 W. Main Street
Mystic, CT 06355
Contact:
Jack Steel
(203) 536-4189

Contemporary American crafts

_____

CONTEMPORARY CRAFTS &
GALLERY
P.O. Box 246, Route 20
Riverton, CT 06065
Contact:
Grace Butland, Owner/Director
(203) 379-2964

Functional and decorative
crafts in all media; original art

_____

THE ELEMENTS
14 Liberty Way
Greenwich, CT 06830
Contact:
Lisa Hampton
(203) 661-0014

_____

ENDLEMAN GALLERY
1014 Chapel Street
New Haven, CT 06510
Contact:
Sally-Ann Endleman
(203) 776-2517

Contemporary artist-designed
jewelry, Native American
jewelry and blown glass

EVERGREEN FINE CRAFTS
23B Water Street
Guilford, CT 06437
Contact:
Sharon Silvestrini
(203) 453-4324

Fine American crafts: jewelry,
wood and ceramics; limited
edition prints

_____

FISHER GALLERY
Farmington Valley Arts Center
25 Bunker Lane
Avon, CT 06001
Contact:
Linda Ronis-Kass
(203) 678-1867

Craft in all media

_____

GALLERY/SHOP AT WESLEYAN
POTTERS
350 S. Main Street
Middletown, CT 06457
Contact:
Maureen LoPresti, Director
(203) 344-0039

Pottery, weavings, baskets,
jewelry, glass and wood

_____

MENDELSON GALLERY
Titus Square
Washington Depot, CT.06794
Contact:
Carol Mendelson
(203) 868-0307

Specializes in wood and clay

_____

SILVERMINE GUILD ARTS CENTER
1037 Silvermine Road
New Canaan, CT 06840
Contract:
Donna Everson, Manager
(203) 966-5617

Paintings, drawings, sculpture,
ceramics, fabric, jewelry and
furniture

_____

WAYSIDE FURNITURE OF
MILFORD
1650 Boston Post Road
Milford, CT 06460
Contact:
Carole R. Greenbaum
(203) 878-1781

Ceramics, glass art, tapestry
and paper art

_____

DELAWARE

THE BLUE STREAK
1723 Delaware Avenue
Wilmington, DE 19806
(302) 429-0506

Contemporary crafts, jewelry,
ceramics, glass and wood

_____

DISTRICT OF COLUMBIA

AMERICAN HAND PLUS
2906 M Street, N.W.
Washington, DC 20007
Contacts:
Ken Deavers, Owner
Dennis Garrett, Manager
(202) 965-3273

Contemporary ceramic vessels,
glass, and wood

JACKIE CHALKLEY
5301 Wisconsin Avenue, N.W.
Washington, DC 20015
Contacts:
Jackie Chalkley,
Owner/President
Ruth Tarbell, Business Manager
Lisa David, Sales Manager
(202) 537-6100

JACKIE CHALKLEY
3301 New Mexico Avenue, N.W.
Washington, DC 20016
Contact:
Lisa Williams, Sales Manager
(202) 686-8882

JACKIE CHALKLEY
1455 Pennsylvania Avenue, N.W.
Washington, DC 20004
Contact:
Stephanie Pilk, Sales Manager
(202) 683-3060

Design-oriented women's
clothing, hand-crafted fashion
accessories and decorative
arts for the home

MAURINE LITTLETON GALLERY
1667 Wisconsin Avenue, N.W.
Washington, DC 20007
Contacts:
Maurine Littleton, Director
R. Ford Singletary
(202) 333-9307

Glass, ceramics and
vitreographs

MOON, BLOSSOMS AND SNOW
225 Pennsylvania Avenue, S.E.
Washington, DC 20003
Contact:
Sharon McCarthy, Owner
(202) 543-8181

Contemporary American
crafts: wearable art, jewelry,
ceramic, glass and wood

SANSAR
4200 Wisconsin Avenue, N.W.
Washington, DC 20016
Contact:
Veena Singh
(202) 244-4448

UPTOWN ARTS
3236 P Street, N.W.
Washington, DC 20007
Contact:
Edward Levine, Director
(202) 337-0600

Contemporary art, pottery and
hand-blown glass

FLORIDA

AMERICAN DETAILS
3107 Grand Avenue
Coconut Grove, FL 33133
Contact:
Sharon Lepak, Manager
(305) 448-6163

American hand-crafted goods:
wood, ceramic, glass, art
jewelry and kaleidoscopes for
collectors

ARTCETERA
3200 S. Congress Avenue, Suite
201
Boynton Beach, FL 33426
Contact:
Gloria Waldman
(407) 737-6953

CHRISTY TAYLOR GALLERY, INC.
5050 Town Center Circle, Suite
243
Boca Raton, FL 33486
Contacts:
Jack Nicks, Owner
Carrie Frifeldt, Director
(407) 394-6387

CHRISTY TAYLOR GALLERY, INC.
Mizner Park
410 Plaza Real
Boca Raton FL 33432
(407) 394-4241

COLLECTORS GALLERY
213 West Venice Avenue
Venice, FL 34285
Contact:
Peaches Haas, Owner
(813) 488-3029

Originals, graphics and limited
editions

FLORIDA CRAFTSMEN GALLERY
235 3rd Street S.
St. Petersburg, FL 33701
Contact:
Michele Tuegel, Executive
Director
(813) 821-7391

GALLERY FIVE
363 Tequesta Drive
Tequesta, FL 33469
Contact:
Paula Coben
(407) 747-5555

Fine crafts and wearables by
150 American artists

HABATAT GALLERIES
608 Banyan Trail
Boca Raton, FL 33431
Contact:
Thomas Boone
(407) 241-4544

HEARTWORKS GALLERY
820 Lomax
Jacksonville, FL 32204
Contact:
Elaine Wheeler, Director
(904) 355-6210

Blown glass, textiles, art
furniture, functional decorative
ceramics and sculptural baskets

HOFFMAN GALLERY
2000 E. Sunrise Blvd., Level 2
Fort Lauderdale, FL 33304
Contact:
William S. Hoffman
(305) 763-5371

RICK SANDERS' GALLERIES
409-411 and 413 St. Armands
Circle
Sarasota, FL 34236
Contacts:
Rick & Diana Sanders, Owners
(813) 388-1000

All media of arts and crafts

**THE SUWANNEE TRIANGLE
GALLERY
Dock Street
P.O. Box 341
Cedar Key, FL 32625**
Contact:
**Clair Teetor, Manager
(904) 543-5744**

Contemporary American fine
art and crafts

GEORGIA

AVERY GALLERY
145 Church Street
Marietta, GA 30060
Contact:
Kip Knauth
(404) 427-2459

Complete restoration services

CONNELL GALLERY
Great American Gallery
333 Buckhead Avenue
Atlanta, GA 30305
Contacts:
Martha and Pat Connell,
Directors
(404) 261-1712

We represent contemporary
American artists, most of whom
work in craft media

HEATH GALLERY, INC.
416 E. Paces Ferry Road
Atlanta, GA 30305
Contacts:
David C. Heath, President
R. Scott McRae, Executive Vice
President
Sean Cook, Vice President
(404) 262-6407

Contemporary art of the 60's,
70's, and 80's

OUT OF THE WOODS GALLERY
22-B Bennett Street N.W.
Atlanta, GA 30309
Contact:
Deb Douglas
(404) 351-0446

Fine crafts, contemporary folk
and tribal in wood, stone,
metal, ceramics, fiber, paper
and glass

RIVERWORKS CRAFT GALLERY
105 E. River Street
Savannah, GA 31401
Contact:
Linda M. Jeanne, Manager
(912) 236-2012

Handmade pottery, jewelry,
fiber, wood, glass; functional
and decorative

**VESPERMANN GLASS & CRAFT
GALLERIES
2140 Peachtree Road, N.W.
Atlanta, GA 30309
(404) 350-9698**

A complex of 6,000 square feet
for the arts! The Glass Gallery
features museum-quality art
glass form America's premier
artists. The Crafts Gallery (next
door) is dedicated to fine
handmade American crafts.

IDAHO

ANNE REED GALLERY
620 Sun Valley Road
Box 597
Ketchum, ID 83340
(208) 726-3036

Idaho continued

GAIL SEVERN GALLERY
620 Sun Valley Road
P.O. Box 1679
Ketchum, ID 83340
Contact:
Gail Severn
(208) 726-5079

ILLINOIS

THE ARKWRIGHT GALLERY
3319 N. Broadway
Chicago, IL 60657
Contact:
Kathleen Zasadil, Owner
(312) 871-7172

Beautiful functional art pieces

ART EFFECT
651 W. Armitage
Chicago, IL 60614
Contact:
Esther Fishman, Owner
(312) 664-0997

Wearables, jewelry and 3
dimensional home accessories

ART MECCA
3352 N. Halsted
Chicago, IL 60657
Contact:
Melanee Cooper, Owner
(312) 935-3255

Decorative and functional art
objects, folk and outsider art;
mostly hand-crafted

THE ART SOURCE
1326 Asbury Avenue
Evanston, IL 60201
Contact:
Kay Mangum, President
(708) 328-2728

Limited edition graphics, oils,
acrylics, monoprints, ceramics,
glass, large-scale sculpture,
fiber, paper

THE ARTISAN SHOP & GALLERY
Plaza del Lago
1515 Sheridan Road
Wilmette, IL 60091
Contact:
Allan Hansen
(708) 251 3775

Contemporary American crafts

THE ARTISTREE
10431 S. Kedzie Avenue
Chicago, IL 60655
Contact:
Fran Salvatori
(312) 455-5880

All American country
hand-made craftwork: jewelry,
wood, floral, weavings, country
decor and glassware

BETSY ROSENFIELD GALLERY
212 W. Superior
Chicago, IL 60610
(312) 787-8020

CROSS CURRENTS ART GALLERY
1446 W. Irving Park
Chicago, IL 60613
Contacts:
Kathleen V. Moga
Tammi L. Phillips
(312) 880-5780

Contemporary art and framing
gallery

CYRNA INTERNATIONAL
12-101 Merchandise Mart
Chicago, IL 60654
Contact:
Cyrna S. Field
(312) 329-0906

DOUGLAS DAWSON GALLERY
814 N. Franklin
Chicago, IL 60610
Contact:
Douglas Dawson, Owner
Nancy Bender, Manager
(312) 751-1961

Ancient and historic textiles
and related ethnographic work

ESTHER SAKS GALLERY
311 W. Superior
Chicago, IL 60610
Contact:
Esther Saks, Director
Jane Saks
(312) 751-0911

Contemporary fine art in craft
material, ceramic sculpture,
paintings and works on paper

FUMIE GALLERY
19 S. La Salle
Chicago, IL 60603
Contacts:
John J. and Fumie Madden
(312) 726-0080

A Modern craft gallery
featuring works by American
artists in jewelry, metal, wood,
ceramics and glass

GIMCRACKS
1513 Sherman Avenue
Evanston, IL 60201
Contact:
Lucile Krasnow, Owner
(708) 475-0900

Folk art, textiles, jewelry, glass,
furniture and lighting

HOKIN KAUFMAN GALLERY
210 W. Superior Street
Chicago, IL 60610
Contact:
Gary F. Metzner, Director
(312) 266-1212

Paintings, sculpture and
artist-designed furniture

JORDAN MCCLANAHAN, LTD.
580 N. Bank Lane
Lake Forest, IL 60045
Contact:
Rebecca McClanahan,
President
Teiko Jordan, Vice President
(708) 295-9670

Jewelry, furniture and
accessories for the home
Jordan McClanahan, Ltd., is a
gallery for fine hand-crafted
and painted furniture which
are one-of-a-kind or limited
editions, as well as home
accessories and jewelry. Our
room vignettes represent over
50 artists and craftspeople.

JUST WONDERFUL STUFF
445 N. Wells Street
Chicago, IL 60610
Contact:
Barbara R. Moss
(312) 222-2225

LILL STREET GALLERY
1021 West Lill
Chicago, IL 60614
Contact:
Angela Murphy
(312) 477-6185

Primarily ceramics, both
functional and sculptural. We
also sell artist made glass,
jewelry, and other gift items

MINDSCAPE GALLERY
1506 Sherman Avenue
Evanston, IL 60201
Contact:
Ron Isaacson
(708) 864-2260

Contemporary American crafts
and sculpture. Discover unique
works in sophisticated,
one-of-a-kind jewelry, studio
glass, ceramics, fiber and
paper wall pieces, wood and
metals Mindscape is one of the
nation's largest and oldest
galleries for contemporary
American crafts and sculpture.
From established craftmasters
to innovative new talents,
Mindscape represents more
than 350 artist. An extraodinary
resource for both private and
corporate collectors.
Affordable, attainable,
extraordinary. Priced from $15
to $15,000.

NINA OWEN, LTD.
212 W. Superior Street
Chicago, IL 60610
(312) 664-0474

Sculpture in all media

OBJECTS GALLERY
230 W. Huron
Chicago, IL 60610
(312) 664-6622

Ceramics, wood, metal and art
furniture

PERIMETER GALLERY, INC.
750 N. Orleans
Chicago, IL 60610
Contact:
Frank Paluch, Director
Linda Glass, Asst. Director
(312) 266-9473

Baskets and ceramics as well as
paintings, sculpture and prints

PIECES ART AND ARTWEAR
644 Central
Highland Park, IL 60015
Contacts:
Lynn, Lori, or Louise
(312) 432-2131

Contemporary dimensional
crafts and wearables

REZAC GALLERY
301 W. Superior Street, 2nd floor
Chicago, IL 60610
Contact:
Suzan Rezac
(312) 751-0481

Contemporary, decorative and
fine arts with an emphasis on
goldsmithing

SCHNEIDER-BLUHM-LOEB GALLERY
230 W. Superior Street
Chicago, IL 60610
(312) 988-4033

Mainly ceramic sculpture,
functional ceramics, jewelry
and some photography

TEXTILE ARTS CENTRE
916 W. Diversey Parkway
Chicago, IL 60614
(312) 929-5655

Fiberworks and classes for
fiberworkers

INDIANA

CENTRE GALLERY
170 E. Carmel Drive
Carmel, IN 46032
Contact:
Susan Musleh
(317) 844-6421

IOWA

IOWA ARTISANS GALLERY
117 E. College
Iowa City, IA 52240
(319) 351-8686

Fine craft and art THE IOWA
ARTISANS GALLERY,
representing almost 200
regional and national artists, is
the primary source for fine
crafts and multi-media art in
eastern Iowa. Custom orders
and rental available.

THE POT SHOP
U.S. 169 South
Humboldt, IA 50548
Contact:
Hiram Shouse
(515) 332-4210

Stoneware, brass, bronze, glass,
wood and custum picture
framing

KANSAS

SILVER WORKS & MORE
715 Massachusetts Street
Lawrence, KS 66044
Contacts:
Jim and Cara Connelly
(913) 842-1460

Ceramics, jewelry, wood, glass,
fiber, metal sculpture

KENTUCKY

KENTUCKY ART AND CRAFT
GALLERY
609 W. Main Street
Louisville, KY 40202
Contact:
Sue Rosen, Director of
Marketing
(502) 589-0102

THE PROMENADE GALLERY
204 Center Street
Berea, KY 40403
Contact:
Kathy West, Manager
(606) 986-1609

All media, musical instruments,
folk art and decorative
accessories

INTERIORS & EXTRAS
324 Metairie Road
Metairie, LA 70005
Contact:
Nancy Hirsch Lassen,
Owner/Designer
(504) 835-9902

Original arts and crafts, from
earrings to sofas

STONER ARTS CENTER
516 Stoner Avenue
Shreveport, LA 71101
Contact:
Linda T. Snider
(318) 222-1780

Contemporary work, ceramics,
glass, jewelry and gift items

MAINE

THE BENSONS - FIBER & WOOD, ETC.
59 Mountain Street
Camden, ME 04843
Contacts:
E.E. "Skip" & Barbara Benson,
Owners
(207) 236-6564

One-of-a kind work
The gallery represents both
recognized and emerging
Maine artists in all media, both
functional and non-functional.
The gallery seeks to show the
finest work available.
Commissions invited.

NANCY MARGOLIS GALLERY
367 Fore Street
Portland, ME 04101
(207) 775-3822

MARYLAND

ART CONNECTIONS
4812 Auburn Avenue
Bethesda, MD 20814
Contacts:
Gayley Knight
Candace Forsyth
(301) 951-1026

ART INSTITUTE & GALLERY
Route 50 & Lemmon Hill Lane
Salisbury, MD 21801
(301) 546-4748

Original artworks, paintings, 3-D
pieces and drawings

BRASSWORKS COMPANY, INC.
1641 Thames Street
Baltimore, MD 21231
Contacts:
Cray Merrill, Owner
Roland Phillips, Owner
(301) 327-7280

Brass and copper refinishing
and sales of home furnishing
and accessories

DISCOVERIES
Columbia Mall
Columbia, MD 21044
(301) 740-5800

Blown glass, pottery,
contemporary dolls, sculpture,
fiber, jewelry and mixed media

DISCOVERIES
8055 Main Street
Ellicott City, MD 21043
(301) 461-9600

Blown glass, pottery,
contemporary dolls, sculpture,
fiber, jewelry and mixed media

THE GLASS GALLERY
4720 Hampden Lane
Bethesda, MD 20814
Contacts:
Sarah Hansen, Director
Diane DiSalvo, Asst. Director

Glass art and sculpture

MEREDITH GALLERY
805 N. Charles Street
Baltimore, MD 21201
Contact:
Judith Lippman, Director
(301) 837-3575

Artist-designed furniture

PIECES OF OLDE
716 W. 36th Street
Baltimore, MD 21211
Contact:
Nancy Wertheimer
(301) 366-4949

Textiles, pillows and
accessories, many from one of
a kind vintage fabrics

TOMLINSON CRAFT COLLECTION
516 N. Charles Street
Baltimore, MD 21201
Contact:
Ginny Tomlinson, President
(301) 539-6585

Original American crafts

TOMLINSON CRAFT COLLECTION
711 W. 40th Street
Baltimore, MD 21211
(301) 338-1572

Original American crafts

ALIANZA CONTEMPORARY
CRAFTS
154 Newbury Street
Boston, MA 02116
Contact:
Karen Rotenberg
(617) 262-2385

BHADON GIFT GALLERY
1075 Pleasant Street
Worcester, MA 01602
(508) 798-0432

CLARK GALLERY
Lincoln Station
P.O. Box 339
Lincoln, MA 01773
Contact:
Jennifer L. Atkinson
(617) 259-8303

THE CRAFTY YANKEE
1838 Massachusetts Avenue
Lexington, MA 02173
Contacts:
Dottie Simpson, Partner
Carla Fortmann, Partner
(617) 863-1219

All hand-crafts: pottery, wood,
glass

DIVINITY'S SPLENDOUR-GLOW
8 Medford Street
Arlington, MA 02174
Contact:
Renuka O'Connell
(617) 648-7100

New England handcrafts:
pottery, jewelry, birch items,
imported cards and painted
clothing

FERRIN GALLERY/PINCH POTTERY
179 Main Street
Northhampton, MA 01060
Contacts:
Mara Superior
Leslie Ferrin
(413) 586-4509

Large selection of
contemporary ceramics, glass
and wood

FIRE OPAL
7 Pond Street
Jamaica Plain, MA 02130
Contact:
Susannah Gordon, Owner
(617) 524-0262

Hand-crafted jewelry,
ceramics, cards, clothings, soft
sculpture, wood objects; very
eclectic and colorful

G/M GALLERIES
Main Street
West Stockbridge, MA 01266
Contact:
Marie J. Bonamici-Woodcock
(413) 232-8519

Fine crafts in glass, wood and
ceramics; also designer jewelry

GROHE GLASS GALLERY
24 North Street
Boston, MA 02109
Contacts:
Arthur Grohe
Gretchen Keyworth
(617) 227-4885

Representing major American
artists working in glass

THE HAND OF MAN
The Curtis Shops
Walker Street
Lenox, MA 01240
Contact:
Stephen D. Barry, President
(413) 637-0632

Jewelry, wood work, metal,
ceramics, glass, fiber and
general visual arts

LIMITED EDITIONS, INC.
1176 Walnut Street
Newton Highlands, MA 02161
Contact:
Jo-Ann Isaacson
(617) 965-5474

All American crafts: glass,
wood and ceramics

REPERTOIRE
207 S. Street Boston, MA 02111
Contacts:
Rick Garofalo
Devin McLaughlin
(617) 426-3865

Hand-crafted metal furniture
and accessories

SALMON FALLS ARTISANS
SHOWROOM
Ashfield Street
P.O. Box 176
Shelburne Falls, MA 01370
Contact:
Nancy Dean
(413) 625-9833

Blown glass, pottery, jewelry,
furniture, turned wood,
sculpture, hand-woven items,
quilts and baskets

SIGNATURE
Dock Square
North Street
Boston, MA 02109
Contact:
Gretchen Keyworth
(617) 227-4885

Glass, jewelry, ceramics, wood
and fiber

SKERA
221 Main Street
Northampton, MA 01060
Contact:
Harriet Rogers
(413) 586-4563

American craft, specializing in
furniture, jewelry and wearables

THE SOCIETY OF ARTS AND CRAFTS
175 Newbury Street
Boston, MA 02116
Contact:
Susan Blake
(617) 266-1810

TEN ARROW GALLERY
10 Arrow Street
Cambridge, MA 02138
Contact:
Betty Tinlot
(617) 876-1117

MICHIGAN

ARIANA GALLERY
386 E. Maple Road
Birmingham, MI 48009
Contact:
Ann Kuffler, Gallery Director
(313) 647-6405

Colorful, contemporary arts
and crafts

DECOART
815 First Street
Menominee, MI 49858
Contact:
Lori J. Schappe
(906) 863-3300

Paintings, hand-made paper,
mixed media, glass, fiber,
jewelry, photography, etchings
and sculpture

HABATAT GALLERIES
32255 Northwestern Highway,
Suite 45
Farmington Hills, MI 48334
Contact:
John Lawson
(313) 851-9090

ILONA AND GALLERY
31045 Orchard Lake Road
Farmington Hills, MI 48018
Contact:
Hirschel Levine
(313) 855-4488

Hand-crafted ceramics, glass,
jewelry, wood and wall
hangings

PEWABIC POTTERY
10125 E. Jefferson
Detroit, MI 48214
Contact:
Mary Roehm, Executive Director
(313) 822-0954

Learning center and producer
of hand-crafted architectural
tile and ceramic art

PINE TREE GALLERY
824 E. Cloverland, US-2
Ironwood, MI 49938
Contact:
Philip J. Kucera
(906) 932-5120

SELO/SHEVEL GALLERY
335 S. Main Street
Ann Arbor, MI 48104
Contact:
Elaine Selo
(313) 761-6263

Contemporary American
blown glass, ceramics, jewelry,
wood and imported folk, art as
well as rare textiles

THE SYBARIS GALLERY
301 W. Fourth Street
Royal Oak, MI 48067
Contacts:
Linda Ross, Director
Arlene Selik, Director
(313) 544-3388

Contemporary art in the media
of clay, fiber, wood, glass and
metal

TOUCH OF LIGHT
23426 Woodward Avenue
Ferndale, MI 48220
Contact:
John Fitzpatrick
(313) 543-1868

MINNESOTA

ANDERSON & ANDERSON
GALLERY
400 First Avenue N., #240
Minneapolis, MN 55401
Contact:
John Anderson Jr, Director
(612) 332-4889

Contemporary sculpture,
drawings and paintings

Minnesota continued

ATAZ
3480 W. 70th Street - Galleria
Edina, MN 55435
Contact:
Patricia Burrets, Owner/Buyer
(612) 925-4883

Casual furniture and
accessories

BOIS FORT GALLERY
130 E. Sheridan Street
Ely, MN 55731
Contact:
Judy Danzl
(218) 365-5066

GEOMETRIE GALLERY
122 N. 4th Street
Minneapolis, MN 55401
Contacts:
Richard Hickenbotham, Partner
Diane Marshall, Partner
(612) 340-1635

Modern design and decorative
arts: art furniture, antiques and
crafted objects

GLASSPECTACLE
402 N. Main Street
Stillwater, MN 55082
Contacts:
Mike Blumer, Owner
Sharon Dorgan, Director
Brenda Hanson, Asst. Director
(612) 439-0757

Contemporary art glass and
collectibles

MADE IN THE SHADE
600 E. Superior Street
Duluth, MN 55802
Contact:
Ruth Ann Eaton
(218) 722-1929

American hand-crafts

MC GALLERY
400 1st Avenue N., #332
Minneapolis, MN 55401
Contact:
MC Anderson, Director
(612) 339-1480

Contemporary glass, ceramics
and mixed media of
mid-career and nationally
known artists

MIXED MEDIA
5041 France Avenue
Minneapolis, MN 55410
Contact:
Nancy J. Shelp, Owner/Director
(612) 922-1712

Fine craft

NORTHERN CLAY CENTER:
THE SALES GALLERY
2375 University Avenue, W
St. Paul, MN 55114
Contact:
Phyllis Edwards, Director
(612) 642-1735

Artworks of clay: sculpture,
functional and jewelry

PERSPECTIVES GALLERY
81 S. Ninth Street, Suite 220
Minneapolis, MN 55402
Contact:
Charles J. Ciali, Director
(612) 336-6076

Contemporary ceramics, glass,
wood, fiber and jewelry

RAYMOND AVENUE GALLERY
761 Raymond Avenue
St. Paul, MN 55114
Contact:
Joseph Brown
(612) 644-9200

Crafts mainly by Minnesota
artists

TECHNIC GALLERY
1055-C Grand Avenue
St. Paul, MN 55105
Contact:
Peter Wood, Owner
(612) 222-0188

Contemporary fine craft by
regional and national artists

TEXTILE ARTS INTERNATIONAL, INC.
400 First Avenue N., Suite 340
Minneapolis, MN 55403
Contacts:
Ellen Wells, Director
Phil Hewett, Sales Manager
Sarah Emmer, Gallery Manager
(612) 338-6776

Textile artworks

THREE ROOMS UP
3515 W. 69th Street
Edina, MN 55435
Contact:
Patricia Burrets, Owner/Buyer
(612) 926-1774

Fine arts with an emphasis on
ceramics

CHIMNEYVILLE CRAFTS GALLERY
1150 Lakeland Drive
Jackson, MS 39216
Contact:
Marjorie Bates, Executive
Director
(601) 981-0019

Fine hand-made crafts:
jewelry, quilts, stained glass,
weavings, baskets,
wood-carvings, furniture and
ceramics

MISSOURI

LEEDY-VOULKOS GALLERY
1919 Wyandotte
Kansas City, MO 64108
(816) 474-1919

Work in all media, painting,
limited edition prints, ceramics,
sculpture and original
contemporary fine art

NEW ACCENTS
506 S. Main Street
St. Charles, MO 63301
Contact:
Christine Raecke, Owner
(314) 723-9398

Weaving, pottery, jewelry, glass
and kaleidoscopes

OBJECTS: ST. LOUIS
5595 Pershing Avenue
St. Louis, MO 63112
Contact:
Marcy Rosenthal, Owner
(314) 361-6670

Contemporary American and
international crafts, jewelry,
ceramics, glass, paper, fiber
and wood

PRO-ART
1214 Washington Avenue, 3rd
floor
St. Louis, MO 63103
Contacts:
Horty Shieber, Managing
Director
Michael Holohan, Artistic
Director
(314) 231-5848

Contemporary American art;
emphasis on vessel and
sculptural clay

RANDALL GALLERY
999 N. 13th Street
St. Louis, MO 63106
Contacts:
William Shearburn
(314) 231-4808

Fine art

MONTANA

ARTISTIC TOUCH
209 Central Avenue
Whitefish, MT 59937
Contact:
Mary Kay Huff
(406) 862-4813

Crafts of merit from
Northwestern artists

NEVADA

MOIRA JAMES GALLERY
2801 Athenian Drive
Green Valley, NV 89014
Contact:
Robin Greenspun, Owner
(702) 454-4800

The Moira James Gallery
features curated exhibitions of
nationally recognized craft
artists and focuses on
contemporary crafts in all
media. Commissions are
welcome and fine art
consultation is available.

NEW HAMPSHIRE

LEAGUE OF NEW HAMPSHIRE
CRAFTSMEN
36 N. Main Street
Concord, NH 03301
Contacts:
Janet H. Dow, Manager
Mary Jane Beardsley, Asst.
Manager
(603) 228-8171

Juried New Hampshire crafts

New Hampshire continued

LEAGUE OF NEW HAMPSHIRE
CRAFTSMEN
13 Lebanon Street
Hanover, NH 03755
Contacts:
Jan Baer, Sales Manager
Marcella Stoelting, Business
Manager

Juried New Hampshire crafts

MCGOWAN FINE ART INC.
10 Hills Avenue
Concord, NH 03301
Contact:
Mary Strayer McGowan
(603) 225-2515

SHOP AT THE INSTITUTE
Manchester Institute
148 Concord Street
Manchester, NH 03104
Contact:
Linda Randazzo, Shop Manager
(603) 623-0313

Fiber, metal, ceramics, paper
and jewelry

NEW JERSEY

BY HAND FINE CRAFT GALLERY
142 Kings Highway E.
Haddonfield, NJ 08033
Contact:
Marjorie Harris
(609) 429-2550

Functional and decorative
pottery, fiber, wood, metal and
jewelry

CONTRASTS
49 Broad Street
Red Bank, NJ 07701
Contact:
Rosalie Rosin
(201) 741-9177

Decorative and functional
work in ceramics, glass, fiber
and wood

THE ELVID GALLERY
41 E. Palisade Avenue
Englewood, NJ 07631
(201) 871-8747

Contemporary mixed media

SHEILA NUSSBAUM GALLERY
358 Millburn Avenue
Millburn, NJ 07041
Contact:
Sheila Nussbaum
(201) 467-1720

Contemporary art, American
fine art and jewelry

STREICHLER GALLERY OF
SCULPTURAL ART
46 N. Dean Street
Englewood, NJ 07631
Contact:
Ronnie Streichler, Owner
(201) 567-8120

Fine sculptural art and fine
crafts in all medias

NEW MEXICO

BELLAS ARTES
653 Canyon Road
Santa Fe, NM 87501
Contacts:
Charlotte and Bob Kornstein,
Directors
(505) 983-2745

Major ceramic and fiber art,
only original works of art

GARLAND GALLERY
125 Lincoln, Suite 113
Santa Fe, NM 87501
Contact:
Karen Garland, Director
(505) 984-1555

Contemporary glass

HANDCRAFTERS GALLERY LTD.
227 Galisteo Street
Santa Fe, NM 87501
Contact:
Peter J. Kahn, Owner
(505) 982-4880

One-of-a-kind ceramics, cast
paper and furniture

RUNNING RIDGE GALLERY
640 Canyon Road
Santa Fe, NM 87501
Contact:
Carol Sorenson
(505) 988-2515

TWINING WEAVERS &
CONTEMPORARY CRAFTS, LTD
Taos Ski Valley Road
P.O. Box 237
Arroyo Seco, NM 87514
Contact:
Sally Bachman, Owner
(505) 776-8367

Handwoven rugs, pillows and
other production crafts

NEW YORK

A SHOW OF HANDS
531 Amsterdam Avenue
New York, NY 10024
Contact:
Christine H. MacKellar
(212) 787-0924

AARON FABER GALLERY
666 Fifth Avenue
New York, NY 10019
Contact:
Patricia Kiley Faber
(212) 586-8411

Vintage Watches, American
studio goldsmiths and 20th
century design

AFTER THE RAIN
149 Mercer Street
New York, NY 10012
(212) 431-1044

Kaleidoscopes, musical
instruments and other fine crafts

AMERICA HOUSE GALLERY
OF CONTEMPORARY CRAFTS
466 Piermont Avenue
Piermont, NY 10968
Contact:
Susanne Turino Casal, Owner
(914) 359-0106

Jewelry, ceramics, glass fiber
and wood

ALEXANDER F. MILLIKEN INC.
98 Prince Street
New York, NY 10012
Contact:
Carol Craven, Director
(212) 966-7800

Contemporary American,
European and Japanese
painting and sculpture

ART ET INDUSTRIE
106 Spring Street
New York, NY 10012
Contacts:
Rick Kaufmann
Kim Kuzmenko
(212) 431-1661

Functional objects

AUSTIN HARVARD GALLERY
50 State Street
Pittsford, NY 14534
Contact:
Adele Elmer, Director
(716) 383-1472

Traditional to contemporary,
including pre-Columbian. 100
artists represented

THE CENTER FOR TAPESTRY ARTS
167 Spring Street, 2nd floor
New York, NY 10012
Contact:
Jean West, Director
(212) 431-7500

THE CLAY POT
162 Seventh Avenue
Brooklyn, NY 11215
Contacts:
Robert and Sally Silberberg
(718) 788-6564

Glass, ceramics, jewelry, wood,
fiber and metal

CONTEMPORARY PORCELAIN
105 Sullivan Street
New York, NY 10012
Contact:
Lanie Cecula
(212) 219-2172

Showcase for national and
international ceramic design,
emphasis placed on functional
and decorative objects

THE CRAFTSMAN'S GALLERY, LTD.
16 Chase Road
Scarsdale, NY 10583
Contact:
Sybil Robins, Director
(914) 725-4644

Contemporary American craft
art, large scale ceramics and
wall hangings

New York continued

CROSS HARRIS FINE CRAFTS
979 Third Avenue, 3rd Floor
New York, NY 10022
Contacts:
Fredda Harris
Rise Cross
(212) 888-7878

Designer sources for fine crafts. Broad selection from America's finest crafts people, directly from our showroom or through commissions

DAWSON GALLERY
349 East Avenue
Rochester, NY 14604
Contacts:
Beverly McInerny
Shirley Dawson
(716) 454-6966

Fine craft and sculptural work

THE ELDER CRAFTSMEN, INC.
846 Lexington Avenue
New York, NY 10021
Contact:
Ann Kronenberg, Managing Director
(212) 861-3294

Items hand-crafted by people 55 years of age or older

THE ENCHANTED FOREST
85 Mercer Street
New York, NY 10012
(212) 925-6677

Beasts, books and hand-made toys

GARTH CLARK GALLERY
24 W. 57th Street
New York, NY 10019
Contact:
Mark Del Vecchio
(212) 246-2205

THE GRATEFUL GIFT
42 W. Park Avenue
Long Beach, NY 11561
Contacts:
Nancy and Don Terry
(516) 431-9159

Hand-made contemporary American crafts

GREENHUT GALLERIES
Stuyvesant Plaza
Albany, NY 12203
Contacts:
John Greenhut, Director
Gary Weitzman,
(518) 482-1984

Original art and sculpture, hand-made paper, multiple originals and one-of-a-kind unique works

HELEN DRUTT GALLERY
724 Fifth Avenue, 9th floor
New York, NY 10019
(212) 974-7700

HELLER GALLERY
71 Greene Street
New York, NY 10012
Contacts:
Douglas Heller, Director
Michael Heller, Vice President
(212) 966-5948

Museum quality work of contemporary glass art

HOLTHOUSE FIBER ART GALLERY
7 Irma Avenue
Port Washington, NY 11050
Contact:
Mary Ann Holthouse
(516) 883-8620

A wide range of work in fiber

HUDSON RIVER GALLERY
217 Main Street
Ossining, NY 10562
Contact:
Pat Lawrence, Director
(914) 762-5300

Contemporary art and craft including ceramics, glass, wood. sculpture and fiber Contemporary art/craft: elegant touches that make a statement about a space. Let Hudson River Gallery's unique combination of artists and consultants make your inimitable statement. HRG: the dynamic choice!

HUMMINGBIRD DESIGNS
29 Third Street
Troy, NY 12180
Contacts:
Kathy and John Bloom
(518) 272-1807

Contemporary crafts, one of a kind jewelry and custom designed art pottery

JOEL SCHWALB GALLERY
12 S. Broadway
Nyack, NY 10960
Contact:
Joel Schwalb, Owner
(914) 358-1701

Ceramics, stained glass,
jewelry, wood, lighting and
blown glass

JOHN CHRISTOPHER GALLERY
43 Main Street
Cold Spring Harbor, NY 11724
Contact:
John Chandler
(516) 367-3978

JOHN CHRISTOPHER GALLERY
131 Main Street
Stony Brook, NY 11790
Contact:
Christopher DeVeau
(516) 689-1601

LEO KAPLAN MODERN
969 Madison Avenue, 3rd floor
New York, NY 10021
Contacts:
Scott Jacobson, Director
Lynn Millinger, Asst. Director
(212) 535-2407

Contemporary studio glass and
furniture

**MARI GALLERIES OF
WESTCHESTER, LTD.
133 E. Prospect Avenue
Mamaroneck, NY 10543**
Contact:
**Carla Reuben
(914) 698-0008**

Fine art craft MARI is a
multi-media gallery celebrating
its 25th year. Our unique craft
plan includes a small fee for
the extent of each show (4-5
weeks), selling at artist's price.

OPUS II
979 Third Avenue
New York, NY 10022
Contact:
Irv Frank
(212) 980-1990

Opus II, located in the
decoration and design
building, is New York City's
primary source for designer
and architects interested in
obtaining contemporary
American sculpture, ceramics,
glass, fiber and mixed media.

SWEET NELLIE
1262 Madison Avenue
New York, NY 10128
Contact:
Pat Ross
(212) 876-5775

Hand-crafted decorative
home accessories

SWEETHEART GALLERY
34C Tinker Street
Woodstock, NY 12498
Contacts:
Norman and Lila Bacon
(914) 679-2622

TREADLES, N.Y.
351 Bleecker Street
New York, NY 10014
Contact:
Lisa Wagner
(212) 633-0072

All handwoven textiles

WEST END GALLERY
87 W. Market Street
Corning, NY 14830
Contacts:
Thomas Gardner, President
Elizabeth Staight, Director
(607) 962-8692

Studio glass from 1960 to the
present

NORTH CAROLINA

CONTINUITY, INC.
P.O. Box 999, U.S. Hwy. 19
Maggie Valley, NC 28751
Contact:
Elizabeth Lurie
(704) 926-0333

All media

FINE LINES
304 S. Stratford Road
Winston-Salem, NC 27103
Contact:
Sandra S. Steele
(919) 723-8066

Ceramics, glass, wood, jewelry,
soft sculpture, lighting, floor
cloths

HODGES TAYLOR GALLERY
227 N. Tryon Street
Charlotte, NC 28202
Contact:
Christie Taylor
(704) 334-3799

MORNING STAR GALLERY
Rt. 1, Box 292-10
Banner Elk, NC 28604
Contact:
Maggie Wilson
(704) 898-6047

Paintings, etchings, silkscreens,
tapestries functional pottery,
quilts, jewelry, blown glass,
turned wood and baskets

THE MOUNTAIN POTTERY
Church Street
Dillsboro, NC 28725
Contact:
Rick Urban
(704) 586-9183
(704) 293-9406

Functional and decorative
work by over 45 different potters

NEW ELEMENTS GALLERY
216 N. Front Street
Wilmington, NC 28401
Contact:
Merrimon Long Kennedy
(919) 343-8997

Fine art and contemporary craft

TAR HEEL TRADING CO.
Sea Holly Square
P.O. Box 1036
Kill Devil Hills, NC 27948
Contact:
Mary E. Ames, President
(919) 441-6235

Functional and decorative
American crafts and prints.
Ceramics, metal, glass, wood
and some fiber

URBAN ARTIFACTS
413 Forum IV
3200 Northline Avenue
Greensboro, NC 27408
Contacts:
Jan Detter, Owner
JoAnne Vernon, Owner
(919) 855-0557

Work by American craftsmen
and designers, primarily
ceramics, glass, wood and
jewelry

OHIO

AMERICAN CRAFTS GALLERY
13010 Larchmere
Cleveland, OH 44120
Contacts:
Sylvia Ullmann
Marilyn Bialosky
(216) 231-2008

Contemporary, hand-made
American crafts: ceramics,
sculpture, wood, furniture,
blown and stained glass, wall
hangings and weavings

ART BANK GALLERY
317 W. 4th Street
Cincinnati, OH 45202
(513) 621-7779

Arts and crafts

BENCHWORKS GALLERY
2563 N. High Street
Columbus, OH 43202
(614) 263-2111

Contemporary crafts

GALLERY '400'
4659 Dressler Road N.W.
Canton, OH 44718
Contacts:
Jimmie Ivan
Barbara Levy
(216) 492-2600

Original paintings, prints, fine
art crafts and custom framing

THE MURRAY HILL MARKET
2181 Murray Hill Road
Cleveland, OH 44106
Contact:
Thomas Houser
(216) 791-9679

American hand-crafts: textiles,
wood, glass, ceramics and
jewelry

OMNI GALLERY
46 The Arcade
401 Euclid Avenue
Cleveland, OH 44114
Contacts:
Stuart and Patricia Zolten
(216) 781-3444

Contemporary American
crafts: ceramics, glass, wood,
sculpture and jewelry

POTTERY HANDWORKS
537 E. Maple Street
North Canton, OH 44720
Contact:
Muriel Meray, Studio Artist
(216) 494-3736

Pottery, jewelry and textiles

RILEY HAWK GLASS GALLERY
2026 Murray Hill Road,
Room 108
Cleveland, OH 44106
Contacts:
Tom and Linda Riley
(216) 421-1445

Glass art sculptures

RILEY HAWK GLASS GALLERY
642 N. High Street
Columbus, OH 43215
Contacts:
Sherrie and Tom Hawk
(614) 228-6554

Glass art sculptures

OKLAHOMA

CRAIN/WOLOV GALLERY
8146-D S. Lewis
Tulsa, OK 74137
Contact:
Nancy Wolov
(918) 299-2299

Contemporary crafts,
exclusively

M.A. DORAN GALLERY, INC.
3509 S. Peoria
Tulsa, OK 74105
Contact:
Mary Ann Doran
(918) 748-8700

Contemporary American
realism and contemporary
crafts

OREGON

CONTEMPORARY CRAFTS
GALLERY
3934 S.W. Corbett Avenue
Portland, OR 97201
Contact:
Marlene Gabel, Executive
Director
(503) 223-2659

The finest art in craft media
from the following disciplines:
glass, ceramics, wood, fiber
and metal

MAVEETY GALLERY
842 S.W. 1st Avenue
Portland, OR 97204
Contact:
Billye Turner
Selby Key
(503) 224-9442

THE REAL MOTHER GOOSE
GALLERY
901 S.W. Yamhill Portland, OR
97205
Contact:
Stan F. Gillis
(503) 233-9510

Contemporary American fine
craft and art in all media

PENNSYLVANIA

AART VARK GALLERY
The Warwick
17th at Locust
Philadelphia, PA 19103
Contact:
Lynne Fankel, Owner
(215) 735-5600

Paintings, prints, jewelry, glass
and ceramics

THE BLUE SKY GALLERY INC.
6022 Penn Circle South
Pittsburg, PA 15206
Contact:
Mimsie Stuhldreher
(412) 661-3600

Fine art, collector quality crafts

THE CLAY PLACE
5416 Walnut Street
Pittsburg, PA 15232
Contact:
Elvira Peake
(412) 682-3737

Ceramics, pottery, sculpture,
jewelry and some glass

THE COUNTRY STUDIO
Rd #1, Box 1124
Hadley, PA 16130
Contact:
Lynn Linton
(412) 253-2493

Pottery, paintings, etchings,
jewelry, wood and glass

CRAFTSMEN'S GALLERY
Star Route 2, Box 16E Route 6
East
Hawley, PA 18428
Contact:
Rose-Marie Chapman, Partner
(717) 226-4111

All categories of handmade
American crafts, also fine art
and photography

DINA PORTER GALLERY
3900 Hamilton Boulevard
Allentown, PA 18103
Contact:
Susan H. Coker
(215) 434-7363

American crafts, all media
including original art and
limited edition prints

GALLERY 500
Church and Old York Roads
Elkins Park, PA 19117
Contacts:
Rita Greenfield
Harriet Friedberg
(215) 572-1203

2 and 3 dimensional work,
paintings, sculpture, fiber,
ceramics, glass, art jewelry and
wood
Gallery 500 established for 21
years, exhibiting fine art and
contemporary American crafts.
Our artists are professionally
juried to show exclusively with
us. Corporate consultations
and commissions presented by
our knowledgeable staff.

GALLERY RIGGIONE
Mallard Creek Village
130 Almshouse Road
Richboro, PA 18954
Contacts:
Joseph and Adelina Riggione
Adelina Riggione
(215) 322-5035

Jewelry, ceramics, glass, wood
and mixed media

GLASS GROWERS GALLERY
701 Holland Street
Erie, PA 16501
Contact:
Deborah G. Vahanian
(814) 453-3758

American crafts (multi-media)
and fine arts

IMAGINE GALLERY & GIFTS
3330 W. 26 Street
Village West #1
Erie, PA 16506
Contacts:
Gene and Nancy Ware
(814) 838-8077

Arts and crafts, art photography

LATITUDES GALLERY
4325 Main Street
Philadelphia, PA 19127
Contact:
Joan Castronuovo, Owner
(215) 482-0417

Fine contemporary crafts,
pottery, jewelry and wall fiber

THE OTTER CREEK STORE
106 S. Diamond Street
Mercer, PA 16137
Contact:
Nancy Myal Griffin
(412) 662-2830

Vessels, wood sculpture,
handwoven floor coverings
and textiles, decorative glass

OWEN/PATRICK GALLERY
4345 Main Street
Philadelphia, PA 19127
Contacts:
James Gilroy
Gary Pelkey
(215) 482-9395

Multimedia, fine art and craft

THE SANDE WEBSTER GALLERY
2018 Locust Street
Philadelphia, PA 19103
Contacts:
Sande Webster, President
Cheryl Sutton, Associate
Director
(215) 732-8850

Contemporary painting,
sculpture, drawings and craft

SNYDERMAN GALLERY
307 Cherry Street
Philadelphia, PA 19106
Contact:
Rick Snyderman
(215) 238-9576

THE STUDIO IN SWARTHMORE
14 Park Avenue
Swarthmore, PA 19081
Contact:
Lee Gilbert
(215) 543-5779

Fine craft and original art
including pottery, glass, wood,
metal, fiber and paintings in all
media

THE WORKS GALLERY
319 South Street
Philadelphia, PA 19147
Contact:
Ruth Snyderman, Director
(215) 922-7775

Works in all medium: ceramic,
glass, wood, metal, fiber and
jewelry

SOUTH CAROLINA

BOHEMIAN
2112 Devine Street
Columbia, SC 29205
Contact:
Bruce Schultze
(803) 256-0629

Contemporary and folk art,
furniture, lighting, fine crafts
and Santa Fe style

CAROL SAUNDERS GALLERY
927 Gervais Street
Columbia, SC 29201
(803) 256-3046

Functional and non-functional
crafts, paintings and studio
jewelry

THE CRAFTSELLER
216 West Street
Beaufort, SC 29902
Contact:
Sandra Williams
(803) 525-6104

American hand-crafted items,
pottery, jewelry, glass and
wood

TENNESSEE

THE BROWSERY
2794 Wilma Rudolph Boulevard
Clarksville, TN 37040
Contact:
Lou Ann Brown
(615) 552-2733

Functional and decorative,
contemporary and traditional
fine crafts. Jewelry, clay,
metal, glass and fiber

THE METALWORKS GALLERY
109 Court Avenue
Memphis, TN 38103
Contact:
Pamela Petterson
(901) 521-9440

Jewelry, pottery, wood, paper,
paintings, photography and
sculpture

TEXAS

CREATIVE ARTS GALLERY
836 North Star Mall
San Antonio, TX 78216
Contact:
Luann Cohen
(512) 342-8659

Contemporary American
crafts, ceramics, glass, metal
and wood

CULLER CONCEPTS INC.
109 Mandalay Canal
Irving, TX 75039
Contact:
Donna Hurd
(214) 869-1937

Ceramics, glass, fiber, wood
and jewelry

ECLECTIONS
3408-B Camp Bowie Boulevard
Fort Worth, TX 76107
Contact:
Barbara Mabli
(817) 332-4407

Ceramics, fiber, metal and
art-to-wear

Texas continued

HEARTLAND GALLERY
4006 South Lamar, Suite #950
Austin, TX 78704
Contact:
Holly Plotner, Owner
(512) 447-1171

Contemporary crafts, all
media: pottery, glass, jewelry,
wood and fiber

JUDY YOUENS GALLERY
2631 Colquitt Street
Houston, TX 77098
(713) 527-0303

Studio art glass, paintings and
sculpture

ROCK HOUSE GALLERY
1311 West Abram
Arlington, TX 76013
Contact:
Jo Ann Bushart
(817) 265-5874

Original craftwork by American
artisans

R.S. LEVY GALLERY
3 Republic Plaza
333 Guadalupe
Austin, TX 78701
Contacts:
Rebecca Levy
Alise Mullins
(512) 473-8926

Contemporary American
paintings, drawings, sculpture
and fiber work

SPICEWOOD GALLERY
1206 W. 38th Street
Austin, TX 78705
Contact:
Jackie Depew
(512) 458-6575

Original art in hand-blown
glass, woods, ceramics and
functional pieces. Also paintings

WILLIAM CAMPBELL
CONTEMPORARY ART
4935 Byers Avenue
Ft. Worth, TX 76107
Contact:
Pam and Bill Campbell
(817) 737-9566

Ceramics, weaving, paintings
and works on paper

VERMONT

DESIGNER'S CIRCLE
21 Church Street
Burlington, VT 05401
Contact:
Dennis Bosch
(802) 864-4238

Jewelry, blown glass, pewter,
fine porcelain and quilts

HANDWORKS
Village Square
Stratton Mountain, VT 05155
Contact:
Barbara Nashner
(802) 297-0090

Contemporary crafts

THE VERMONT STATE CRAFT
CENTER
Frog Hollow
Middlebury, VT 05753
Contact:
Pamela Siers, Executive Director
(802) 388-3177

Handcrafts by Vermonts finest
artists in the media of wood,
metals, fiber, glass and
ceramics

VIRGINIA

THE CAVE HOUSE CRAFT SHOP
279 E. Main Street Abingdon,
VA 24210
Contact:
William Gable, Director
(703) 628-7721

Traditional, contemporary,
mixed media

COUNTRY HERITAGE ANTIQUES
AND CRAFTS
Main Street
P.O. Box 148
Washington, VA 22747
Contact:
Nancy Thomasson, Owner
(703) 675-3738

Antiques and American
hand-crafts

CUDAHY'S GALLERY
1314 E. Cary Street
Richmond, VA 23219
Contact:
Helen Levinson, Director
(804) 782-1776

Original art in all media, fine
crafts in glass, wood metal and
ceramics

ELECTRIC GLASS GALLERY
823 W. Pembroke Avenue
Hampton, VA 23669
Contact:
Bobo Vines
(804) 722-6300

Contemporary art glass and
lighting

FIBER DESIGNS
Higgins House
Main Street
P.O. Box 614
Wellfleet, VA 02667
Contact:
Rebecca Smith, Owner
(508) 349-7434

All media

GALLERY 3
213 Market Street
Roanoke, VA 24011
Contact:
Andy Williams
(703) 343-9698

Contemporary crafts

PAULA LEWIS, COURT SQUARE
216 4th Street N.E.
Charlottesville, VA 22901
(804) 295-6244

American folk art

QUILTS UNLIMITED
Merchants Square
440-A Duke of Gloucester Street
Williamsburg, VA 23185
Contact:
Joan Fenton, President
(804) 253-8700

New and antique quilts

SIGNET GALLERY
212 5th Street, N.E.
Charlottesville, VA 22901
Contact:
Priscilla F. Bosworth
(804) 296-6463

Jewelry, ceramics, glass and
wood

TACTILE
105 N. Union Street
Alexandria, VA 22314
Contact:
Jean Thompson
(703) 549-8490

Collage, fans and screens

VISTA FINE CRAFTS
8 N. Madison Street
P.O. Box 2034
Middleburg, VA 22117
Contact:
Sherrie Posternak, Owner
(703) 687-3317

Contemporary crafts in
ceramics, metal, wood, fiber
and glass

WHISTLE WALK CRAFTS GALLERY
7 S. King Street
Leesburg, VA 22075
Contact:
Velda A. Warner
(703) 777-4017

Contemporary crafts

YORKTOWN ARTS FOUNDATION
ON THE HILL CULTURAL ARTS
CENTER
121 Alexander Hamilton Blvd.
P.O. Box 244
Contact:
Helen Stevenson, Executive
Director
(804) 898-3076

WASHINGTON

ARTWORKS GALLERY
155 S. Main
Seattle, WA 98104
Contact:
Mary Jane Rehm,
Owner/Director
(206) 625-0932

Contemporary craft

BELA BELLENA LTD.
8825 N. Harborview Drive
Gig Harbor, WA 98335
Contact:
Pat Semon
(206) 858-7434

Contemporary American crafts

CARNEGIE CENTER, INC.
109 S. Palouse
Walla Walla, WA 99362
Contact:
Christine Bishop, Director
(509) 525-4270

Gallery exhibitions, drawings,
paintings, sculpture and fiber

CORPORATE ART WEST, INC.
1600 124th Avenue N.E.
Bellevue, WA 98005
Contact:
Carol A. Young
(206) 454-2595

Original and limited editions
and prints

CRACKERJACK
CONTEMPORARY CRAFTS
1815 N. 45th Street, #212
Seattle, WA 98133
Contact: Kathleen D. Koch,
Owner
(206) 547-4983

Jewelry, glass, fiber, ceramics,
metal and wood

FIREWORKS GALLERIES
Westlake Center
Seattle, WA 98101
and
Pioneer Square
210 1st Avenue S.
Seattle, WA 98104
Contact:
Michele Manasse
(206) 682-8707

Ceramics, jewelry, furniture,
children's toys and clothes
A browse through the two
vastly different galleries
representing over 170 artists in
a variety of media is the best
introduction to some of the
choicest works by regionally
and nationally acclaimed craft
artists. Special orders, welcome.

FLYING SHUTTLE
607 First Avenue
Seattle, WA 98104
Contact:
Judy Jester
(206) 343-9762

Handwoven clothing,
contemporary jewelry and
rugs, pillows and throws for the
home

FOSTER/WHITE GALLERY
311 1/2 Occidental Avenue S.
Seattle, WA 98104
Contact:
Donald Foster, Owner
(206) 622-2833

GLASS EYE GALLERY
1902 Post Alley
Seattle, WA 98101
(206) 441-3221

Art glass

GLASSHOUSE ART GLASS
GALLERY
311 Occidnetal Avenue S.
Seattle, WA 98104
Contact:
Eric Brakkon, Owner
(206) 682-9939

Hand-blown art glass

MIA GALLERY
314 Occidental Avenue S.
Seattle, WA 98104
Contact:
Mia McEldowney
(206) 467-8283

Contemporary fine art, folk art,
jewelry and furniture

NORTHWEST GALLERY OF FINE
WOODWORKING
317 N.W. Gilman Blvd.
Issaquah, WA 98027
Contact:
Cheryl Peterson, Director
(206) 391-4221

Contemporary hand-made
furniture and wood artistry

**NORTHWEST GALLERY OF FINE
WOODWORKING**
**202 1st Avenue S.
Seattle, WA 98104**
Contact:
**Cheryl Peterson, Director
(206) 625-0542**

Exquisite contemporary
furniture, sculpture,
wood-turning, and gifts for the
discerning collector. Our
nationally-recognized and
cooperatively owned gallery
represents the work of 35
owner/members, as well as the
work of the finest wood artisans
today.

WILLIAM TRAVER GALLERY
2219 4th Avenue
Seattle, WA 98121
Contact:
William Traver
(206) 448-4234

WOOD MERCHANT
707 South 1st Street
La Conner, WA 98257
Contacts:
Stuart and Laurie Hutt
(206) 466-4741

A gallery of fine wood working

THE SHOP
The Cultural Center
Charleston, WV 25305
(304) 348-0690

A showcase for West Virginia
crafts

AVENUE ART
10 College Avenue
Appleton, WI 54911
(414) 734-7710

A wide range of originals, prints
and pottery

BRIDGE ROAD GALLERY
N70 W6340 Bridge Road
Cedarburg, WI 53012
Contacts:
Pat and David Eitel
(414) 375-2600

Fine crafts in a variety of media

THE FANNY GARVER GALLERY
230 State Street
Madison, WI 53703
Contacts:
Fanny Garver, Director
Jack Garver, Craft Manager
(608) 256-6755

Glass, jewelry, wooden objects,
ceramics and fine art

THE HANG UP GALLERY
204 W. Wisconsin Avenue
Neenah, WI 54956
(414) 722-0481

A wide range of originals, prints
and pottery

KATIE GINGRASS GALLERY
241 N. Broadway
Milwaukee, WI 53202
Contact:
Pat Brophy
(414) 289-0855

Contemporary American art
and fine craft

POSNER GALLERY
207 N. Milwaukee Street
Milwaukee, WI 53202
Contact:
Judith Posner
(414) 273-3097

RED BALLOON GALLERY
P.O. Box 606, Highway 35
Stockholm, WI 54769
Contact:
Mark Edwards, Owner
(715) 442-2504

Pottery, sculpture, serigraphs,
original watercolors, baskets
and jewelry

Adachi, Karen 159
Adams, B.J. 127
Adams, Carol 193
Aguero, Michael 64, 249
Aiello, Rosemary 275
Alden, Lincoln 35
Alden Design 35
Allan, Ruth E. 276
Andrew Pate Design 36
Angel-Wing, Dina 259
Architectural Ceramics 236
Art in Fiber 127
Art in Fiber 137
Artfocus, Ltd. 162, 163
Askew, Sandy 128
Athari, Shawn 260, 261
Atleson, Carol 97
Axelsson, Chris 21
Axelsson Metalsmith 21
AZO Inc. 185
Bach, Susan 194
Barkley, Teresa 113
Barron, Barbara 129
Belfor, Christine 229
Bender, Laura 77
Berek, Cynthia 232
Bergman, Eric W. 37
Bess, Nancy Moore 262
Big Sur Handwovens 142
Bisceglia, Therese 161
Bissett, Tim 277
Blocksma, Carter Gustav 38
Bobin, Chris 114
Bolesky, Mark T. 39
Bonciolini, Diane A. 248
Boney, Nancy 130
Boyd, Douglas 288
Bracci, Pamela 87
Bracci and James 87
Bradford Woodworking 69
Braen, Jeanne 131
Brendler, Linda 284
Breton, Lynette 41
Breton Flannery Woodworks 41
Brian Russell Designs 28
Brothers, Lynda 98
Bruce Smith Designs 195
Buxton, Kerri L. 245

Buxton/Taylor Design 245
Cabaniss, Michael 42
Cabitt, Stephen M. 43
California Glass Studio 280
Camp, James M. 44
Carey, Joyce Marquess 132
Carolyn Cole Studios 164
Carther, Warren 45
Chatelain, Martha 162, 163
Chia Jen Studio 92
Christine Belfor Design Ltd. 229
Clarke, Tony 46
Clarke Fine Furniture 46
Claudia Zeber, Inc. 224
Cohen, Jacqueline M. 297
Cole, Carolyn 164
Colella, Janis 196, 48, 49
Contemporary Maine Textiles 110
Cooper, Jeffrey 47
Cooper, Kathy 88
Creative Textures 269
Culin, Ray 48, 49
Culin Colella 48, 49
Cunningham, Liz 281
Cunningham, Beth 165
Custom Carpentry 39
Cynthia Nixon Studio, Images in Fabric 144
Dabrowski, Laura 78
Dalton, Pamela 166
Dalton, Anne Lanford 89
Davies, D. Joyce 115
Dawson, Jeanne 133
de Rham, Jeremiah 50
de Rham Custom Furniture 50
DeNicola, Joy 167
Design Works, Inc. 230, 231
Designer of Sculptural Furnishings in Wood 47
Designforms 38
Diane McKenzie Design 105
Diefenbacher, Ron 51
Dillon, Allester 278
Dimensional Works of Art 193
Double Vision Studio 179
Dudchenko, Nancy Weeks 197
Dudchenko Studios 197
Duffy, Thomas J. 52
Duffy's General &
Specific Millwork 52

Earley, Kevin 53
Early, John 77
Egen, Su 134
Emmons, Michael 54
England, Susana 116
Epstein, Ann 135
Ewing, Susan 253
Fauna Collections 25
Feller, Lucy G. 136
Fiber Design Studio 99
Firebird Inc. 232
Firedrake Studios 239
Fisher, Linda 196
Flanders, Pamela 168
Flanders Fine Art 168
Flannery, Ann 41
Fleming, Ron 279
Fleming, Penelope 246
Fletcher, Barbara F. 169
Forth, Marilyn 90
Fox, Rosemary 79
Fry, Logan 263
Fuerst, Wayne A.O. 170
Fused Glass Studio 221
Garvelink, Frank 56
Gary Upton Woodworking Inc. 73
Gekht, Rita R. 107
Goldstein, Judith E. 264
Goodman, Johanna Okovic 80
Granek, Al 137
GrayWing Arts 218
Grebow, Marion 234
Greenwood, Brad 55
Greenwood Designs 55
Gregory Sheres Studio 83
Griffin, Joan 99
Grychczynski, Mark 265
Hammond, Marcia 138
Hand Built Porcelain 199
Handler, Peter 22
Handwoven Originals 108
Hansen, Michael K. 280
Hanson, Harriet 171
Harris, Lisa 198
Hayashi, Yoshi 81
Hearthstone Studios 279
Hein, John 57
Heine, Martha 100

Heller, Nancy 235
Herd, Carol 172
Hewitt, William 58
Heyden, Silvia 101
Hill, Pamela 117
Hill, Glenn J. 266
Hoblitzell, Jean 118
Holt, Georgina 199
Hughto, Margie 200
Hulsey/Trusty 124
Hutchison, Boyd A. 59
Hutchison Woodworking 59
Inter-Ocean Curiosity Studio 186
Interior Graphics 84
J. Camp Designs 44
J.E. Jasen 201
Jacoby, Victor 102
James, Kathy 87
James, Valarie Lee 281
Jaqua, Russell C. 23
Jasen, June E. 201
Jeffrey Sass: Metal Work 29
Jensen, Eric L. 282
Johnson, Rob 24, 247
Johnson, Will 283
Jones, Norman 82
Joseph, Pamela 202
Joyce Lopez Studio 206, 207
Kanter, Janis 139
Kastaris, Rip 203
Kastaris Studio 203
Keer, AIA, Ira A. 60
Ken Sedberry Studio 219
Klein, K.H. 119
Kline, Vivian 204
Knox, Christine 267
Kopchik, Joan 173
Kuemmerlein, Janet 140
Kuemmerlein Fiber Art Inc. 140
La Mountain, Melba 120
LaFollette, Curtis K. 253
Laico, Colette 174
Laughing Willows 54
Laura D's 78
Laurence, Pamela 268
Len's Wood Specialties 225
Leonard, Elle Terry 236

Lester, Michelle 103
Lewing, Paul 237
Lewis, Ray 25
Leznicki, Bojana H. 107
Lhotka, Bonny 205
Lilienthal, Wendy 175
Lill St. Studios 198
Lill Street Studios 282
Linda Brendler Studios 284
Lopez, Joyce P. 206, 207
Lowden, Antonia 104
Loy D. Martin Furniture 61
Lubin, Nancy 91
Lyon, Nancy 141
Mackey, Jennifer 92
MacNaughton, Wendy 84
Maginniss, Irene 177
Main Avenue Pottery 296
Malakoff, Peter 82
Malakoff & Jones 82
Mann, Richard 209
Martin, Loy Davis 61
May, Therese 122
Maynard, Peter 62, 63
McKenzie, Diane 105
McLeod, La Verne 142
McLeod, Jennifer 143
Medford, Bobby J. 285
Meeker, J. Wade 210
Meier, Ann Mayer 269
Mesmer, Gregg S. 248
Mesolini Glass Studio 248
Metal Paintings, Inc. 202
MIA Gallery 31
Middleton, Gordon 286
Modern Objects 64, 249
Moore, Dottie 121
Morgese, Marcella 178
Moritz, Andrew 211
Mountain Glen Wind Harps 266
Mylynne, Cyndi 179
Nancy Heller Design Originals 235
Neon Art 215
Neophile Inc. 37
New Expressions In Clay 217
New York Tapestry Artists 107
Nimba Forge 23
Nixon, Cynthia 144

Nordgren, Elizabeth 145
O'Heron, Faith 180, 181
Oaks, Susan M. 287
Okovic/Goodman Studio 80
Orchard House Floorcloths 88
Orchid Studios 170
Orient & Flume Art Glass 288
Osborn, Kevin 289
Owen, Carol 182
Paladino, Nina 280
Palanza, William 238
Palanza Mosaic Co. 238
Paley, Albert 26
Paley Studios, Ltd. 26
Pappageorge, Louise 212
Parker, Leroy Wheeler 183
Parsley, Jacque 270
Pate, Andrew 36
Patterson, Cynthia 251
Paul Lewing Custom Tile 237
Pearson, Charles 290
Peartree, Arline 213
Pepper-Pot Pottery, Inc. 293
Petaja, Dean 214
Peter Handler Studio 22
Peter Maynard and Associates 62, 63
Petersen, Norman 65
Photo Linens 136
Pinciotti, Michael Rocco 215
Plummer, Beverly 184
Ponsler, David A. 27
Puckett, Ronald C. 66, 67
R.E.A. Studio 276
Radca, Tom 216
Red Top Design 255
Renaissance Fibres 156
Renner, Robin 291
Renner Clay & Beadwork 291
Richard Mann Studio 209
Richardson, Amanda 146, 147
Richardson Kirby 146, 147
Richert Sandy 271
Rob Johnson Furniture 24, 249
Roeder, Timothy 290
Rogovin, Harold 253
Ron Diefenbacher Design 51

Ronald C. Puckett & Company 66, 67
Ross, Betsy 292
Rowley, Mathers 239
Russell, Jude 149
Russell, Brian F. 28
Sabiston, Carole 150, 151
Sarti, Michael 64, 249
Sass, Jeffrey 29
Sattler, Lois 250
Saxe-Patterson 251
Sayre, William B. 74
Scarpa, Siglinda 240
Scarpa Design Studio 240
Schell, Toar 293
Scherenschnitte 166
Schloss, Julia 108
Schmitt, Carl 217
Schuh, Victoria 218
Sculpture and Design Studio 272
Searls, Fred 252
Searls Design Group 252
Sears, Martha 68
Sedberry, Kenneth 219
Sharp, Kathleen 123
Shawn Athari's, Inc. 260, 261
Sheres, Gregory 83
Shore, Sally 152
Sievert, Mary-Ann 107
Singer, Karen 241
Singleton, Susan 185
Site Painters 77
Smith, Brad 69
Smith, Steve 30
Smith, Vaughan 297
Smith, Bruce F. 195
Smithwork Studio 30
Society of American
Silversmiths 253
Souder, Ned 220
Special Creations in Metal 211
Spiegel, Mamie 70
Steele, Elinor 109
Stenstrom, David 71
Stephen M. Cabitt Company 43
Stevens Design Associates 222

Stone, Judy 254
Strange, Nick 72
Studio 1617 223
Sullivan, Robert 221
Svoboda, Michelle 255
Swanson, Brian 31
The Art of Calabash 281
The Century Guild 72
The Quilt Connection 120
The Studiospace 171
Tim Bissett Designs Inc. 277
Tolpo, Carolyn Lee 153
Tomasso, Raymond D. 186
Tomchuk, Marjorie 187
Trusty, Ann 124
Twycross-Reed, Pamela 154
Upton, Gary 73
Van Gelder, Lydia 155
Van Leunen, Alice 188
Van Noppen, David 294
Van Noppen Glass, Inc. 294
Vera, Betty 107
Vermont Paperworks 189
Vesper, Kerry 272
Walsh, Eva S. 295
Warren, S. M. 189
Warren, Jackque 222
Warren Carther Glass Studio 45
Weber, Timothy 296
Westcote Bell Ceramics 297
Western Maine Weavers 91
Wheeler, Bill 223
White, Judi Maureen 156
White, Larry 256
Whitehead Street Pottery 290
Wilcox, Jill 93
Wines-DeWan, Nancy 110
Witticks Design 58
Wittig, Irene 242
Wm. B. Sayre, Inc. 74
Wonderland Products, Inc. 27
Wooldridge, Stephen E. 32
Wooldridge Sculpture Studios 32
Woven for the Wall,
Contemporary Design 104
Wright, David 230, 231
Young, Nancy J. 190
Zeber, Claudia 224
Zeoli, Len 225
Zheutlin, Dale 226
Zimmerman, Lee 298
Zinkel, Barbara 94

INDEX BY STATE OF CRAFT ARTISTS AND COMPANIES

ALABAMA

Main Avenue Pottery, 296
Timothy Weber, 296

ARIZONA

Art in Fiber, 137
Su Egen, 134
Al Granek, 137
Bobby J. Medford, 285
Kevin Osborn, 289
Renaissance Fibres, 156
Sculpture and Design Studio, 272
Kerry Vesper, 272
Judi Maureen White, 156

CALIFORNIA

Karen Adachi, 159
Dina Angel-Wing, 259
Artfocus, Ltd., 162, 163
Shawn Athari, 260, 261
Chris Axelsson, 21
Axelsson Metalsmith, 21
Laura Bender, 77
Big Sur Handwovens, 142
Douglas Boyd, 288
Linda Brendler, 284
Lynda Brothers, 98
Michael Cabaniss, 42
California Glass Studio, 280
Martha Chatelain, 162, 163,
Chia Jen Studio, 92
Liz Cunningham, 281
Diane McKenzie Design, 105
Allester Dillon, 278
John Early, 77
Michael Emmons, 54
Susana England, 116
Fauna Collections, 25
Firedrake Studios, 239
Pamela Flanders, 168
Flander's Fine Art, 168
Fused Glass Studio, 221
Gary Upton Woodworking Inc., 73
Brad Greenwood, 55

Greenwood Designs, 55
Mark Grychczynski, 265
Michael K. Hansen, 280
Yoshi Hayashi, 81
Pamela Hill, 117
Victor Jacoby, 102
Valarie Lee James, 281
Will Johnson, 283
Norman Jones, 82
Laughing Willows, 54
Ray Lewis, 25
Wendy Lilienthal, 175
Linda Brendler Studios, 284
Loy D. Martin Furniture, 61
Jennifer Mackey, 92
Peter Malakoff, 82
Malakoff & Jones, 82
Richard Mann, 209
Loy Davis Martin, 61
Therese May, 122
Diane McKenzie, 105
La Verne McLeod, 142
Gordon Middleton, 286
New Expressions In Clay, 217
Faith O'Heron, 180
Orient & Flume Art Glass, 288
Nina Paladino, 280
Leroy Wheeler Parker, 183
Norman Petersen, 65
Red Top Design, 255
Richard Mann Studio, 209
Mathers Rowley, 239
Lois Sattler, 250
Carl Schmitt, 217
Fred Searls, 252
Searls Design Group, 252
Kathleen Sharp, 123
Shawn Athari's, Inc., 260, 261
Site Painters, 77
Judy Stone, 254
Studio 1617, 223
Michelle Svoboda, 255
The Art of Calabash, 281
Gary Upton, 73
Lydia Van Gelder, 155
Bill Wheeler, 223
Larry White, 256

COLORADO

Inter-Ocean Curiosity Studio, 186
Bonny Lhotka, 205
Vincent Tolpo, 153
Carolyn Lee Tolpo, 153
Raymond D. Tomasso, 186

CONNECTICUT

Michael Aguero, 64
Jeanne Braen, 131
Bruce Smith Designs, 195
Beth Cunningham, 165
Judith E. Goldstein, 264
Interior Graphics, 84
Wendy MacNaughton, 84
Modern Objects, 64, 249
Michael Sarti, 64, 249
Bruce F. Smith, 195
Marjorie Tomchuk, 187

DISTRICT OF COLUMBIA

B.J. Adams, 127
Art in Fiber, 127
Handwoven Originals, 108
Julia Schloss, 108

FLORIDA

Architectural Ceramics, 236
Susan Bach, 194
Creative Textures, 269
Jeanne Dawson, 133
Gregory Sheres Studio, 83
Hand Built Porcelain, 199
Georgina Holt, 199
Elle Terry Leonard, 236
Ann Mayer Meier, 269
Carol Owen, 182
Charles Pearson, 290
David A. Ponsler, 27
Timothy Roeder, 290
Gregory Sheres, 83
Eva S. Walsh, 295
Whitehead Street Pottery, 290
Wonderland Products, Inc., 27

GEORGIA

Double Vision Studio, 179
Cyndi Mylynne, 179

ILLINOIS

Harriet Hanson, 171
Lisa Harris, 198
Nancy Heller, 235
Carol Herd, 172
Eric L. Jensen, 282
Joyce Lopez Studio, 206, 207
Janis Kanter, 139
Lill St. Studios, 198
Lill Street Studios, 282
Joyce P. Lopez, 206, 207
Nancy Heller Design Originals, 235
Louise Pappageorge, 212
The Studiospace, 171

INDIANA

Stephen E. Wooldridge, 32
Wooldridge Sculpture Studios, 32

KANSAS

Hulsey/Trusty, 124
Janet Kuemmerlein, 140
Kuemmerlein Fiber Art Inc., 140
Ann Trusty, 124

KENTUCKY

Jacque Parsley, 270

MAINE

Lynette Breton, 41
Breton Flannery Woodworks, 41
Contemporary Maine Textiles, 110
Ann Flannery, 41
Nancy Lubin, 91
David Stenstrom, 71
Western Maine Weavers, 91
Nancy Wines-DeWan, 110

MARYLAND

Jean Hoblitzell, 118

MASSACHUSETTS

Pamela Bracci, 87
Bracci and James, 87
Stephen M. Cabitt, 43
Tony Clarke, 46
Clarke Fine Furniture, 46
Jeremiah de Rham, 50
de Rham Custom Furniture, 50
Barbara F. Fletcher, 169
Wayne A. D. Fuerst, 170
William Hewitt, 58
Boyd A. Hutchison, 59
Hutchison Woodworking, 59
Christine Knox, 267
Curtis K. LaFollette, 253
Marcella Morgese, 178
Orchid Studios, 170
William B. Sayre, 74
Martha Sears, 68
Stephen M. Cabitt Company, 43
Witticks Design, 58
Wm. B. Sayre, Inc., 74

MICHIGAN

Sandy Askew, 128
Carter Gustav Blocksma, 38
Designforms, 38
Ann Epstein, 135
Frank Garvelink, 56
Barbara Zinkel, 94

MINNESOTA

Ira A. Keer, AIA, 60
Ned Souder, 220

MISSOURI

Ron Diefenbacher, 51
Rip Kastaris, 203
Kastaris Studio, 203
Ron Diefenbacher Design, 51

NEVADA

Antonia Lowden, 104
Contemporary Design,
Woven for the Wall, 104

NEW HAMPSHIRE

Jeffrey Cooper, 47
Designer of Sculptural Furnishings
in Wood, 47
Kathy James, 87
Nancy Lyon, 141
Peter Maynard, 62, 63
Elizabeth Nordgren, 145
Peter Maynard and
Associates, 62, 63

NEW JERSEY

Cynthia Berek, 232
Nancy Boney, 130
Firebird Inc., 232
John Hein, 57
Harold Rogovin, 253

NEW MEXICO

Therese Bisceglia, 161
Cynthia Patterson, 251
Robin Renner, 291
Renner Clay & Beadwork, 291
Saxe-Patterson, 251
Nancy J. Young, 190

NEW YORK

Rosemary Aiello, 275
Andrew Pate Design, 36
Carol Atleson, 97
Teresa Barkley, 113
Barbara Barron, 129
Christine Belfor, 229
Eric W. Bergman, 37
Nancy Moore Bess, 262
Chris Bobin, 114
Christine Belfor Design Ltd., 229

New York continued

Janis Colella, 196
Janis Colella, 48, 49
Ray Culin, 48, 49
Culin Colella, 48, 49
Laura Dabrowski, 78
Pamela Dalton, 166
Thomas J. Duffy, 52
Duffy's General & Specific
Millwork, 52
Lucy G. Feller, 136
Fiber Design Studio, 99
Linda Fisher, 196
Marilyn Forth, 90
Rosemary Fox, 79
Rita R. Gekht, 107
GrayWing Arts, 218
Marion Grebow, 234
Joan Griffin, 99
Margie Hughto, 200
J.E. Jasen, 201
June E. Jasen, 201
Rob Johnson, 24, 247
Pamela Joseph, 202
Colette Laico, 174
Laura D's, 78
Pamela Laurence, 268
Michelle Lester, 103
Bojana H. Leznicki, 107
Jennifer McLeod, 143
Metal Paintings, Inc., 202
Neon Art, 215
Neophile Inc., 37
New York Tapestry Artists, 107
William Palanza, 238
Palanza Mosaic Co., 238
Albert Paley, 26
Paley Studios, Ltd., 26
Andrew Pate, 36
Arline Peartree, 213
Photo Linens, 136
Michael Rocco Pinciotti, 215
Rob Johnson Furniture, 24, 247
Betsy Ross, 292
Siglinda Scarpa, 240
Scarpa Design Studio, 240

Scherenschnitte, 166
Victoria Schuh, 218
Sally Shore, 152
Mary-Ann Sievert, 107
Mamie Spiegel, 70
Pamela Twycross-Reed, 154
Betty Vera, 107
Jill Wilcox, 93
Dale Zheutlin, 226

NORTH CAROLINA

Kathy Cooper, 88
Martha Heine, 100
Silvia Heyden, 101
Ken Sedberry Studio, 219
Orchard House Floorcloths, 88
Beverly Plummer, 184
Kenneth Sedberry, 219
Nick Strange, 72
The Century Guild, 72

OHIO

Carol Adams, 193
Mark T. Bolesky, 39
Claudia Zeber, Inc., 224
Jacqueline M. Cohen, 297
Custom Carpentry, 39
Dimensional Works of Art, 193
Susan Ewing, 253
Logan Fry, 263
Vivian Kline, 204
Irene Maginniss, 177
Tom Radca, 216
Sandy Richert, 271
Steve Smith, 30
Vaughan Smith, 297
Smithwork Studio, 30
Westcote Bell Ceramics, 297
Claudia Zeber, 224

OKLAHOMA

Ron Fleming, 279
Hearthstone Studios, 279

OREGON

Carolyn Cole Studios, 164
Carolyn Cole, 164
Glenn J. Hill, 266
Andrew Moritz, 211
Mountain Glen Wind Harps, 266
Jude Russell, 149
Special Creations in Metal, 211
Alice Van Leunen, 188

PENNSYLVANIA

Bradford Woodworking, 69
James M. Camp, 44
Images in Fabric,
Cynthia Nixon Studio, 144
Nancy Weeks Dudchenko, 197
Dudchenko Studios, 197
Penelope Fleming, 246
Johanna Okovic Goodman, 80
Peter Handler, 22
J. Camp Designs, 44
K.H. Klein, 119
Joan Kopchik, 173
Cynthia Nixon, 144
Okovic/Goodman Studio, 80
Peter Handler Studio, 22
Karen Singer, 241
Brad Smith, 69

RHODE ISLAND

Society of American
Silversmiths, 253
David Van Noppen, 294
Van Noppen Glass, Inc., 294

SOUTH CAROLINA

Dottie Moore, 121